Cantonese Love

*An English translation of Jiu Ji-yung's
Cantonese songs of the early 19th century*

Peter T. Morris

Hong Kong University Press
香港大學出版社

Published by Hong Kong University Press
University of Hong Kong
139 Pokfulam Road, Hong Kong

© HONG KONG UNIVERSITY PRESS 1992

ISBN 962 209 284 5

All rights reserved. No portion of this publication may be reproduced or transmitted in any form or by any means, electronic or mechanical, including photocopy, recording, or any information storage or retrieval system without permission in writing from the copyright owner.

Printed in Hong Kong by Elite Printing Co. Ltd.

This book is dedicated to my wife Helen (凱徵) and my children, Edwin (欣榮) and Loretta (欣恒); to all my Chinese teachers and Chinese friends (to me these words are synonymous: my friends are my teachers; and my teachers, my friends); and to non-Chinese who want to know something more about the Chinese people, their culture and language.

My sincere thanks are due to Miss Lai Wing-yin (黎詠妍), my former post-graduate student in Translation in the Chinese University of Hong Kong, for expertly helping me to translate lines I found difficult to construe and to avoid mistranslating some of the many racy Cantonese expressions in the text.

Peter T. Morris
June 1991

ACKNOWLEDGEMENTS

The translator gratefully acknowledges permission to reprint extracts from the following works:

A Golden Treasury of Chinese Poetry. Translated by John A. Turner (S.J.), compiled and edited by John J. Deeney, Renditions Paperbacks, Hong Kong, 1989.

Brocade River Poems. Selected writings of the Tang Dynasty Courtesan Xue Tao. Translated and introduced by Jeanne Larsen, Princeton University Press, 1987.

Gems of Classical Chinese Poetry in Various English Translations. Edited by Lu Shu-xiang and Xu Yuan-zhong, Joint Publishing (H.K.) Company Ltd., Hong Kong, 1988.

The Nineteen Ancient Poems. Ho, Kenneth P. H., Kelly & Walsh, Hong Kong, 1977.

The publisher is grateful for permission to use the painting on the front cover:

Lady in the Lotus Pond. Painted by Zhu Meicun and relatives, courtesy of Han Mo Xuan Company Ltd., Hong Kong.

CONTENTS

Introduction	1
Prefaces	41
Author's preface	43
Second preface	43
Third preface	45
Fourth preface	46
Fifth preface	47
Sixth preface	48
Seventh preface	50
Eighth preface	50
Ninth preface	52
Tenth preface	54
Eleventh preface	55
Songs	57
1. Dispel your sorrows (Parts 1–2)	59
2. Choosing a true heart	60
3. Do not die	61
4. Listening to the oriole in spring	62
5. Thoughts arise	63
6. Ungenerous fate	65
7. The world of flowers	66
8. The farewell banquet	67
9. Woe is me	67
10. Infatuation	68
11. Lamenting the ill-fated (Parts 1–5)	69
12. Passion is killing me (Parts 1–6)	76
13. Flowers are ever the same (Parts 1–2)	82
14. Ill-fate and passion	84
15. It is hard to hold back my tears	85
16. The geese of the rivers Siu and Seung	86
17. Concord grass	87
18. Flowers are beautiful	88
19. How can I be patient?	90

20. This weary world	91
21. Flowers are happy	92
22. Regrets of spring	93
23. The tender moon	94
24. The heartless moon	94
25. My heart	96
26. The moon on the rim of the sky	97
27. The moon over the house	98
28. The lone-flying goose	99
29. The letter-carrying goose	100
30. The passionate geese	101
31. The region of mist and flowers (Parts 1–2)	101
32. Willow blossoms	103
33. Flowers in the mirror	104
34. Flowers shed tears	105
35. How easy it is (Parts 1–6)	106
36. The ebbing tide	111
37. Flowers fall easily	112
38. The butterfly dream	113
39. It is hard for the moon to keep its roundness	114
40. On pre-ordained fate	115
41. Repentance	116
42. Virtuous woman and passionate man	117
43. Do not be too much on fire	117
44. Detain your guest	118
45. Reassure yourself	119
46. I am waiting for you	120
47. A lament for 'Autumn Joy'	121
48. Wounded spring	123
49. The flirting butterfly	123
50. The lamp moth	124
51. Long dreams	125
52. Do not dream	126
53. The bonds of love	126
54. The tree of love	127
55. The love knot	128
56. The tears of parting (Parts 1–3)	128
57. Unfeeling words	130
58. Unfeeling eyes	131

59. Songs without feeling	132
60. The debt of three lives	133
61. The single-hearted palm tree	134
62. Unending	134
63. Facing the weeping willow	135
64. Hearing the cry of the goose	136
65. Born beautiful	137
66. Not all that beautiful	137
67. Why are you so thin?	138
68. My darling	138
69. No easy task	139
70. Half a life's bitterness	141
71. It is hard to conduct oneself	141
72. Utterly helpless	142
73. Sent far away	143
74. Spring-flowers-autumn-moon (Parts 1–4)	144
75. The one word 'passion'	147
76. The passionate willow (Parts 1–2)	148
77. The sorrow I cannot dispel	149
78. In the depths of sorrow	150
79. What is the best thing to do? (Parts 1–2)	150
80. Only one body	152
81. Do not be afraid of ungenerous fate	153
82. Lamenting the shortness of life	153
83. Unhurt by the wind	154
84. The cable of love	155
85. Lovesickness	155
86. Soul-dissolving willow	156
87. The region of mist and flowers	157
88. The mandarin drake and duck	158
89. The fan	159
90. Knitting the silken fabric	160
91. Facing the lonely lamp	161
92. The peach-blossom fan	162
93. The waves at the prow	162
94. Hearing the cawing of the crow	163
95. Dressing the hair	164
96. Paying the flower-debt	165
97. Burn pure oil	166

Appendices   **167**

Appendix I : The original prefaces in Chinese   169
Appendix II: The original songs in Chinese   171

Bibliography   **195**

Index   **199**

Introduction

Romanization of Chinese names, places, dynasties

In these introductory pages and throughout the translation and notes appended, I have romanized the Chinese ideographs in their Cantonese pronunciation, to allow non-Cantonese speakers to pronounce them in the Cantonese way. Of the many available Cantonese–romanization systems I chose the one used by Sidney Lau in his *A Practical Cantonese–English Dictionary* as being the one that makes it somewhat easier to pronounce Cantonese words, because they are pronounced more or less as they are spelt. Needless to say, any romanization can only approximate to (and at times but distantly) the accepted Cantonese pronunciation.

Canton and the Cantonese language

Canton (廣州, *Gwong Jau*) is the capital of the *Gwong Dung* (廣東) province which is the southernmost of the 21 provinces of the People's Republic of China covering an area of 211 500 square kilometers (81 000 square miles), and is the largest city of South China. Since the 3rd century AD, the Chinese name of the city has been *Gwong Jau*. However, to Westerners the city is commonly known as Canton, a name that derives from that of the *Gwong Dung* province whose anglicized form gives Canton. Archaeology has revealed that the site of the city during the Chun (秦, *Ch'in*, 221–206 BC) and the Hon (漢, *Han*, 206 BC–AD 220) dynasties was slightly to the north of the present one. Today, Canton is situated just upstream of the head of the Pearl River Estuary, more than 90 miles (145 km) inland, west of the South China Sea. Canton, because of its geographical position, was the first port to be regularly visited by European traders and since the 3rd century AD has been the gateway for foreign influence.

During the Southern Sung (南宋, 1127–1279) dynasty Chinese seamen and traders sailed to Southeast Asia, thus opening the way for Chinese emigration in subsequent ages. In the late 13th century and throughout the 14th century, many Chinese families from North China moved into the *Gwong Dung* region in the wake of the Mongol conquest. A booming economy ensued as the Yuen (元, *Yüan*, 1206–1368) dynasty rulers encouraged maritime trade. The population of the *Gwong Dung* province, according to the *China Population Statistics Yearbook 1989* (中國人口統計年鑑, *Chung-Kwok Yan-Hau Tung-Kai Nin-Kaam*), was 59 283 134 in 1989, or about 5.5% of China's total population of 1 086 540 493 (men: 559 838 516; women: 526 701 977).

Not only noted as a historical centre of learning, Canton was also the centre of Sun Yat-sen's political activities; the cradle of the Nationalist revolution.

Cantonese (粵, *yuet*) is the variety of Chinese spoken in *Gwong Dung* and the southern *Gwong Sai* (廣西) provinces, including the important cities of Canton, Hong Kong and Macao, and by large numbers of overseas Chinese, the majority of whom are from areas where Cantonese is spoken. Cantonese preserves more features of ancient Chinese than do other major Chinese dialects, retaining most of the final consonants of the older languages. It has nine tones, in contrast to the four tones of *Putonghua* (普通話), Modern Standard Chinese, to distinguish meaning between words or word-elements that have the same arrangement of consonant and vowel sound; it has fewer initial consonants than Modern Standard Chinese and about twice as many distinctively different syllables. Numerous monosyllabic words are still used by the Cantonese people, while in *Putonghua* they have been ruled out in favour of disyllabic words. Many of these Cantonese monosyllabic words only appear in classical Chinese. *Colloquial Cantonese and Putonghua Equivalents* makes a number of interesting comparisons between Cantonese and Putonghua.

Why did I translate these songs?

Three reasons seemed compelling. My first reason: this is a collection of 97 love songs (or folk songs or ballads) in Cantonese, a language that is spoken but not 'written'. But when written, as in these songs, Chinese characters have frequently to be 'invented' or modified for ideas and words; and words and expressions can have their own Cantonese meaning, unintelligible to non-Cantonese. There have not been wanting, to use an understatement, those who decried Cantonese as a poor relative of the Chinese language; a rough, somewhat uncouth, less than educated tongue. Such linguistic chauvinism is not worth refuting. Nevertheless, with the wider use of *Putonghua*, it is possible that Cantonese in the years to come will decline as the spoken language of so many millions, and hence this small book of Cantonese songs be relegated (because Cantonese is not the official language) to a literary limbo. An English translation of them may go some way towards preserving this collection of emotionally powerful and dramatic songs.

My second reason: I translated these Cantonese songs to give a wider audience the opportunity of reading these songs in English; songs which were written in Cantonese over 160 years ago by Jiu Ji-yung (招子庸), and which enjoyed a long popularity. Jiu Ji-yung in his *Author's Preface* said these songs were 'written in the ninth month of the sixth year of the reign of Emperor Do Gwong (道光) (i.e. 1828)'. Do Gwong was born on 16 September 1782 in Peking (today's Beijing) and died there on 25 February 1850. His reign as the sixth emperor of the Ching dynasty (1644–1911) lasted from 1821 to 1851. A historical aside. In 1838 the emperor's attempts to stop the opium trade carried on by Western merchants resulted in the First Opium War between Britain and China (1839–42). Do Gwong died just as the great political-religious upheaval known as the Taiping Rebellion (1850–1864) was beginning to sweep South China.

My third reason: considering these songs to be of real value (they are in no sense a marginal work) I judged a re-translation was due. Good works should be regularly re-translated (could one say, every twenty years?) to make them more available to the contemporary reader.

I say 're-translation' because I have to hand two books brought out in 1904 by Cecil Clementi, 'MA (Late Demy of Magdalen College, Oxford, Member of the Land Court for the New Territory, Hong Kong)' and later to become Sir Cecil Clementi, Governor of Hong Kong (1925–30). One is the Chinese text of these songs (粵謳, *Yuet Au*), together with a small glossary of difficult words and expressions; the other is his own translation of them into English, under the title of *Cantonese Love Songs*, with explanatory notes. After a lapse of over 80 years, another slightly more up-to-date translation is needed. In recent years I have seen very few reprints of the original Cantonese text and no copy of a translation into English.

The translation of these songs

While (partially) agreeing with my late friend, J A Turner, S J (1909–71) who translated Chinese Tong (唐 , *T'ang,* 618–907) dynasty poetry into English poetry, that to translate poetry, even with verbal accuracy, into anything less than poetry, is simply not to translate poetry, nevertheless, not being a poet, I have not dared to attempt translating these songs into English poetry (or songs). Thus the rhythm of the songs is necessarily lost; the rhyming of the last syllable in each line is lost; the melodic element of Cantonese is lost; much is lost. Indeed, much of the original is necessarily lost in any translation. The artist may paint the flower but not the scent. I am fully aware that a translation can no more be definitive than the interpretation of a piece of music. An 'ideal translation' is unreal; translations can always be improved. I would be very pleased if this work led others to translate these songs more satisfactorily. However, I would like to think all is not lost. Although no translation can do what the original songs do, maybe in this new English translation something like the voice of the singer will ring in your mind's ear. I am sure that even in the prose translation the reader will savour something of the original songs. Their essence and spirit and moving insight do come through: the love given and spurned; the disappointment, the yearning, the hopes; the singer's passionate insistence on her constancy; the frenzied passion and thoughts of suicide; the ambivalent emotions of love and hatred for her lover — all expressed with the utmost delicacy, and very frequently both through symbols and through allusions to the classics, history, legend, poetry and other aspects of Chinese culture. Footnotes (with Arabic numerals) at the end of each song explain the allusions and indicate where a similar idea, emotion, or topic is dealt with elsewhere in the songs. Square brackets [i.e. . . .], (which are not part of the original songs), within the translated version clarify the meaning of certain words or phrases. When I refer to the works of William Frederick Mayers (*The Chinese Reader's Manual*) and Herbert Allen Giles (*A Chinese Biographical Dictionary*) I do so by giving a number, e.g., Mayers # 660, Giles # 2070, because in both of these works individual entries are numbered with Arabic numerals.

The prefaces

The songs are preceded by the author Jiu Ji-yung's own short preface, by ten dedicatory prefaces written pseudonymously, and lastly by a twelfth preface. This last preface, dealing with the 'notation of the Chinese pipa music' which accompanies these songs, I have omitted for the practical reason that it is less than clear to readers not familiar with this musical instrument.

The ten dedicatory prefaces sketch the theme of these songs and are almost as full of allusions as the songs themselves. They praise very highly their author Jiu Ji-yung (who is compared to previous 'great poets' and even to the classics) for his poetic excellence; for composing these songs in Cantonese; for his unerring understanding and vigorous delineation of the women in the 'houses of entertainment' he writes of; and finally for giving us 'a glimpse of the whole world'.

The theme of the songs

The author of the Fourth Preface (line 4) writes:

> These songs sing of mutual grief, mutual tenderness; now ridiculing, now warning; they fear to sing of happiness, loving to sing of sorrow.

This is true. On the surface, we have nothing of the passionate fire of love, the ecstaticism we find in Western cultures; nothing approaching Sappho, Horace or Ovid. But through the sorrow and suffering, anguish and disappointment the singer experiences, we do see what requited love would have meant for her: a love no whit less ardent, vibrant, passionate and sublime. Throughout there is the constant theme of sorrow and parting, abandonment and dejection. Her suffering overwhelms her, because her love is so passionate. She calls on the traditional love of the phoenix and its companion, the fidelity of the mandarin drake and duck, the two fish that swim together, the birds that fly in pairs, to accentuate her own unreciprocated love.

The songs tell the story of her rejected love and her unquenchable yearnings. Because of this I suggest that the best way to read them is as if you were reading a book. On your first reading, do not choose a song at random as you might choose a poem in an anthology. Rather take this collection of songs as the unfolding of the tragic and piteous story of a young courtesan, forced to live in a 'house of entertainment' until she can either ransom herself or be ransomed by another or, failing that, to remain there for as long as she is lucrative to the its owner, that is, her keeper. The more you read them, the more they grow on you; the more you identify with the emotions of the singer. Read them slowly, check the allusions and references, and you will realize how perfectly the author has interpreted the mind and feelings of these 'lost women in the houses of entertainment'. Then go back and re-read your favourite songs.

The word 'courtesan' in English, while strictly meaning a 'court-mistress', was very frequently a euphemism for prostitute. The courtesan in China, however, was not a prostitute in the usual sense of the word. In Europe a courtesan or mistress had neither legal status nor legal rights, but in China she had. Until 1911, when it was legally abolished in China, concubinage had been an age-old institution evolved in a patriarchal society to provide sons. If a wife was barren or only had daughters, the husband could, without his wife's consent, and his action was sanctioned by custom and law, take a concubine and hope to prolong the patrilineal line. The young woman (or sometimes more than one) was taken into the household where she became a fully accepted member of the family, as a kind of secondary wife. If the concubine gave birth to a son, her prestige increased. Ideally, concubinage was to produce children, male preferably. But motives for taking a concubine were not always the purest. The motive could be infatuation or lust or perhaps the need for pleasing female company. It is said the practice did, however, serve as a safety-valve in a society where marriages were arranged:

a man was free to choose his own concubine. The courtesan who sings these songs hopes her lover will ransom her and take her either as his wife or concubine. A concubine was sometimes chosen from among the sing-song girls, the courtesans, the polished *musiciennes* or the 'hostesses' in houses of entertainment. Pretty girls are always in demand.

This term 'sing-song girl' was coined by foreigners resident in China who did not know how otherwise to describe her. Her main accomplishment was singing, but she also entertained during feasts and banquets where the guests were almost exclusively men. She was not a prostitute in the usually accepted sense, and these houses of entertainment were not strictly brothels, although the difference at times could be marginal. The institution of 'sing-song girl', far younger than that of concubinage, was created about 2000 years ago by an emperor of the Hon dynasty who, in extending his empire to central Asia, saw the need of providing female entertainment and amusement for his troops.

In his historical novel covering the years 1895–1904, *The Fabulous Concubine*, Chang Hsin-hai describes how these sing-song girls were purchased, and how they could win their freedom. Golden Orchid, the heroine of the novel, and at this point mistress of a sing-song house of entertainment, was accused of murdering Phoenix Bell, one of her sing-song girls. As part of her defence she explains how Phoenix Bell had come to work for her. Phoenix Bell had previously been employed in a cheap house of entertainment, where she had a met a man who wanted to marry her. Her keeper demanded a very high ransom fee before she would release Phoenix Bell, but all the man could afford was seven hundred dollars, and so nothing came of it. The owner came to hear that the man in question had said he would abduct the girl and save himself the seven hundred dollars. It was then that Phoenix Bell's keeper visited Golden Orchid offering to sell Phoenix Bell, to avoid a financial loss if the man were true to his word. Golden Orchid agreed to pay this woman one thousand dollars for Phoenix Bell, and an additional two hundred dollars to the man who had acted as go-between. The plight of the singer of these songs is hardly different. She hopes her lover will soon return to ransom her from the infernal house of entertainment.

These songs are simple, direct, almost conversational. Nothing forced or artificial, no striving for effect despite the frequent use of euphemism. Simply the outpouring of emotion deeply felt. We come to understand the stark reality behind the delicate euphemisms used throughout for the courtesan, the house of entertainment, the behaviour of its patrons, and their attitude to the young 'flowers' they hope will entertain them for a while. One Chinese euphemism for brothel/house of entertainment is: 煙花地, *yin fa de*i, literally translated as the 'smoke-flower region' (suggesting that a courtesan's life, like smoke or mist, obvious symbols of transitoriness, is dissipated in the house of entertainment); another is: 花叢, *fa chung*, in literal translation, 'the flower groves'. Yet another euphemism for brothel/house of entertainment is 青樓, *ching-lau*. The single character 青, *ching*, covers all shades of colour from dark grey through blue to green, and even at times can mean black. The character 樓, *lau*, refers to a storeyed building, a tower, an upper storey. However, while almost all dictionaries give the meaning of *ching-lau* as 'brothel', the *ching-lau* was not strictly speaking a brothel, but merely a place of entertainment (perhaps something like the modern pleasure-seeker's club?). Obviously there would always be male patrons who, not completely satisfied by the young ladies' musical accomplishments, had their eye on other less subtle forms of 'entertainment'. These three expressions in literal translation would suggest the tenderness of a romantic love; unfortunately not the horrifying reality the euphemisms referred to.

The Fourth Preface continues in lines 7 and 8:

> Listening to Jiu Ji-yung's songs you choke with grief and distress; you are excited and roused; you are crushed and oppressed. Why, even the fish and the dragons come out from the sea!
>
> Do you know why? Because his songs sing of human feelings and give us a glimpse of the whole world.

The background against which the songs unfold is indeed harrowing. The young girl or young wife was sold by her parents or by her husband to the house of entertainment for a number of years, in many cases to pay a debt. The keeper of the house of entertainment would try to resell at a profit or failing that would train her in the arts of seduction (pretty well of prostitution). The young girl or wife must save enough money to redeem herself from this way of life, or she must find a true-hearted lover to pay the ransom for her, and take her as his wife or concubine. No other escape was open to these unfortunate women. In a few of the Songs it appears she adopts the role of a man to encourage her sister-courtesans to escape from this hell upon earth.

A brilliant young scholar whose studies have called him to Peking is the object of the singer's love. On him she places her hopes. Into his hands she trustingly gives herself. She will not let her love for him stand in the way of his advancement, and she hopes he will come back to her covered in academic glory.

Before he leaves they spend time together and she entreats him to write to her, to be constant to her. He promises he will. But no word comes from him. She almost echoes Shakespeare's Proteus (*Two Gentlemen of Verona*):

> O Heaven! were man
> But constant, he were perfect. That one error
> Fills him with faults . . .

Lonely and inconsolable, bruised with adversity, her thoughts are those of Ophelia:

> And I, of ladies most deject and wretched,
> That suck'd the honey of his music vows . . .

In secret she cries, not wanting to tell others of her distress for fear they should come to know of her infatuated yearning for her absent lover. The house of entertainment, despite its outward showiness and splendour, is hell on earth, a place that as an innocent child she never thought she could sink to. Although she still has to entertain her 'guests', continue her life in 'the region of mist and flowers', she is more than ever alone, with no-one on whom she can rely for support. She looks carefully at her lamp for an omen from its snuff that will tell her of her lover's imminent return. Even in the depths of despair, she dreams of rising pure as the lotus out of stagnant water; of becoming with her lover 'the virtuous woman and passionate man'.

Time is running out and he has not returned to ransom her. She knows full well:

> The flowers anew, returning seasons bring!
> But beauty faded has no second spring.
> (Ambrose Philips. c.1674–1749)

Looking in the mirror she sees 'Grief that's beauty's canker' (*The Tempest*) and wonders where is the face that once was reflected there. Half the years of her life wasted. Nothing to show for them. No-one to rely on, to save and redeem her, to support and protect her. All she can do is to call on *Gwoon Yam* (觀音) for help.

Distraught, her thoughts fly in all directions; and in certain songs we feel the lack of logical coherence between one idea and the next. But her emotional state is perfectly delineated. Now she hates her lover but still cries in secret for him to return. Now she never wants to see him again; but strains her eyes watching for his return. Now she decides to rid herself of him forever and be happy without him; in the next line she tells us she will meet him in her dreams and passionately embrace him. The Tong poet Wai Jong (韋莊, graduated 902) expresses her mood of secret sorrow and, in her dreams, her secret solace.

> The seventeenth of the fourth moon —
> It was this day last year —
> I saw you last.
> I bowed my head, but shed no tear;
> My brows were knitted fast.
>
> My heart was broken, if you but knew!
> But still in dreams I follow you.
> Except the moon
> In the far sky
> None knows of this but I.

(Translation by John Turner, in *Gems of Classical Chinese Poetry in Various English Translations*.)

四月十七

正是去年今日

別君時

忍淚佯低面

含羞半斂眉

不知魂已斷

空有夢相隨

除卻天邊月

沒人知

While she believes that everything has been pre-ordained, she nevertheless rails against ungenerous fate. Why me? Why do I have to suffer so much? She echoes what the anonymous poet of the Eastern Hon dynasty (AD 25–220) had written and whose poem is found in the collection entitled: *Nineteen Ancient Poems* (古詩十九首), # 15.

> The years of a lifetime do not reach a hundred,
>   Yet they contain a thousand years' sorrow.

(Translation by Arthur Waley, in *Gems of Classical Chinese Poetry in Various English Translations*.)

生年不滿百

常懷千歲憂

Why does fate separate people, especially those in love? If only fate had decreed that 'separation' would never exist! She fully understands the line from *The Elegies of Chor* (楚辭):

> No sorrow is greater than the parting of the living.

悲莫悲兮生別離

Indeed, the thoughts expressed by the poet Lui Boon-jung (呂本中) are exactly hers:

> I wish you were like the moon on the river.
> South, north, east, or west,
> South, north, east or west,
> You'd always be near and never part.
>
> I wish you weren't like the moon on the river.
> Full for a time, it wanes again.
> Full for a time, it wanes again.
> How long the wait for a full reunion?

(Translation by Hans Frankel, in *Gems of Classical Chinese Poetry in Various English Translations*.)

> 恨君不似江樓月
> 南北東西
> 南北東西
> 只有相隨無別離
>
> 恨君卻似江樓月
> 暫滿還虧
> 暫滿還虧
> 待得團圓是幾時

Symbols and symbolism

The French poet, Charles Baudelaire (1821–67) in his *Correspondences*, has the following lines:

> La nature est un temple ou de vivants piliers
> Laissent parfois sortir de confuses paroles;
> L'homme y passe a travers des forets de symboles
> Qui l'observent avec des regards familiers.
>
> (Nature is a temple in which living columns
> Sometimes emit confused words;
> Man approaches it through forests of symbols
> Which observe him with familiar glances.)

In these songs, the reader also passes through a forest of symbols, whether these be flowers or trees or fruit or mountains or rivers or birds or fish or butterflies or bees or moths, the full moon, the stars, the seasons (Love is typified by spring with its wealth of flowers in blossom, the stirring of the sap; old age is autumn with its falling leaves and sere complexion . . .), or even the way she adorns her hair. One might say that almost every object is taken as a symbol in these songs.

What is meant by the word 'symbol' which is used so frequently in reference to Chinese ideographs? To paraphrase C G Jung (from his *Man and His Symbols*): A word or a picture (painting) is symbolic if it contains more than can be grasped at first glance. Wolfram Eberhard in his *A Dictionary of Chinese Symbols* refers to *On the Language of Symbolism in Chinese Art* by Ferdinand Lessing who says the 'symbolic language' of the Chinese is a second form of language which penetrates all communication in Chinese. This symbolic language is, as it were, a second-tier communication level, of greater potency than ordinary language, and extremely rich in nuances.

In the following paragraphs I deal with some of the more common symbols used in these songs. In fact, everything: rocks, water, clouds, animals, trees, flowers, etc., have not only their own 'surface' meaning but also this second-tier meaning beyond themselves. Everything is imbued with symbolic meaning. One example: the standard one (but which does not occur in these songs) is that of the bird, the bat. In Chinese the word for 'bat' is 蝠, *fuk*, and the word for 'happiness' is 福, *fuk*; both words are pronounced in exactly the same way. So the bat is taken as a symbol of happiness, good fortune, good luck. Five bats therefore suggest the Five Blessings: a long life, riches, health, love of virtue and a natural death.

The Chinese developed through symbols an enormously rich sensual imagery to express their sensuality and erotic impulses. For example 'jade-fluid' is semen or vaginal secretion, 'playing with jade' is a metaphor for sexual intercourse. A young girl has a 'jade bearing' and 'jade thighs', and her breasts can be likened to 'warm jade'. The female bust is 'the jade mountain'. 'Fragrant clouds' refers to a woman's hair when it falls free. 'Cloud mist' refers to a woman's ample breasts. A woman's pubic hair is 'in the depths of the willow shade'. The sexual orgasm can be described as 'the soul flying over the heavens'. The 'well' character stands for the vagina. 'Willow feelings and flower wishes' are sexual desires. In my opinion these songs contain a number of euphemistic references to objects and activities that can best be described as erotic.

The second-tier meaning of butterfly and bee occurs frequently in these songs. The butterfly is the symbol of a lover sipping nectar from the calyx of a flower (a female symbol). Sexual intercourse can be described as the activity of the 'loved-crazed butterfly and wild bee'. The bee also represents a young man in love; the flower round which it flies the girl he loves.

The moon as symbol

An important symbol is the moon. In addition to its 'lunar reality' and legends attached to it, the full moon is a symbol of the perfection and fulfilment of true love. About the symbolism of the moon, Mircea Eliade in his *The Myth of the Eternal Return* writes:

> The moon is the first of the creatures to die, but also the first to live again. We have shown elsewhere the importance of lunar myths in the organization of the first coherent theories concerning death and resurrection, fertility and regeneration...
>
> The phases of the moon-appearance, increase, wane, disappearance, followed by reappearance after three nights of darkness, have played an immense part in the elaboration of cyclical concepts...
>
> This assimilation is important not only because it shows us the 'lunar' structure of universal becoming, but also because of its optimistic consequences: just as the disappearance of the moon is never final, since it is necessarily followed by a new moon, the disappearance of man is not final either...

For Eliade the moon symbolizes the cyclical view of life (continual rebirth until Nirvana is attained) which is opposed to the Judaeo-Christian linear one. The Moon Festival is one of the three great annual Chinese feasts, and it takes place on the fifteenth day of the eighth month, at the full moon of the autumn equinox. Traditionally Chinese families gather together (even coming from very great distances) to celebrate their chief festival: the Lunar New Year, which is also calculated by the moon.

The moon is inhabited by a person who is considered the moon 'goddess': Seung Ngoh (嫦娥). She was the wife of the mythological archer Hau Ngai (后羿). It was believed that originally there were ten suns, one for each hour of the day, but that one day all ten appeared simultaneously in the sky threatening to burn up the earth with their heat. Hau Ngai brought down nine of these suns with his magic bow. However, one day he arrived home to find that his wife had drunk the elixir of immortality the gods had given him. So angry was he that the frightened Seung Ngoh fled to the moon, with her husband in pursuit. She asked protection of the Hare who fought with Hau Ngai and made him desist from punishing her. Seung Ngoh has lived in the moon ever since. She is represented as a very beautiful young woman and her name is often mentioned in novels and poems, and also in these songs. (See Song 24, Line 12, note.)

The full moon is round. For the Chinese, roundness is perfection. Hajime Nakamura, in his *Ways of Thinking of Eastern Peoples: India-China-Tibet-Japan*, says that when the Buddhist scriptures were translated into Chinese, the Indian word 'perfect' was rendered as 'round and filled'.

The perfect doctrine in Buddhism was, in certain systems, translated as 'the round doctrine' (圓教, *yuen gaau*) meaning complete, whole, 'full-orbed', comprehensive. This equivalence between 'perfection' and the 'circle or the quality of roundness' is peculiar to the Chinese. The circle (or wheel) does not have an exactly similar meaning for the Indians.

By Moonlight, written by the Tong dynasty poet Jeung Gau-ling (張九齡, 673–740), will help the reader to appreciate the author's use of the full moon as a symbol in these songs:

> Over the sea the round moon rises bright,
> And floods the horizon with its silver light.
> In absence lovers grieve that nights should be,
> But all the livelong night I think of thee.
> I blow my lamp out to enjoy the rest,
> And shake the gathering dewdrop from my vest.
> Alas! I cannot share with thee these beams.
> So lay me down to seek thee in my dreams.

(Translation by Herbert A Giles, in *Gems of Classical Chinese Poetry in Various English Translations*.)

望月懷遠

海上生明月　天涯共此時
情人怨遙夜　竟夕起想思
滅燭憐光滿　披衣覺露滋
不堪盈手贈　還寢夢佳期

Another of the *Nineteen Ancient Poems*, # 19, epitomizes the singer's agitated state of mind:

> How white the clear moon shines!
> Shines through the silk curtains of my bed.
> Racked by sorrow I cannot sleep;
> I take my robe, pace to and fro,
> My absent lover may rejoice in travel,
> But I would wish his early return.
> I stand outside, alone, uncertain.
> To whom can I disclose my grief?
> I stare about me, return to my room,
> My robe wet with falling tears.

(Translation by Kenneth P H Ho, in *The Nineteen Ancient Poems*.)

明月何皎皎
照我羅牀幃
憂愁不能寐
攬衣起徘徊

客行雖云樂
不如早旋歸
出戶獨彷徨
愁思當告誰
引領還入房
淚下沾裳衣

Another poem by Jeung Gau-ling (張九齡) captures her mood when she compares herself to the waning moon:

> Ever since the day
> You went,
> And left me here alone,
> My lord,
> The world is changed!
>
> Upon the loom
> The web, half woven, hangs
> Untouched.
>
> My thoughts
> Are all of you,
> And I am like you silver moon,
> Whose glory wanes
> And grows more pale
> Each night!

(Translation by Henry H Hart, in *Gems of Classical Chinese Poetry in Various English Translations*.)

自君之出矣
不復理殘機
思君如滿月
夜夜減清輝

During the Tong dynasty pearls were seen as tiny moons. In fact, in ancient times pearls were considered the concrete essence of the moon distilled through the secret workings in nature of 陰, *yam*, the feminine or secondary principle as opposed to 陽, *yeung*, the masculine or primary principle associated with the sun) within the shell of the mussel which produced it. The symbolic relationship between pearls and women is expressed by the Tong poet Sit To (薛濤) (see Ninth Preface, line 6, note 27):

> White as the moon,
> round, bright,
> translucent to the core.
>
> Its brilliance seems reflected
> from the crystal lunar keep.

(Translation by Jeanne Larsen, in her *Brocade River Poems*.)

皎潔圓明內外通
清光似照水晶宮

In contrast, for Juliet the moon was a symbol of inconstancy:

(To Romeo): O! Swear not by the moon, the inconstant moon,
That monthly changes in her circled orb,
Lest that thy love prove likewise variable.

The flower as symbol

Perhaps the most commonly used symbol in these songs is the flower. In Chinese, as in many other cultures, the flower symbolizes a beautiful woman. And in these songs the flower symbolizes her fragrance, youth, attractiveness, delicacy, tenderness, loveliness and, forebodingly, frailty and transience. In Chinese culture many flowers have their own symbolic meaning. The willow supplied poets of the Tong (618–907) and painters of the Sung (960–1279) dynasties with a never-failing motif. Because of the willow's beauty and suppleness, it has become the emblem of the female sex. Moreover, the whole body of a beautiful woman should look like a willow: slim, supple and curved. Taoists take the white plum blossom as the symbol of winter; the peony, of spring; the lotus, of summer; the chrysanthemum, of autumn.

The pine and the bamboo symbolize longevity; the narcissus and the peony, good fortune. The bamboo is particularly rich in symbolism and women can easily identify themselves with this plant. The bamboo is self-contained, growing by itself and not intermixed with other species. The bamboo is spiritually noble and modest, with its empty heart (虛心, *hui sam*), suggesting not only the hollow stalk of the plant but Buddhist and Taoist philosophical detachment from worldly affairs. The bamboo is constant, remaining green all winter. The Chinese character for the joints or nodes between sections of the bamboo is 節, *jit,* and this same character means moral integrity, chastity. Each month also had its symbolic flower. In addition, the Chinese plum-tree together with the bamboo and the pine were designated as the 'Three Friends of Winter': they do not die, they remain constant and they blossom before the spring comes. They symbolize hardiness and purity. Particularly popular is the plum blossom because its five petals symbolize the 'Five Blessings'.

Jeung Chiu (張潮) in his essay: *Sweet Dream Shadows* (幽夢影) writes about the moon and flowers and beautiful women, topics referred to constantly throughout these songs. The following passage is taken from *Gems From Chinese Literature Rendered Into English* by Lam Yue-tong (林宇堂):

One should not see flowers wither, should not see the moon decline below the horizon, or see a beautiful woman die in her youth. One should see flowers when they are in full bloom, after planting the flower; should see the moon when it is full, after waiting for the moon . . .

One should see a beautiful woman when she is gay and happy. If one loves beautiful women with the same heart that he loves flowers, he feels a special charm in them; if one loves flowers with the same heart that he loves beauties, he feels a special tenderness and protective affection.

One feels tender towards even a good potted flower that he has just bought; how much more should he be tender towards a 'talking flower'.

Beautiful women are better than flowers in that they understand human language, and flowers are better than beautiful women in that they give off fragrance; but if one cannot have both at the same time, he should forsake the fragrant ones and take the talking ones.

Most of the flowers that are seductive and beautiful are not very fragrant, and most flowers that have layers upon layers of petals do not bear fruit. Alas, rare is a perfect personality. Only the lotus has fragrance and fruit.

The plum flower makes a man feel high-minded; the orchid make a man feel like a recluse; the chrysanthemum makes a man simple-hearted, the lotus make a man quiet or mild-tempered; the peony makes a man generous, the bamboo and the banana tree make a man charming, the pine tree makes a man romantic, the phoenix tree [See Song 11, Part 4, note] makes a man lucid; the willow makes a man sentimental.

If a beauty should have the face of a flower, the voice of a bird, the soul of the moon, the expression of a willow, bones of jade and skin of snow and ice, the charm of an autumn lake and a heart of poetry, I should be perfectly satisfied.

論花與美人

花不可見其落，月不可見其沉，美人不可見其夭。

種花須見其開，待月須見其滿 ⋯ 美人須見其暢適。

以愛花之心愛美人，則領略自饒別趣；以愛美人之心愛花，則護惜倍有深情。

買得一本好花，猶且愛護而憐惜之；矧其為"解語花"乎！

美人之勝於花者，解語也；花之勝於美人者，生香也。二者不可得兼，舍生香而解語者也。

凡花色之嬌媚者多不甚香，瓣之千層者多不結實。甚矣全才之難也！兼之者，其惟蓮乎。

梅令人高，蘭令人幽，菊令人野，蓮令人淡，牡丹令人豪，蕉與竹令人韻，松令人逸，桐令人清，柳令人感。

所謂美人者，以花為貌，以鳥為聲，以月為神，以柳為態，以玉為骨，以冰雪為膚，以秋水為姿，以詩詞為心，吾無間然矣。

Talented men who are at the same time handsome, and beautiful ladies who at the same time can write, Jeung Chiu suggests, can never live a long life. This not only because the gods are jealous of them, but also because such persons are the treasure not of one generation alone, but of all ages. The creator does not want to leave them in this world too long, for fear of sacrilege.

Concluding this passage, Jeung Chiu refers to an ancient writer who had said that if there were no flowers and no moon and no beautiful women, he would not want to be born into this world.

The Chinese have numerous phrases about flowers, a few of which are given here to help the reader appreciate more fully the many references to 'flowers' in these songs:

> Amid the moonlit flowers (花前月下, *fa chin yuet ha*) in olden times referred to the meeting-place of lovers.
> Fair like a flower, beautiful as jade (花容玉貌 , *fa yung yuk maau*) refers to a young girl's beautiful face.
> No flower is in bloom for hundred days (花無百日紅 , *fa mo baak yat hung*) refers to the transiency of flowers, the transiency of beauty.
> The mind's flower in full bloom (心花怒放 , *sam fa no fong*) refers to being wild with joy, elated, extremely happy.
> The flower in bloom, the moon full round (花好月圓 , *fa ho yuet yuen*) is an expression used to greet newly-weds. The fuller text reads:
> (I wish) flowers to retain bloom; man to retain health; the moon to retain roundness (願花長好　人長健　月長圓 , *uen fa cheung ho, yan cheung kin, yuet cheung yuen*).

I conclude this part of the Introduction with words spoken by Marina who had been sold to a brothel-keeper (*Pericles, Prince of Tyre*). They summarize in another language and from another age and culture the feelings of frustration expressed in these Cantonese songs:

> For me,
> That am a maid, though most ungentle fortune
> Have placed me in this sty . . .
> O, that the gods
> Would set me free from this unhallow'd place.

Buddhism

In this Introduction are some pages on Buddhism to help the reader with the many references and allusions to Buddhism contained in the songs. Indeed, without some knowledge of Buddhism, in which the author or at least the singer firmly believes, these songs can scarcely be understood, much less appreciated. Should the reader not be familiar, even in a general way, with Buddhism, then I hope the pages on Buddhism will help towards understanding something about the Buddha himself and his teaching; his assistant *bodhisattvas,* one of whom is the most popular Chinese 'goddess' *Gwoon Yam*; his exhortation to perform good deeds and to show universal compassion; accepting one's *karma* of a previous existence; the cycle of re-birth; this 'dusty world'; prayer and meditation; praying to Buddhist images; reaching the isles of the Blest. Obviously most Chinese will be familiar with the teaching and practice of Buddhism in China.

The spread of Buddhism to China

The home of Buddhism lies in what is now South Behar, west of Bengal and south of the Ganges.

The historical Buddha, Siddhartha Gautama, died in either 480 or 380 BC. During the first two centuries of its existence Buddhism was confined to the Ganges valley. Initially, Buddhism consisted of small, scattered communities of monks, subject to simple disciplinary rules. It then spread rapidly throughout India and beyond. In the middle of the 3rd century BC it began to expand in all directions: southwards across the sea to Sri Lanka, and from there to what is now Burma, Indonesia, Thailand and Indo-China; northwards to Kashmir in northwest India, from where it spread to (and by the 1st century was already established in) Central Asia, and was first introduced into China during the reign of Emperor Ming (AD 68–75) of Eastern (or Later) Hon dynasty.

Juk Faat-laan (竺法蘭, the Chinese transliteration of his name: Indu-dharmaraksa), was a monk from Central India who is said to have first brought Buddhism to China in AD 67, at the request of Emperor Ming. He lived at White Horse Temple (白馬寺, *Baak Ma Chi*) near Lok Yeung (洛陽), said to be the first Buddhist temple in China, built by the emperor for Juk Faat-laan and the other Indian monk who accompanied him, and there he translated five sutras. The temple was so called because the two Indian monks were said to have brought the Buddhist scriptures from India on the backs of white horses. In China the Hon (漢) dynasty (206 BC–AD 220) was in power, and during the 1st century AD at least three centres of Buddhism were in existence: at Paang Sing (彭城) in the lower Yangtze region of East China; at Lok Yeung where foreign monks organized a translating centre; at Tonkin (now in Vietnam). Both Hinayana and Mahayana sutras were translated into Chinese soon after the first introduction of Buddhism. The worship of Avalokitesvara, whose name became in Chinese: 觀音, *Gwoon Yam*, was introduced into China as early as the 1st century AD, and by the 6th century had already entered all Buddhist temples.

From China, by way of Korea, Buddhism spread to Japan. It has been accepted that the official date for the introduction of Buddhism into Japan was AD 522.

In the course of its early development splinter groups emerged from the 'body of the elders', followed by further subdivisions in varying degrees from the parent body. Margaret and James Stutley in their *A Dictionary of Hinduism* note that history records only the decline and virtual disappearance of organized Buddhism in India: in the home of the Buddha, Buddhism entered into and became an integral part of the Hindu culture.

Buddhist influence on Chinese culture

Propagating Buddhism in China was not easy. It met with a millenary culture, a tradition of rationalism (as in Confucianism), a solid social structure, the cult of the family, and the authority of the state. Buddhism had necessarily to develop slowly, being often obstructed by a completely different mode of thought and expression. For example, the doctrine of *karma* (業 , *yip*), past actions determining one's existence in the present, and present actions determining one's existence in the future, was incomprehensible to the Chinese. Furthermore, the Buddhist monastic organization represented a dangerous innovation that allowed or even encouraged men to withdraw from the service of the state; such a withdrawal being detrimental to the national economy.

It had to cope with Taoism which in its literary and speculative form was reserved for the few, in its magical form for the many. At first, ambiguities and misunderstandings plagued both Buddhists and Chinese. Translation into Chinese of the Buddhist Mahayana works in the 2nd century had used Taoist expression for key Buddhist concepts, and certain Buddhist schools were formed whose discussions had to be understood on the basis of a Taoist vocabulary. Despite the Indian origin of the new religion, some circles identified Lo Ji (老子), one of the founding fathers of Taoism, with the Buddha.

Although gaining strength during the 2nd century crisis in Confucianism, Buddhism remained on the outside, isolated in small communities. However, by the 4th century it had brought about a new ferment of ideas in China.

Buddhism exerted a tremendous influence on Chinese culture. A number of Buddhist ideas stimulated the development of neo-Confucianism. Although the neo-Confucianists continued to use terms found in the Confucian classics, they interpreted them in the light of Buddhism, thus making the neo-Confucianist system incomprehensible to anyone not versed in the Buddhism of the age. Buddhism allied itself closely with Taoism and borrowed from it. And the reverse happened. The Taoists admitted their practice of making statues and images had been borrowed from the Buddhists. Even the Taoist canon, modelled on the Buddhist Tripitaka (三藏, *Saam Chong*), now consists of three sections, each section divided into twelve categories. Buddhist words and phrases found their way into the Chinese language. Finally and most important of all, the doctrine and practices of the Buddhists, their pantheon and their ceremonies affected profoundly the religious life of the Chinese. The Buddhist aspiration towards serenity and peace, strengthened by a total rejection of violence, were easily understood by Taoist masters. Offering a new hope to all in the *Bodhisattva* (菩薩, *Po Saat*) ideal, and a way to an easy salvation as promulgated by the devotional schools, the Buddhist gospel could not fail to attract.

In literature, the Chinese learned the art of imaginative and descriptive story-telling from the Indians, being greatly influenced by the style of the Mahayana sutras. They began to give freer rein to their imagination. The Chinese novel, *A Record of a Trip to the West* (西遊記, *Sai Yau Gei*) from the Ming dynasty (1368–1644), is but one example. Other examples of rich, imaginative and romantic literature could be drawn from the novels and short stories of the Ming and Ching (1644–1911) dynasties.

The new terms coined by the Buddhists and which found their way into the Chinese language can be divided into two classes:
1. those which translate Buddhist concepts, for example: bitter sea (苦海, *foo hoi*), western paradise (西天, *sai tin*), ignorance (無明, *mo ming*), destiny or *karma* (業, *yip*), to leave one's home to become a monk or nun (出家, *chut ga*);
2. those which transliterate Pali or Sanskrit words, for example: pagoda (in Chinese 塔, *taap*) from *thupa*; idol (in Chinese 菩薩, *po saat*) from *bodhisattva*; jasmine (in Chinese 茉莉, *moot lei*) from *mallika*; monk (in Chinese 僧, *jang*) from *sangha*; naam mo (in Chinese 南無, *naam mo*) from *namas*.

The Buddhist concept of 'emptiness'(空, *hung*) influenced Chinese landscape artists, for whom all nature is to be converted to an unsubstantial plane: mountains, trees and rivers are but the creation of the mind and are subject to the laws of impermanence. In the Sung dynasty (960–1279) landscape mountains are to be seen as if floating in the distance having no real existence. In this way is illustrated the basic Mahayana doctrine of emptiness.

Sculpture, of all the Arts, received the greatest impetus from the introduction of Buddhism to China during the Hon dynasty; from the expansion of Buddhism during the Six Dynasties (AD 220–582) and during the Tong (618–907) period. Statues and carved relics of Buddhas and *bodhisattvas* were made by the thousands and these represent the pinnacle of Chinese religious art.

Buddhism, through its pantheon of the compassionate Buddhas and *bodhisattvas* offering refuge to those in need, enriched, deepened and broadened Chinese religious life, making it more meaningful in terms of human sympathy, love and compassion for all living creatures. One by-product was the establishment of charitable institutions such as hospitals, orphanages, dispensaries and rest-houses or homes for the aged.

In the course of time various *bodhisattvas* took on a Chinese appearance. *Maitreya* (彌勒 , *nei lak*), meaning 'friendly, benevolent', the future Buddha, became the well-fed, pot-bellied, stomach-bared, laughing, genial figure holding a sack who greets visitors to the temple. He is known as the Laughing Buddha, or as the Cloth-bag Monk (布袋和尚 , *Bo Doi Woh Seung*). Avalokitesvara (觀音, *Gwoon Yam*) was transformed into a Chinese female deity.

The historical Buddha

According to a Buddhist tradition in China and Japan, the Buddha, Siddhartha Gautama, the historical founder of Buddhism, was born on 8 April 1029 BC and died on 15 February 949 BC. Western studies, however, place him about 500 years later; and his dates are given as either: 560–480 BC or 460–380 BC. The future Buddha's conception was miraculous. Queen Maya, who was forty-five years of age and childless, saw in a dream the future Buddha enter her womb in the shape of a lovely little elephant as white as snow. At this moment the whole universe showed its joy: musical instruments played without being touched, rivers stopped flowing to contemplate the Buddha, trees and plants were covered with flowers and the lakes with lotuses. When the time of his birth drew near, Queen Maya went to the Lumbini Gardens (in what is now Paderia in southern Nepal) and there, standing and holding on to a branch of a tree with her right hand, she gave birth to her son who came through her right side without causing her pain. He began at once to walk and a lotus appeared as soon as his foot touched the earth. The lotus is of almost unique importance in Chinese symbolism, largely, it would seem, because of Buddhist influence. The lotus comes out of the mire, but itself is not sullied; it is inwardly empty but outwardly upright; it has no branches but it smells sweet. It is the symbol of purity.

Five days after his birth he received the significant name of

Siddhartha, meaning 'One who has achieved his goal'. On the seventh day after his birth, his mother died of joy and was re-born amongst the gods. He was the son of Shuddhodana, King of the Sakyas, a small tribe whose kingdom was located in the foothills of the Himalayas, south of what is now central Nepal. His family name was Gautama (meaning 'best cow'). He is also referred to as Sakyamuni (釋迦牟尼 , *Sik Ga Mau Nei*, from *Sakyas*, the name of the tribe he belonged to, and *Muni*, meaning a sage: the wise man from the Sakyas tribe). Although raised amid the pleasures of the court, Siddhartha very soon was aware of and troubled by the problem of human suffering. As a young man he married the beautiful Yashodhara who bore him a son Rahula. In his determination to seek a solution to the four inescapable sufferings: of birth; of old age; of sickness; of death, he renounced his princely state and embarked on the life of a religious mendicant, undertaking traditional ascetic practices. These, however, were abandoned when he decided to seek his own path to enlightenment.

One day he sat cross-legged under a pipal tree and began to meditate, determined not to rise without finding enlightenment. His vow: 'Here, on this seat, may my body dry up, may my skin and flesh waste away if I raise my body from this seat before I have attained the knowledge it is hard to attain during numerous cycles.' But enlightenment did not come without a struggle. Mara (魔 , *moh*; 魔羅 , *moh loh*), the evil one, the tempter, the Lord of the world of passion, was determined to defeat Gautama and prevented him from attaining enlightenment. *Mara* derives from Sanskrit and means 'robber of life'. The most formidable of devils, Mara personifies evil. (In Buddhism, devils are interpreted to mean functions that work to block or hinder people in their Buddhist practice.) With his hideous demonic hordes, he approached Gautama who seated upright, was unmoved in his meditation, supported only by the Ten Virtues he had perfected during innumerable past lives as a *bodhisattva* (one of whose meanings is, a Buddha-to-be) in order to attain enlightenment. The ten virtues are: charity, morality, renunciation, wisdom, effort, patience, truth, determination, universal love, and equanimity. Mara was vanquished and fled with his evil spirits. In the Buddha's life this episode had been mythologized as the internal struggle between good and evil.

Under the pipal tree he did achieve enlightenment and became the Buddha. Buddha is not a proper name, but rather a title (comparable to, for example, the Messiah) given by the adherents of Buddhism to their founder. The word Buddha comes from the Sanskrit *buddha* meaning 'the enlightened one, the awakened one', from the verb *budh* meaning 'to know, to awake, to perceive'. Later on, because of this incident, the pipal (in Sanskrit: *pippala*) tree was called the bodhi tree (菩提樹, *po tai sue*).

The Buddha is one who perceives the truth of all phenomena and who leads others to achieve the same enlightenment. In India the word Buddha was originally a common noun meaning 'the awakened one', but in Buddhism it came to mean 'The one who has become awakened to the ultimate truth of life'.

In the forty-five years between his enlightenment and his death at the age of eighty, Sakyamuni travelled through many parts of India disseminating his teachings, which during his own lifetime spread not only to central India but also to more remote areas, and people of all classes were converted to Buddhism. His final words (it is said) as he lay dying were: 'Decay is inherent in all composite things. Work out your salvation with diligence.' His body was cremated seven days later. The ashes were divided into eight parts, and eight stupas (塔, *taap*) were erected to enshrine them. Two more stupas were built to house the vessel used in the cremation and the ashes of the fire. The stupa which originated from a burial mound, is usually dome-shaped or mound-shaped. It is said that the Mahayana movement began with a group of Buddhists who practised stupa worship.

Background to Buddhism

The Buddha claimed that his enlightenment was due to neither inspiration nor divine illumination. It was by his own unaided efforts he discovered this unheard-of doctrine: the new way to salvation which puts an end to all pain. Although new, Buddhism was expounded and expressed in the concepts of the Hindu world of the 6th century BC, and as it developed it took for granted all the Hindu conceptions and views on nature and the world that were not in conflict with its own.

Brahmism was the system in which Buddhism originated. The Indians at the time of the Buddha were a highly sophisticated, civilized race with sophisticated ideas about religion and salvation. Brahmism held that the accumulation of merit and the gods' beneficence all depended on the correct performance of rituals prescribed in the Hindu Vedas (the supreme sacred knowledge contained in the four collections, called Vedas), even to the extent of making the gods do the will of men. This invested them with tremendous authority. Others, referring to the teaching of the Upanishads (one of the speculative metaphysical treatises forming a division of Vedic literature) advocated intellectual means.

They sought for a unity between the impersonal *Brahma* (the first person of the Hindu trinity, the creator of the universe, the father of gods and men, the Lord of wisdom from whose heads the four Vedas are said to have sprung; the cosmic principle pervading the entire universe) and the *atman* (the self, oneself; it designates what is manifested in the fact of consciousness as being the thinking principle; the word derives from an Indo-European root meaning 'to breathe'; the soul or inner essence of man). Once man reached this unity, he was released from the endless cycle of re-births. Others again taught salvation was to be attained through constant self-mortification and torture of the body.

The Buddha established a system that repudiated the Brahminic claim of the Vedas to be the divine and infallible source of spiritual truth; that rejected the rituals as sole means of salvation; that disapproved of the intellectual means of the Upanishad. Nevertheless he did incorporate the 'doctrine' of *karma* and re-birth into his system. Buddhism was indeed 'heretical'. It was far less concerned with giving mankind power over nature than in freeing mankind from what it considered the basis of existence: the law of transmigration. Buddhism is a doctrine of salvation, laying no claim to revelation or earthly authority. In the beginning it contained no dogma, no rites, only a law and an example.

The Buddha welcomed into his community not only high-caste Brahmins and warriors but also traders and artisans and women and outcasts. His way to salvation was based on a rigorous code of personal spiritual behaviour with the emphasis on conduct as the chief means to salvation. Steering a middle course between austerity and gratification, he called his teaching: The Middle Path.

The Buddha's teaching

The Buddha hesitated for some time about explaining to the world what he had just realized. The world, he said, was like a lotus pond, where there are some lotuses still under water; others have reached only water level; there are some that stand above the water and are untouched by it. In a similar way, in this world men are at different levels of development. Only some of them would understand the truth. The lotus (蓮花, *lin fa*) is still a symbol of the pure wisdom of the Buddha, unsullied in the midst of the world. As a symbol of purity — purity in stagnant water — the lotus is frequently referred to in these Cantonese Love Songs. A Chinese phrase says the lotus 'rises out of the mire but is itself unsullied': 出污泥而不染, *chut wu nai yi bat yim*.

It may be said the Buddha based his entire teaching on the fact of human suffering. Existence is painful. The conditions that make an individual are precisely those that cause suffering. Individuality implies limitation; limitation gives rise to desire; desire inevitably causes suffering, since what is desired is transitory, changing, perishable. It is the impermanence of the object of our craving that causes disappointment and sorrow. By following the Buddha's 'path' the individual can dispel the 'ignorance' that perpetuates suffering. Enlightenment shines beyond the transitoriness of human existence.

In what is the present Benares was a Deer Park and it was in this Deer Park that the Buddha preached his first sermon. The origin of the name is interesting. The Lord of Varanasi used to hunt and kill deer on this land. The deer-king pleaded with him to stop and promised that every day he would give the Lord whatever number of deer he required. One day the deer-king was faced with the problem of sending a pregnant deer. Rather than sacrifice her and the unborn deer, he went to the Lord to offer his own flesh. The Lord was so touched by the deer-king's compassion that he gave him the whole piece of land; from that time on it was called the Deer Park. It was here that the Buddha spoke of the man who has left home and gone into the world. He should not follow the extremes of either self-indulgence or self-mortification. The Tathagata (如來, *Yue Loi*), one of the more common of the eighty-one titles given to the Buddha and the name by which he referred to himself, meaning 'one who returned from the world of truth', had discovered the middle path leading to vision, to knowledge, to calmness, to awakening, to salvation, to Nirvana.

How is man to achieve this salvation? The classical formulation was given by the Buddha in his first sermon. He enunciated Four Noble Truths (四聖諦 , *Sei Sing Dai*), four 'dogmas', truths, axioms, considered to be primary and fundamental. The doctrines of: 苦 , *foo*; 聚 , *jui*; 滅 , *mit*; 道 , *do*):

苦 , *foo*, suffering. Life is suffering;

聚 , *jui*, aggregation. Suffering stems from a craving for existence and sensual pleasures.

滅 , *mit*, extinction of desire. Emancipation, freedom, liberation from all suffering, in Nirvana. The 'extinction' would seem to refer to the extinction of re-birth and of the passions that cause suffering.

道 , *do*, 'the way'. To attain Nirvana, one must follow the Eightfold Right Path (八正道 , *Baat Jing Do*).

This Eightfold Right Path is usually divided into three categories comprising the whole of Buddhist discipline: moral conduct (戒 , *gaai*), meditation (定 , *ding*) and wisdom (慧 , *wai*).

'Right' (正 , *jing*) in the following categories is used to distinguish the teachings of the Buddha from those that were not his; in other words, Buddhist orthodoxy. Anything contrary to this is heterodox: 邪, *che*.

The first category (dealing with moral conduct)

Right speech (正語, *jing yue*): refraining from falsehood, malicious talk, and abusive language;

Right action (正業, *jing yip*): refraining from stealing, killing, and unchastity;

Right livelihood (正名, *jing ming*): abstaining from earning a living by improper means, such as killing living beings, making astrological forecasts, practising fortune-telling. It also embraces loving friendship, compassion, sympathetic joy and equanimity.

Discipline (戒, *gaai*) will ward off bodily evil.

The second category (dealing with mental discipline)

Right effort (正精進, *jing jing jun*), right aspiration (正思, *jing si*), right concentration (正定, *jing ding*): its objective is the control of the mind. To the Buddhist the root of all evil is a craving: a craving for sensual pleasures and material possessions. Such cravings require two elements: the organs of sense, and external objects. External objects are too numerous to be ignored and they impinge on our senses from all sides. Buddhism does not encourage austerities that torture the senses. We can control the mind and discipline it so that it will not foolishly take the unpleasant, the impure and the impermanent for the pleasant, the pure and the permanent.

Meditation (定, *ding*) will calm mental disturbances.

The third category (dealing with intuitive wisdom)

Right views (正見, *jing gin*), *right intentions* (正念, *jing nim*): this consists in taking the right view of things, namely, holding to these truths: all existence is suffering, all existence is impermanent, there is no permanent self or soul in man. Belief in a permanent self breeds attachment; attachment breeds egoism; egoism breeds a craving for existence, pleasure, fame, and fortune — all of which keep man tied to the endless cycle of re-birth. The Buddha said he looked everywhere for a permanent self, but could only find a conglomeration of five aggregates: material body, sensation, perception, pre-disposition, and consciousness. We are a combination of physical matter and mental energies, and as these are continually changing, so is the composition. Once we deny the permanent self, we destroy all selfish desires and self-interest; we give up egotistical pursuits; we abandon the craving and the quest for personal pleasures and gains; we overcome hankering and dejection.

Wisdom (慧, *wai*) will free us of delusions.

An allied concept is 'emptiness': entities have no fixed or independent nature. Because phenomena arise and continue to exist only by virtue of their relationship with other phenomena, they have no fixed substance and cannot exist in absolute independence of other things or arise of their own accord. Phenomena have as their true nature only 'emptiness'. Practical implications lie in the rejection of attachments to transient phenomena and to the egocentricity of envisioning oneself as being absolute and independent of all other existences. The 'emptiness' of a person means that one is no more than a temporary union of five components; one cannot be said to have an absolute self.

The belief in re-birth, in an endless series of worldly existences repeated by every being, was already in pre-Buddhist India associated with the Hindu doctrine of *karma*. The primary meaning of the Sanskrit word *karma* was 'action'. Then more particularly it referred to the potential energies residing in the inner realm of life which manifest themselves as various results in the future. In Buddhism, *karma* was interpreted to mean mental, verbal and physical actions, that is: thoughts, (意, *yi*), words (口, *hau*), and deeds (身, *san*). Every action, be it good or evil, imprints its stamp on one's life. My actions in the past have shaped me as I am at present. In turn, my actions in the present determine my future existence. Every being is what he has made himself, and will become what he deserves to become according to the kind and quality of his actions. Death cannot annihilate the individual existence, because after it, retribution for things done must be endured. Heavens and hells merely designate relative and temporary conditions. It is the *karma* in past lifetimes that accounts for the differences with which we are born into this life. I am what I am because of my previous *karma*; I will be what I will be because of my present *karma*. *Karma* can be either mutable or immutable. Immutable: it never fails to produce a fixed result. Mutable: what result will come about is not absolutely fixed.

Karma operates automatically without any 'god' sitting in judgement and meting out rewards and punishments. For the Indians, *karma* means the deed (cause) and the result (effect) that ensues. The Buddha held that *karma* involved not just the deed and its reward or punishment. What is most important of all is the intention behind the deed.

Karma is only generated when there is deliberate intention. If an action is unintentional, no *karma* is generated. Once there is the intention to perform the deed, *karma* is generated, even if the intended action is never carried out.

According to their *karma* of the past, living beings will undergo repeated re-births, and assume a different form in each re-birth. Some *karmas* bear fruit in the same life in which they are committed; others in the immediately succeeding one; others again in future lives more remote. The Buddha formulated that one condition arises out of prior condition, deriving in a chain or series of causes. The original condition is 'ignorance': 無明, *mo ming*: the state of illusionment, unenlightenment, of not possessing Buddha-wisdom. A liberating purification is effected by following, with a sincerity reinforced by continual meditation, the Eightfold Right Path. In these Cantonese Love Songs, the singer admits that her present plight is due to failing to cultivate virtue in a former existence.

For the follower of the Eightfold Right Path, salvation consists in an escape from the endless cycle of re-birth and in the realization of Nirvana. Nirvana is the end of re-birth (無後生死 , *mo hau sang sei*), the cessation of suffering.

One of the Buddha's fundamental beliefs was that so long as we are caught up in this endless cycle of re-births we are continually subject to suffering, misery, sorrow and anguish. In his very first sermon the Buddha had said that birth is suffering, old age is suffering, death is suffering, separation from loved ones is suffering, not realizing ones wishes is suffering. The living process is compared to a fire burning. The sole remedy is the extinction of that fire: the fire of illusion, passion and craving. The Buddha, the enlightened one, is no longer enkindled or inflamed.

According to Buddhist teaching, the universal aim (the Buddha did not recognize any essential differences between men, therefore Buddhism is open to all) is salvation, enlightenment, the attainment of Nirvana, which requires a great span of time. The important thing is that the way has been found, that one has set out on the right path. In a word, then, the state of the Buddha, the state of the perfectly enlightened one is Nirvana, and it is a state from which one is not re-born. In Sanskrit, Nirvana is derived from the verb *nirva* meaning 'to be extinguished', from *nir* meaning 'out', and *va* meaning 'to blow'. In English the transliterated Sanskrit word has been fully accepted. In Chinese Nirvana has been transliterated as 捏盤 , *nip poon*, and translated as 滅 , *mit*, meaning to extinguish; as 解脫 , *gaai tuet*, meaning release; as 寂滅 , *jik mit*, meaning tranquil extinction; as 無為 , *mo wai*, meaning inaction; as

安樂, *on lok*, meaning calm joy; as 極樂, *gik lok*, meaning extreme happiness; as 圓寂, *yuen jik*, meaning perfect rest. Sometimes the English explanation of Nirvana is given as 'dying out': the dying out (in the heart) of the fierce fire of the three cardinal sins of sensuality, of ill-will, and of infatuation. The Buddhist does not seek either annihilation or non-existence. Rather what is sought is the eternal, the immortal. Nirvana should not be considered negatively but rather as an ideal state, as happiness, as bliss. A state in which all illusions and desires and the cycle of rebirth are extinguished. Many poetic terms describe Nirvana: the harbour of refuge, the cool cave, the place of bliss, the further shore, the shore of peace, the island amidst the floods, and the true panacea. The aim of the Buddha is to break the cycle of re-birth at some point, so that living beings need no longer be re-born and again suffer in their new existence. Once true enlightenment, Nirvana, is achieved, transmigrating comes to an end.

Mahayana and Hinayana Buddhism

These words refer to two schools (that might loosely be termed the progressive and the conservative schools) of Buddhism and their respective doctrines. In Sanskrit *Maha* means 'great' and *Hina* means 'small, inferior'; *Yana* means 'vehicle' or 'conveyance'. Mahayana (大乘, *daai sing*) is frequently translated as 'The Great Vehicle', and Hinayana (小乘, *siu sing*) as 'The Lesser Vehicle'. 'The Great Vehicle', indicating universalism, refers to the teaching which can lead all people to enlightenment; 'The Lesser Vehicle' refers to teaching that seeks only personal enlightenment.

As Buddhism developed in India dissatisfaction arose over what were considered shortcomings in the traditional doctrine of the elders. One of the two schools formed by the first schism in Buddhism, which took place about a hundred years after the Buddha's death, was called The Theravada School (上坐部, *Seung Jor Bo*, Teaching of the Elders), and it rejected a proposal to modify five points of doctrine. The Theravada School retained the allegiance of the older monks and was more conservative, stressing strict adherence to the precepts, together with a literal interpretation of doctrine. Our knowledge about Theravada Buddhism comes from the Pali canon (Pali: an ancient Indian literary language) which was written about the 1st century BC — four or five hundred years after the death of the Buddha. Because of this time-lag scholars said the Pali canon did not represent the original teaching — much less the *ipsissima verba* of the Buddha; it merely reflected the views of the monastic communities of the 1st century BC. As time went on, more schisms appeared in Buddhism. Monks of these varying schools tended to withdraw from the lay community and lived in monasteries, losing sight of the original purpose of Buddhism: the enlightenment of all people. Theravada Buddhism, narrow and individualistic, exemplified this tendency. It was essentially a discipline undertaken by the individual for his own personal salvation; a salvation open only to those who join the monastic order. The monk was intent on accumulating meritorious *karma* for himself alone. Such *karma* could not be transferred to anyone else.

Towards the end of the 1st century BC and at the beginning of the 1st century AD, out of dissatisfaction with the self-complacent and monastic elitism of Theravada Buddhism, a reforming group of believers emerged who called their Buddhism Mahayana (The Great Vehicle), whose sacred literature is written in Sanskrit. Its followers coined and contemptuously applied the term Hinayana (The Lesser Vehicle) to Theravada and similar schools of Buddhism. *A Dictionary of Buddhist Terms and Concepts* notes that eighteen (or perhaps twenty) Hinayana Schools were formed by schisms.

In the early periods of Chinese Buddhism missionaries introduced both Mahayana and Hinayana Buddhism. However, in later periods only Mahayana Buddhism spread through and was followed in China. Perhaps the specific ways of thinking of the Chinese mind was the reason for the acceptance of Mahayana Buddhism over its counterpart, Hinayana. (Mahayana Buddhism is also widespread in Tibet, Mongolia, Korea and Japan, whereas Hinayana Buddhism is still extant in Sri Lanka.) Mahayana Buddhism compromised with the faiths of the common people and adopted charms and prayers as expedient teaching methods. Spells and charms became a part of Chinese Buddhism. After all, Mahayana Buddhism had come into being as a religion for ordinary people. It was this Buddhism that was introduced to, and would flourish for some ten centuries or more in China until the Ming dynasty (1368–1644) and even later.

Mahayana Buddhism offers salvation to all sentient beings, as all sentient beings are capable of being enlightened. It emphasizes that enlightenment is to be achieved mainly by faithful devotion to the Buddha, and love for all fellow men manifest by compassion, charity and altruism. The *bodhisattva*, the being destined for enlightenment, epitomizes Mahayana virtues. While the *bodhisattva* is 'qualified' to enter Nirvana, he chooses to defer his final entry (into Nirvana) in order to remain in the world until he has brought every sentient being across the sea of misery to the calm shore of enlightenment. (The word *bodhisattva* is derived from *bodi*, meaning 'enlightenment', and *sattva*, meaning 'sentient being'; the *bodhisattva* makes sentient beings enlightened.) This he can do by transferring some of his own inexhaustible stock of merits to less fortunate beings so they too may share in the reward. Contrasting starkly with the narrow spiritualization of Theravada Buddhism is the universal compassion of the Mahayana *bodhisattva*.

The *bodhisattva* is considered to be a personification of a particular trait in the Buddha's personality. As there are many different traits, so there are many different *bodhisattvas*. Avalokitesvara (觀音, *Gwoon Yam*), for example, representing the compassion of the Buddha, can abrogate the law of *karma*; he visits numerous hells to lighten the miseries of the suffering; and he is especially on the look-out for people facing danger from water, fire, demons, swords and enemies.

The nature of the Buddha is different in both Theravada and Mahayana Buddhism. In Theravada Buddhism, the Buddha is regarded as a human teacher who lived on earth, carried out his mission, and passed into Nirvana. In Mahayana Buddhism, the Buddha is regarded as an eternal being who is the embodiment of universal and cosmic truth. In the Lotus Sutra (法華經, *Faat Wa Ging*), the Buddha denies that he first attained enlightenment in India, and discloses that his original enlightenment took place in the unfathomably remote past. 法華經, *Faat Wa Ging*, is strictly The Dharma-flower Sutra, but is also called The Lotus Sutra (妙法蓮華經, *Miu Faat Lin Wa Ging*). Dharma (in Chinese 法, *faat*) is law, truth, religion, anything Buddhist. Strictly, it is 'that which is held fast or kept, usage, custom'; duty, morality.

The Buddha was never born nor will he ever die; he lives from eternity to eternity. To save suffering mankind from evil, this eternal Buddha became incarnated as the historical Siddhartha Gautama. The eternal Buddha had countless such 'theophanies' on earth in the past, and will continue to appear in the future. As the earthly Sikamuni is considered to be an illusory being, an incarnation of the eternal Buddha, the facts of his (earthly, historical) life are of less importance than speculation about the eternal Buddha.

It is interesting to note that the cult of Mahayana Buddhism came into existence on the borders of Iran in lands where there had been interpenetration of Hellenic, Persian and Indian influences. The Graeco-Syrian gnosis, the Iranian religion of light, and Vishnu sectarianism played their part in it. Perhaps also to some extent the faith of the Semites, and Manichaeism.

Representations of the Buddha also indicate Western influence. Native art never depicted the Buddha's features, but most frequently symbolized him by an empty throne. When it was decided to give him a plastic form, the Greek type was chosen. Western sculptors living in Bactriana represented him as Apollo. Scholars have demonstrated the gradual degrees by which the Buddha evolved from a Greek Buddha to the most Oriental of Buddhas.

The Mahayana teachings are divided into two:

1. True Mahayana (實教, *Sat Gaau*), another name for The Lotus Sutra, elucidates the Buddha's enlightenment itself, and is expounded irrespective of the people's capacity to receive it. In it the Buddha is endowed with the three virtues of sovereign (to protect all living beings), of teacher (to instruct and lead them to enlightenment) and of parent (to compassionately nurture and support them);
2. The Provisional Mahayana (權教, *Kuen Gaau*) contains teachings preparatory to the perfect teaching (of 1). It leads people to the True Mahayana teaching, and helps them understand what is revealed in The Lotus Sutra.

Hajime Nakamura, op. cit., suggests that the Chinese bent for the individual and the concrete as opposed to the universal or abstract is one reason for their accepting Sakyamuni as a historical person, when the Bhagavadgita (the famous religious book of India) says that the Buddha is the incarnation of Krishna.

All beings may attain the state of Buddhahood: a state of perfect freedom in which one is awakened to the eternal and ultimate truth that is the reality of all things. It is characterized by boundless wisdom and infinite compassion. This state is achieved by becoming a *bodhisattva*, and the *bodhisattvas* came to be the main objects of religious enthusiasm. They are individualized as half-mythical beings who undertake to save the world. The advantages of worshipping them and winning their favour is extolled rather than the task of becoming such a saviour. The Buddhas and *bodhisattvas* are conceived as wonderfully beneficent beings rivalling the gods of the surrounding Hinduism. They are not gods in the strict sense of being the supreme divinity, the ultimate reality. But popular devotion seeking objects of worship found what they wanted in the Buddhas and *bodhisattvas*. Thus was the element of 'devotion' introduced into Buddhism. Perhaps, it has been said, these 'deities' were no more than a transference of Krishna-worship, Siva-worship from Hinduism.

'The Lotus of the True Doctrine' is the Mahayana sutra which deals with the *bodhisattva* doctrine and the new mythology of Buddhist belief.

The Sanskrit word *sutra* apparently has four meanings: a string; a mat; a well-rope; wise teaching. In the present context *sutra* has combined the first and the fourth senses, giving 'a thread on which jewels (of wise teaching) are strung', and was applied to that part of the Buddhist canon which contained the dialogues and discourses of the Buddha. In the Mahayana school, no claim is made that its sutras contain the words of the Buddha. All save one part, however, are put into the mouth of the Buddha.

The three divisions of the Buddhist canon are called the Tripitaka (三藏, *Saam Chong*). Tripitaka is a Sanskrit combination of 'Tri-' meaning 'three', and 'Pitaka', meaning a box or basket, indicating a collection of writings. The three divisions are:

1. the Sutras (經, *Ging*, meaning scripture, canon, classics), the Buddha's doctrinal teachings;
2. the Vinays (律, *Lut*, meaning the law), the rules of discipline for monks and nuns;
3. the Abhidharma (婀比達磨, *Oh Bei Daat Moh*) merely a transliteration of the Sanskrit word which means the law behind the law, which goes beyond the law, translated into Chinese as: 論, *lun*, meaning discourses, doctrinal commentaries on the sutras and the vinaya.

The Pure Land School

The many schools of Buddhism that developed in China show the intense intellectual ferment the introduction of Buddhism brought about. Some of these schools (The Pure Land School (淨土宗, *Jing To Jung*, is an example) were the product of the Chinese response to Buddhism and indicate how the Chinese mind took over certain basic Buddhist principles and re-shaped them to suit the Chinese temperament. These schools were no longer of Indian Buddhism, but of indigenous Chinese Buddhism.

Originally the Pure Land teaching did not have charms and spells, did not possess magical elements. When the Chinese translated the Pure Land teachings they made use of the special terminology of Taoism. They also infused the thought of superhuman beings into the Pure Land teaching by adopting Taoistic words and phrases which could not be found in the original Sanskrit. Chinese Pure Land teaching since the time of its first introduction from India and Central Asia has been under the influence of Taoism. Chinese Buddhism today is generally the teaching of the Pure Land, and it is this Pure Land teaching that permeates these Cantonese songs.

Perhaps the most important person associated with this school and considered one of the great patriarchs is Wai Yuen (慧遠 , 344–416). In 402 he founded a religious group the White Lotus Society (白蓮社 , *Baak Lin Se*), called after the white lotus pond (白蓮池 , *baak lin chi*) in his monastery. The society was composed of over a hundred monks who devoted themselves to the Pure Land practices. This was the origin of the Pure Land school in China. Once he had studied Buddhism, Wai Yuen declared that Confucianism and Taoism were empty; Buddhism alone showed the way to the profound mystery.

Buddha Amitayus / Buddha Amitabha

The Pure Land School based its teaching on The Pure Land Sutra, (honoured above all other sutras, because it teaches that women can attain Buddhahood) in which there is a dialogue between Sakyamuni and Ananda. Sakyamuni tells how, aeons ago, a certain monk named Dharmakara went to a former Buddha and asked for a description of both the ideal Buddha and the Buddha land. Having heard it, Dharmakara promised in the eighteenth of his forty-eight vows that once he achieved his Buddhahood, all those who believed in him and called on his name would be born into his Land of Pure Bliss and live there until they had achieved Nirvana. This Land of Pure Bliss is not the same as Nirvana, nor is it a substitute for the goal of enlightenment. Dharmakara fulfilled his vow and presided as the Buddha Amitabha or the Buddha Amitayus — his name indicates an idealization of eternal life and light rather than that of an historical personality — over the Western Paradise (ten billion Buddha-lands to the west). This paradise is also known as the Pure Land, the Land of Pure Bliss. The Buddha Amitabha is the great 'saviour-deity' of Buddhism, presiding over a paradise of light inhabited by pure, stainless beings who are reborn there after invoking his name.

'Pure land' (淨土 , *jing to*) contrasts with 'impure land' (穢土 , *wai to*), which refers to the present world defiled by suffering and illusion. Some sutras teach that one should hate this present impure world and aspire to re-birth in the pure world; while others hold that any land is pure or impure depending on the enlightenment or delusion of those who live there. When one purifies the heart, the world one lives in becomes a 'pure land'. To the pure, all things are pure.

There are two versions of this sutra: the long version and the short version. And the difference between the versions is indeed far-reaching. The long version emphasizes that re-birth in the Land of Perfect Bliss is the result of meritorious actions coupled with faith and devotion to the

Buddha Amitabha. In contrast, the short version states very clearly that to attain this re-birth only faith and prayer are necessary, as indicated by repeatedly uttering the formula of faith: *Namas Amitabha*, meaning: 'Thee I honour and in thee take refuge, Amitabha.'

Up to the Sui dynasty (581–618) the Chinese used the translated name of the Buddha Amitayus, the Buddha of infinite life: 無量壽佛, *Mo Leung Sau Fat*; or the translated name of the Buddha Amitabha, the Buddha of infinite light: 無量光佛, *Mo Leung Gwong Fat*. The word Buddha was transliterated in a variety of ways, some of which were: 佛, *fat*; 佛陀, *fat toh*; 浮陀, *fau toh*; 浮圓, *fau yuen*; 浮頭, *fau tau*. Today 佛, *fat*, or 佛陀, *fat toh*, are the accepted transliterations. After the Tong dynasty (618–907) the Pure Land teaching spread widely and the element Amita— (of either Amitayus or Amitabha) was transliterated as 阿彌陀, *oh nei toh*, and became widely adopted. (The form Amida is the Japanese transliteration of both Amitayus and Amitabha.) One suggested reason is that a translation of the Buddhist invocation of his name in the Sanskrit phrase: *Namas-Amitabha*, would not sound smooth in Chinese where it would have become: 南無無量壽佛, *naam-mo mo leung sau fat*. The Sanskrit word *'namas'* (transliterated into Chinese as 南無, *naam mo*) meant 'devotion', 'to offer one's life to the Buddha'. And the invocation could be translated as, 'Thee I honour and in Thee take refuge, Amitabha'. It appears there were two objects of 'devotion': one, the person of Sakyamuni; two, the Law, which was the Lotus Sutra. So complete transliteration was decided upon: 南無阿彌陀佛, *naam mo oh nei toh fat*. While not having any meaning in Chinese, this transliteration of Indian words suggested the exotic, the mysterious. The Pure Land sects assert that one can attain rebirth in the Pure Land of Amitabha Buddha by chanting this phrase.

Oh nei toh fat's image most frequently depicts him as a standing, ageless Buddha with one very long arm and hand reaching down below his knee and the other of normal size holding a golden tower or pagoda in the palm of his hand at waist level. His other features include a head slightly larger that one would expect, short curly hair, and the 'bump of wisdom' on the forehead.

Avalokitesvara

In this land of Pure Bliss resides Avalokitesvara, whose name was translated as: 觀音, *Gwoon Yam*. He (or later, she) is the most merciful and compassionate of *bodhisattvas* (personification of particular traits of the eternal Buddha Amitabha) who out of profound compassion assumes thirty-three different forms and manifests himself anywhere in the world to save people from danger or suffering and bring them to the Land of Perfect Bliss. He/she is possibly the most beloved of any deity throughout the Buddhist world.

According to legend, The Buddha Amitabha's head once split with grief at realizing the number of wicked beings yet to be saved in the world. He caused each of the pieces to become a whole head and then he placed them on his son (Avalokitesvara) in three tiers of three; then a tenth, and topped them all with his own image. Sometimes the eleven-headed Avalokitesvara is represented with thousands of arms, outspread like the fanned-tail of a peacock. In paintings, he is usually shown in white; and his consort is the 'goddess' Tara. His images are frequently placed on hilltops, because of the very meaning of his name, and possibly also because his traditional residence is the mountain Potalaka (補陀落迦 山 , *Bo Toh Lok Ga Saan*), said to be located on the southern coast of India. Inside houses his image must be placed in a high, overlooking position.

Avalokitesvara is the earthly manifestation of the self-born, eternal Buddha Amitabha, whose figure is represented in his headdress. He guards the world in the interval between the departure of Sakyamuni and the appearance of the future Buddha, Maitreya. Avalokitesvara protects against shipwreck, fire, assassins, robbers and wild beasts. He is the creator of the fourth world: the actual universe we now live in.

The meaning of the name Avalokitesvara (an approximate transliteration of the Sanskrit word) has caused some problems. In Sanskrit, *Avalokita* means 'looking on', from the verb *Avalokayati* meaning 'to look at, to survey', and *Isvara* meaning 'self-existent, sovereign, absolute, lord'. His name in Sanskrit has been variously interpreted as: 'the Lord of compassionate glances', 'the Lord who looks in every direction', and 'the Lord of what we see'. Avalokitesvara, just like the eternal Buddha, 'surveys' the world in his compassion for all beings, and could be called 'the Lord who surveys'.

In Chinese, Avalokitesvara has been translated by the two characters 觀音, *Gwoon Yam*. The literal meaning of the first of these characters is 'one who looks at or watches or observes', and of the second is 'sound or sounds'. Another translation was 觀世音, *Gwoon Sai Yam*, literally meaning 'one who looks at or watches or observes the sounds (i.e. prayers) of the world'. At first sight, the Chinese characters would appear to mis-translate the Sanskrit: the translator had read Avalokitasvara instead of Avalokitesvara, for '*svara* does mean 'sound or voice' in Sanskrit. Interestingly enough, in a copy of the Lotus Sutra dated AD 5th century and discovered in Eastern Turkestan, the name Avalokitasvara appears five times on the same page, suggesting it was not simply a misspelling. All early translators wrote *Gwoon Yam* or *Gwoon Sai Yam*. It was not until Yuen Jong (玄壯 , 602–664, who had left China in 629 to study Buddhism in the original Sanskrit and to visit the places associated with Sakyamuni, and had carried back with him after his seventeen-year journey 650 Buddhist texts packed in 520 suitcases) dedicated himself to the task of translating the rich stores of sutras he had acquired, that the characters 觀自在 , *Gwoon Ji Joi* (自在 , *ji joi*, translating the *isvara* element of the name), the Onlooking Lord, the correct translation of Avalokitesvara, were first used. However, the translation, *Gwoon Yam*, had come to stay.

The 3rd–7th century saw the height of Avalokitesvara's veneration in northern India. His images in China prior to the Sung dynasty (960–1126) were unmistakably masculine. Later images, however, show characteristics of both sexes. One interpretation has it that Avalokitesvara is neither male nor female, but transcends sexual distinction. In statues and paintings, the flowing garments and soft contours of the body have been intentionally combined with a very visible moustache to emphasize the absence of sexual identity. The Lotus Sutra relates that Avalokitesvara can assume whatever form is required to relieve suffering; and also has the power to grant children.

As early as the 7th century, the idea of Avalokitesvara as a female began to emerge, and she was said to protect women in childbirth. During the Tong (618–907) dynasty the concept of a Madonna-like figure clad in white was gaining ground; from the 10th century on, painters began to paint this (female) figure, which was called 'The white-clad *Gwoon Yam*' (白衣觀音 , *baak yi Gwoon Yam*). Avalokitesvara's change of sex took place, it has been suggested, because the cult had superimposed on Avalokitesvara the qualities of a mother-goddess, and in the popular mind from about the 11th or 12th century Avalokitesvara was increasingly conceived of as female. Indeed, *Gwoon Yam* is the great saviour 'goddess' particularly in East Asia and often eclipses the eternal, celestial Buddha in the personal devotion she inspires.

The original text

The original text of the Prefaces and the Cantonese Songs appears in the Appendices at the end of this book, hence giving the readers the chance to savour the drama, the poetry, the symbolism and indeed the raciness of the these songs; in a word, the idiosyncracy of the Cantonese mind.

Prefaces

Author's Preface

Scholars who follow the path of virtue[1] will take pleasure in learning of the tender devotion which these Cantonese songs describe. Please accept this small book as an attempt to rescue from torment all who in this world are sunk deep in the sea of desire.

    Written in the ninth month of the sixth year [i.e. 1828] of the reign of Emperor Do Gwong [1821–51],[2] in the 'Blue Sky' bookshop.

The Second Preface

The Preface of Sek, the Taoist

In the autumn[3] of 1828, Meng Saan [i.e. the non-de-plume of the author of these songs: Jiu Ji-yung], a retired official, kindly visited me. The crickets were chirping at my door and the cool wind was rustling my curtains. Meng Saan was quiet and seemed depressed as he remarked:

    'These autumn sounds make me more gloomy and depressed. Is there anything you can do for me?'

    'Yes, yes!' I replied.

    Meng Saan continued:

    'My son, you see the Pearl River, its fragrance wafts for more than ten *li* [i.e. about 3.5 miles]. You see the fields covered in jasmine, the red-sandalwood houses. Out there, hundreds of 'Pearl boats' [i.e. Cantonese flower boats] hang up their red lanterns when the sun sets in the west. As the mist descends it sucks up the perfume of the flowers. 'Pearl young ladies' [i.e. who live on the flower boats] and 'Pearl young men [i.e. 'guests' who frequent the flower boats], whether they be plump or slender, appear in all their finery — the pendant ornaments at their girdle jingling and tinkling. They play most exquisitely on the Jiu [i.e. modern *Saan Sai*, 山西] zither. Some time later, a little heated with wine, they change to Chun [i.e. modern *Sim Sai*, 陝西] songs. Are you fond of these?'

    'Oh, great! But they're not what I like to hear.'

    Meng Saan went on:

---

[1] 'The path of virtue': the 'Way' (道 , *Do*) proposed by Lo Ji (老子) in the *Do Dak Ging* (道德經). Scholarly opinion puts the composition of the *Do Dak Ging* somewhere between the 8th–3rd century BC, as the book contains no references to other writings, persons, events, or places that might provide a clue for the dating of this work.

[2] See Introduction, p. 5.

[3] Strictly speaking, the fifteenth day of the eighth moon.

'When the Lo Lung [north-east of *Wai Jau*, 惠州] houseboats recede with the ebbing tide, and the flower boats become fewer, and the cold moon shines brightly, then the young ladies coiffed with the top-not put the lotus roots on ice and with slender fingers offer oranges. All your cares vanish! Then they begin singing Ng-country [i.e. modern *Gong So*, 江蘇] ballads, and other beautiful songs follow. The bright lanterns make a resplendent scene as the bamboo pipes of Choh [i.e. modern Hunan and Hupei, 湖南 , 湖北] are played. Immediately, voices are hushed. Do you enjoy this?'

'Beautiful, beautiful. But that's not what pleases me.'

Meng Saan continued:

'When the Three Stars are in the heavens[4], and everything is silent as the water, the ladies remove their adornments and there is a slight scent of fragrant ointment: looking back to the slowly passing years, cherishing the peace and quiet of the long nights. They want to recapture the past but they thrill to their present passion. As these southern songs are poured out, as a forlorn hope is painted, as the voice swells to the beat, as the melody ebbs and flows, you choke with emotion and hold back your grief; the harmony soothing your broken heart. At such a time, when the moon on the water would fade, and the clouds are stilled, then do they lament their inexorable fate. Can anyone dispel such feelings?'

I said:

'These southern songs thrill men through and through. Their music is exactly as you say it is. Can you compose such songs?'

Immediately Meng Saan sang the words he had written, his rich voice prolonging the notes. The burden of his songs was gentle and plaintive; graceful and heart-rending, like those songs that Fan Yam[5] had said were sad enough to pierce a man to the core, piteous enough to melt even the most cantankerous beauty.

You will not have to wait for the songs of Hoh Moon[6], for already your green garments[7] will be wet through with your tears.

---

[4] A quotation from the Book of Songs (詩經 , *Si Ging*) Part 1, Book X, Ode 5, describing the joy of a husband and wife at their unexpected union. The reference is possibly to the group of stars in Orion which is visible in the tenth month. And the tenth month for Chinese is an auspicious one for marriage.

[5] Fan Yam's (繁欽) literary talent and powers of argument made him famous even as a youth. His songs and poems were widely known.

[6] During the reign of Emperor Tong Yuen Jung (唐玄宗 , 742–56), the singer Hoh Moon (何滿) was considered a rare genius whom the poet Yuen Jan (元稹) praised highly. Mayers, # 961; Giles, # 2543.

[7] See Songs 12 (Part 4), Line 4, note; 60.

The Third Preface

Four stanzas on the theme of the Cantonese Love Songs by 'the cultivator of the plum blossom'

We who were born and bred in the Southern villages speak our own rough tongue. But singing our unpolished words demands the greatest care. The music of the pipa breaks and re-unites, as the notes sob in silence. Jiu Ji-yung makes his verses long or short as he pleases, as in the Juk Ji songs.[8]

Innumerable are the sorrows of parting; innumerable too the passions of love. As in a dream, predestined fate is not yet clear. At the banquet [i.e. the entertainment of which the banquet formed a part], can anyone remain unmoved?

Men are like willow catkins; young ladies are like the willow fibre. Famed ladies in their boudoirs sing the songs that once were heard in So Toi[9]. The infatuated and the heart-broken have no one to rely on. You who read this, do not doubt it.

---

[8] The Juk Ji (竹枝) style of poetry originated in Ba Yue (巴渝), a district in the Szechuan (四川, *Sei Chuen*) province. The boys of the Ba country sang them, blowing their short flute, beating the drum and brandishing their sleeves as they danced and sang.

[9] See also the Ninth Preface, Line 2. In 495 BC Foo Chaai (夫差) succeeded his father as king of Ng (吳) country. Until his death in 473 BC, he maintained a struggle with Gau Chin (勾踐), prince of the state of Yue (越). In the beginning he was victorious, and submitted Gau Chin to three years of ignominious treatment before allowing him to return to his native Yue. Once home, Gau Chin with the help of his minister, Fan Lai (范蠡), planned revenge. Were he able to present a beautiful concubine to Foo Chaai, she would take his mind off the affairs of state and Yue would be able to attack with certainty of victory. Fan Lai 'discovered' Sai Si (西施), a girl of peerless beauty but of humble origin. He had her tutored in the arts necessary to make her mission a success when she became Fu Chaai's concubine. Tantalizingly radiant, the *femme fatale* Sai See entered Foo Chaai's palace like a princess of royal blood. Her long black hair shimmering with pearls and kingfisher feathers and smiling a smile that would bring ruin and death. Fu Chaai immediately fell in love with Sai Si; abandoned himself to her; built the tower known as So Toi (蘇臺) for the pleasure of his exquisite concubine. This tower was erected near the present city of So Jau (蘇州), which takes its name from this traditional story. Sunken in dissolute pleasures, Foo Chaai handed over virtually all power to his prime minister, who had already started taking bribes from Yue. Sai Si had anaesthetized him for Yue's surgery. In 485 BC Yue attacked and destroyed Ng. Foo Chaai's life was spared but discovering that Sai Si had disappeared in the tumult, he put an end to his life. Sai Si, despite the role she had played in bringing about the downfall of Ng, could not help remembering Foo Chaai who had laid all his possessions at her feet. It is said she looked for the last time at the reflection of the face that was the envy of the moon, and drowned herself in one of the canals of the city she had 'conquered'. Of the four superlatively beautiful women in Chinese history Sai Si is the peerless queen. Mayers, # 127, 139, 571, 627; Giles, # 540, 576, 679.

The magic brush of Jing Jau's prefect [i.e. Jiu Ji-yung, the author of these songs] flourishes hither and thither, and the ladies wait for the songs that will describe their feelings. Painstakingly he creates his captivating style. Even if you were singing to a group of complete fools, their souls would be touched.

The Fourth Preface

Spring: the revitalizing season, written by the fisherman who lives near the shallows where the red water-pepper grows

The pipa is clasped, the cups of wine put aside, and we listen to the pure music.

Love entwines like the threads of the damask veil that are so hard to part; wide, wide is the sea of lust, and it is not easy to turn one's back on it.

These songs sing of mutual grief, mutual tenderness; now ridiculing, now warning; they fear to sing of happiness, loving to sing of sorrow.

Carefully see through vanity[10] and cast it into the eastward-flowing river to be carried away.

Who composed these songs? Had I earlier met Yue Yeung[11] I would have given him a copy of them to keep.

I think that Gwan Hong[12] melodies although once elegant have now become vulgar; that while Chun songs[13] may be robust, they lack tenderness.

Listening to Jiu Ji-yung's songs you choke with grief and distress; you are excited and roused; you are crushed and oppressed. Why even the fish and the dragons come out from the sea![14]

Do you know why? Because his songs sing of human feelings and give us a glimpse of the whole world.

---

[10] See Song 1 (Part 2), Line 9.
[11] Yue Yeung (漁羊), another name for Wong Si-jing (王士正, 1634–1711), a distinguished statesman and patron of letters. Mayers, # 819; Giles # 2221.
[12] Gwan Hong (崑腔) refers to the name of a class of tunes.
[13] See Second Preface.
[14] 'Listening to Jiu Ji-yung's songs. . .': Baak Gui-yi (白居易, 772–846), the famous Tong poet, describes in his *The Lute Girl's Lament* (See Song 12 (Part 4), Line 3, note) the way this 'Lute Girl' played and sang:

   At length, after much pressing, she came forth, hiding her face behind her lute; and twice or thrice sweeping the strings, betrayed emotion ere her song was sung. Then every note she struck swelled with pathos deep and strong, as though telling the tale of a wrecked and hopeless life, while with head bent and rapid finger she poured forth her soul in melody. Now softly; now slowly, her plec-

The Fifth Preface

The lines of this preface are all excerpted from *Si Ban* (詩品), a poem by Si-hung To[15], and have been compiled by 'The Immortal in the Ninth

---

trum sped to and fro; now this air, now that; loudly, with the crash of falling rain; softly, as the murmur of whispered words; now loud and soft together, like the patter of pearl and pearlets dropping on a marble dish. Or liquid, like the warbling of the mango-bird in the bush; trickling, like the streamlet on its downward course. And then like the torrent, stilled by the grip of frost, so for a moment was the music lulled, in a passion too deep for sound. Then, as bursts the water from the broken vase, as clash the arms upon the mailed horseman, so fell the plectrum once more upon the strings with a slash like the rent of silk.

(Translation by Herbert A Giles, in *Gems of Classical Chinese Poetry in Various English Translations*)

千呼萬喚始出來　猶抱琵琶半遮面
轉軸撥絃三兩聲　未成曲調先有情
絃絃掩抑聲聲思　似訴平生不得志
低眉信手續續彈　說盡心中無限事
輕攏慢撚抹復挑　初為霓裳後六么
大絃嘈嘈如急雨　小絃切切如私語
嘈嘈切切錯雜彈　大珠小珠落玉盤
間關鶯語花底滑　幽咽流泉冰下難
水泉冷澀絃凝絕　凝絕不通聲暫歇
別有幽愁闇恨生　此時無聲勝有聲
銀瓶乍破水漿迸　鐵騎突出刀槍鳴
曲終收撥當心畫　四絃一聲如裂帛

    In Chinese mythology, the Dragon King (the Chinese Neptune) lives in a glorious palace at the bottom of the sea. The dragon has the head of a camel, horns of a deer, eyes of a rabbit, ears of a cow, neck of a snake, belly of a frog, scales of a carp, claws of a hawk, palms of a tiger. The dragon is the Chinese 'god' of water and rain, making the wind blow and bringing down rain for the benefit of mankind.
    There is a Chinese phrase: 下海擒龍 , *ha hoi kam lung* which means: to go down to the ocean to seize a dragon, and is used with reference to a brave man, an able man.

[15] Si-hung To (司空圖) lived during the reign of Jiu Jung (昭宗, 889–905) Although having been given the post of Vice-President of the Board of War, a foot-disease made him seek seclusion on Mount Jung Tiu. When Jue Chuen-jung usurped the throne in 905, he invited Si-hung To to become President of the Board of Rites, but Si-hung To starved himself to death. Another story has it that Si-hung To was depressed because of the evil times he lived in, and he constantly dwelt on the past. His poems were considered pure in tone and coldly austere, like those of a philosopher who had retired from the world.

Heaven'.¹⁶ [Line 1 of the preface is from poem 10 of Si Ban; lines 2, 3 and 4 from poem 3; line 5 from poem 23; line 6 from poem 3; line 7 from poem 11; line 8 from poem 20; line 9 from poem 5; line 10 from poem 3; line 11 from poem 1; line 12 from poem 20; line 13 from poem 6; line 14 from poem 3.]

With head bent over his work, he dashes off a song in a moment.

Under his hand, spring comes alive.

No awakening from passion,

Ever he looks at the beautiful ladies.

He revels in pleasure, but is distressed at its shortness,

As short-lived as the wind or the sun at the water's edge.

He gives himself fully to dissipation,

But it bears the stamp of this world's emptiness.

When his words are beautiful

We realize their truth.

He pierces through outward appearances and

Goes right to the essence of the flowers and herbs.

People say that he is worth reading, and

They compare his new songs to the classics.

The Sixth Preface

Written by the recluse fisherman of the village opposite

Fill up the wine cups! Call the singers! Let joy be unconfined!

If you are really a distinguished person, join in the revelry.

As the red-sleeved young girls stand in two rows holding their silver-white candles,

Reclining drunkenly near the bottle we listen to the Cantonese songs one after the other.

Ships and boats all around are alive with song;

Whenever I hear these songs, I cannot help sighing.

---

¹⁶ The Ninth Heaven (九天) is based on a conception of nine heavens, or nine divisions of the heavenly kingdom. The nine heavens of the Buddhists and the later school of Taoists were conceived as sphere above sphere. Mayers, (Part 2) # 289.

For one gift, I gave her [i.e. a courtesan] three million bales of silk:

As unresisting clay, I am moulded by her side-long glances.

Exchanging a string of pearl-songs for a hank of passion

Won Naam Bo[17] fame in olden times.

The startled swan [i.e. his sweetheart][18] has flown away, without a trace;

All the more reason not to sing the songs of Wai City.[19]

In a previous existence you should have been Do Muk-ji,[20]

Who was accustomed to write new sorrows in new songs.

For ten years I have not dreamed of Yeung Jau,[21] so

It is easy for the autumn frost to whiten the hair at my temples.

---

[17] Nam Bo (南部), a book (whose full title was: Nam Bo Yin Fa Gei (南部烟花記), written by Fung Ji (馮贄) during the Tong dynasty about courtesans in general, about the world of 'Mist and Flowers'.

[18] The wild swan (鴻, hung) is considered a larger member of the wild goose (雁, ngaan) class, which accompanies it on its flights. The ngaan (雁) is supposed to be preeminently the bird of light and virility (陽鳥, yeung niu). It follows the sun as it moves south in the winter and shows an instinctive knowledge of migrations. It always flies with the wild swan (鴻, hung) in pairs, and has therefore become an emblem of the married state. More technically the goose is defined as any large web-footed bird of the sub-family Anserinae, whose family is Anatidae (that to which the swan belongs). Mayers, # 909, 932.

[19] Cheung On (長安) used to be known formerly as Haam Yeung (咸陽). The emperor Go Dai (高帝, 206–194 BC) changed its name to San Sing (新城), and the emperor Mo Dai (武帝, 140–86 BC) changed it to Wai Sing (渭城, Wai City), after the river Wai on which it is situated. When in AD 618 the Tong dynasty was fully acknowledged the capital was removed from Lok Yeung to Wai Sing and it then received its well-known name of Cheung On and it remained the seat of the empire till the fall of the Tong dynasty (905). It is now the modern Sai On Fu (西安府), and it was here that in 1901 the emperor Gwong Sui (光緒) and the empress dowager took refuge. A story has it that a rich man every day on his way home passed a cake-seller who was always singing. One day the rich man gave him '10 000 cash' because he was so poor. But from then on, the rich man never heard the cake-seller sing again. On being asked why he no longer sang, the cake-seller replied: 'The money you gave me was so much, I became very anxious about it, and I simply had no time to sing the songs of Wai City.' Mayers, # 660; Giles, # 1750.

[20] Do Muk-ji (杜牧之, 803–52), a Secretary of the Grand Council, was a celebrated poet and is often spoken of as the lesser Do (小杜) to distinguish him from the great Do Foo (杜甫, 712–70), one of the most renowned of all Chinese poets. Mayers, # 680, 681; Giles, # 2058, 2065.

[21] Yeung Jau (楊州). A poem by Do Muk-ji has the lines:
> For ten years I have dreamed the dreams of Yeung Jau.
> I have earned the name of a frivolous lover in the houses of entertainment.

十年一覺楊州夢　贏得青樓薄倖名

The Seventh Preface

Written by the good-for-nothing who ploughs the mist

I had originally composed these lines as a preface to 'Willow Blossoms' [Song 32] but later decided it should be the preface to the whole of the songs.

One willow blossom, one heart [i.e. a courtesan has a human heart] . . .

When I see ten thousand flowers strewn about, I find it hard to control my anguish.

For my lord's sake, my tears have fretted a thousand channels;

I set my songs of sorrow to music as did Yung Moon,[22] and I again strike the lute.

The Eighth Preface

Written by the retired scholar of the Tek River

The young ladies clash the iron castanets and strike the bronze 'guitars';

The Pearl River is alive with song.

The embroidered bag[23] has the remnants of the songs of yesterday.

If you examine too closely your dusty [i.e. preoccupied with this world] past, your temples will become frost-white.

Your singing took pride of place at the elegant banquet.

His meaning was that although he had frequented the 'houses of entertainment' for ten years, he had never taken a concubine. Yeung Jau was noted for the beauty of its courtesans, as was also So Jau (蘇州) in the same province. (See Third Preface, stanza 3, note). These cities had a reputation similar to that of Corinth in ancient Greece.

[22] The story runs that Mang Seung-gwan (孟嘗君, died: 279 BC) once invited Yung Moon-jau (雍門周) to visit him because the latter played the lute so movingly. 'Can you play the lute so as to move me to tears?' asked Mang Seung-gwan. Yung Moon-yau played exquisitely and when he had finished, he saw that Mang Seung-gwan was indeed weeping. (See Song 12 (Part 4), Line 3, note.) Mayers, # 491; Giles, # 1515.

[23] The Book of Tong (唐書) has it that every single morning Lei Hoh (李賀) went out riding on a pony and was followed by a small page-boy. He carried on his back an embroidered bag, so that when an idea struck him, he wrote it down immediately and threw it into the bag. In the evening when he returned home, he elaborated the thoughts he had jotted down. Another account has it that Lei Hoh when he was only seven years of age was able to write essays. It is said that the famous Hon Yue (韓愈) refused to believe in the prowess of this Tong dynasty (618–907) boy-poet until the boy produced a brilliant poem offhand, under Hon Yue's very eyes. He died at the age of twenty-seven. Giles, # 632, 1132.

The sweet music which So Neung[24] left to us is now scattered like the mist in spring.

Why do you worry that your fingernails are like those of Ma Gwoo?[25]

Why do you fold your hands and pray before Chi Wan, the embroidered Buddha?[26]

In another vein and with a new song, tell the story of Mok Sau[27].

---

[24] So Neung (蘇娘) was a famous courtesan in Chin Tong (錢塘), a district of Chit Gong (浙江). She lived in AD 11th century. She was equally distinguished for her wit and her beauty and she took part in the literary and poetical gatherings in which her famous patron, the poet So Sik (蘇軾), delighted. Mayers, # 618, 623; Giles, # 1779, 1785.

[25] Ma Gwoo (麻姑) is one of the well-known celebrities of Taoist fable. She was believed to be the sister of the Taoist astrologer Wong Fong-ping (王方平) who was in high favour with the emperor Hon Woon Dai (漢桓帝, 147–67). It is said that Wong Fong-ping, accompanied by his sister, appeared to Choy Ging (蔡經), a man of the people whom he had chosen as his disciple and taught to free himself from the bonds of death. She was dressed beautifully, and she waited on her brother and his pupil (Choy Ging) with food served on golden platters. Choy Ging admired her long fingernails, saying to himself that when his back was itchy, how wonderful it would be if Ma Gwoo used her nails to scratch it. For this wish Choy Ging was punished by having his shoulders beaten by an invisible whip. Ma Gwoo has found her way into the language in a phrase which runs, 'as delightful as being scratched by Ma Gwoo'. Her excessively long nails may have given the idea of the wooden back-scratcher that is in use today. Mayers, # 471, 831; Giles # 1476, 1970, 2256.

[26] 'The embroidered Buddha' refers to Maitreya Buddha. Commentators on a poem by Do Foo in which the line occurs,

> So Jun always fasted before the embroidered Buddha
>
> 蘇晉長齋繡佛前

suggest that a Mongol Buddhist monk had given So Jun a scroll on which was embroidered the Maitreya Buddha. The word Maitreya derives from the Sanskrit word for 'friend', and is frequently transliterated in Chinese as 'nei lak' (彌勒), and explained by 'chi wan' (慈雲), meaning literally, 'compassionate (as the rain) clouds': the Buddha-heart, the Buddha's over-spreading cloud of compassion. Maitreya is a Bodhisattva, a principal figure in Sikyamuni's retinue, though not his disciple. It is said that Sikyamuni visited him in Tushita (See Tenth Preface, Line 1, note) and appointed him to come forth as his successor after a period of 5000 years. Maitreya is now the expected 'Messiah' of the Buddhists. (See also Introduction, pp. 23, 36, 37.)

[27] Mok Sau (莫愁) sang beautifully, and a Chinese poet, Mo Yuen-hang (武元衡) has written about her:

> I do not grudge paying a thousand gold pieces to Mok Sau for her singing.
>
> 不惜千金與莫愁

At fifteen she married a certain Lo, and at sixteen she gave birth to Oh Hau (阿侯) and it was said if you wanted to know how beautiful Mok Sau was, you had only to look on Oh Hau's face.

Siu Long [i.e. a generic name for a lover],[28] has become a stranger to her; the azure clouds are dispersed [i.e. his wife is taken away from him];

Under the laurel-wood rafters in the orchid bower, she has married another.

Mok Sau fondles her child Oh Hau who is wrapped in embroidered swaddling clothes adorned with jade.

Do not go to the old-fashioned 'Bridge of Sighs'[29]

At whose head the autumn willows, half-bare, stand desolate.

No one can sing the song of 'The Region of Mist and Flowers',[30]

Wide, wide, and by day and night in full flow, is the sea of sorrow.

The Ninth Preface

Written by an admiring devotee

These new songs, which the very clouds would stop to listen to, make other pleasures insipid.

I remember how formerly I roamed near So Toi;[31]

---

[28] Siu (蕭), her lover. Siu Long (蕭郎) is the popular name of Siu Yin (蕭衍) who in 502 founded the Leung dynasty (梁, *Liang*, 502–57). Today in Chinese Siu Long means no more than merely 'lover'. Mayers, # 863a; Giles, # 720.

[29] 'The Bridge of Sighs' I have used to translate the Chinese 銷魂橋, *Siu Wan Kiu*. Literally the Chinese means 'the bridge where the soul dissolves, melts in sorrow'. In English the word 'sigh' seems to me to cover this idea adequately, as it means prolonged, deep and more or less audible respiration, following on a deep-drawn breath indicating or expressing dejection, weariness, longing, pain, etc. Certainly 'sighing' is what happens at this bridge, indicating the pain and sadness of farewell. To the east of Cheung On (長安) is the Pa Bridge (灞橋). People made it the place of parting; therefore it was called the Bridge of Sighs. Again we read that during the Hon (漢) dynasty friends accompanied their departing guests to this Pa Bridge, snapped off a willow-twig and gave it as a token of farewell, of reluctance to part. The Chinese character for 'willow' (柳, *lau*) and for 'to stay' (留, *lau*) are homonyms. (See also Songs 76 (Part 2) Line 3; 35 (Part 5), Line 8.)

[30] 'The Region of Mist and Flowers' (煙花地, *yin fa dei*). The first of the two Chinese characters, 煙, literally means smoke, vapour, mist, while the second one literally means 'flowers'. Both are symbols of transience, and are constantly used in Chinese poetry and writing as a metaphor for a courtesan: Songs 14, line 9; 31 (Part 2), line 9; 34, line 9; 45, line 3; 55, line 3 ; 57, line 7. Similarly, 'The region of mist and flowers' (煙花地) is a euphemism for a brothel/ house of entertainment: Songs 31 (Part 1); 46, Line 3; 87, Line 1.

[31] See Third Preface, stanza 3, note.

Tonight I am on the Pearl River, with the moon hanging overhead,

And the notes of the flute rippling across the autumn water and sky.

The spume of the water and the play of the wind greet the feasting dancers,

Where gold can scarcely buy the paper Sit To used.[32]

These poems born of passion's frenzy are the record of the mist and flowers;[33]

The author is a genius because he is talented; he is an immortal because he is chivalrous.

Is there any sense in hearing all about pomp and splendour?

With head bent forward [i.e. in concentration] we never tire of listening to those wondrous songs.

No wonder then that these songs can dispel our griefs.

Someone has stolen and given them to Suet Yi to sing.[34]

These pure songs are like those of the young lady that Do Si-Hung and Wai Ying-mat loved so much,[35]

---

[32] Sit To (薛濤), whose dates are put at c. 768–831, was a well-known courtesan with a considerable reputation as a poet in an age of great poets who lived in Seng-do (成都) the capital of Sei Chuen (四川). Today ninety of the poems attributed to her exist, but this is only about a fifth of the number that once were in circulation. Her admirers gave her name to the ornamental paper on which she wrote her poems. This paper she was said to have dipped in a stream from which water had been taken some years before by a concubine of Chui Ning (崔寗) to wash the stole of a Buddhist priest who had fallen into a cesspool. The stream immediately filled with flowers, and was called, 'The Stream of a Hundred Flowers'. It was the water from this stream that Sit To used to make paper of ten colours. It has been suggested that there were not ten colours but only one colour: deep crimson, a colour associated with poetic exchanges between courtesans and their admirers. In AD 806 Sit To, when she took to writing shorter poems, made smaller-sized sheets which were called 'Sit To paper', and this apparently was her chief innovation. Mayers, # 585; Giles, # 743. See Introduction, p. 16.

[33] See Eighth Preface, Line 15, note.

[34] Suet Yi (雪兒), the concubine of Lei Mat (李密), was an accomplished singer and dancer. Whenever Lei Mat came across a good poem by one of his friends, he would give it to Suet Yi to sing. Mayers, # 359; Giles, # 1176.

[35] Wai Ying-mat (韋應物) and Do Si-hung (杜司空; Do, the Minister of Works) would give poems to this singing-girl to sing for them. Wai Ying-mat (of the 8th century) came from Cheung On (長安). Having given up his military career, he entered the civil service, and later became governor of So Jau. His poetry, simple in expression and pregnant with meaning, is said to have been inspired by his lofty character. The Minister of Works, Do Si-hung, was none other than one of China's most celebrated poets: Do Foo (杜甫, 712–70). Although a promising

As enraptured, with sleeves all fragrant, she sings the spring wind tune.

But, I ask you, how many men can really judge a song?

Even today we still admire Jau Long [i.e. a well-known critic].³⁶

The Tenth Preface

Written by an immortal of the Jade Pool [i.e. a heavenly abode]

For those born in the Heaven of Tushita³⁷ the world of appearances no longer exists;

What harm is there, then, in entering the company of silk-clad maidens?

Our poet's carefree mood is not less than that of Baak Sek's.³⁸

Is he unfit to play the bamboo flute with Siu Hung?³⁹

---

youth, he never distinguished himself in the public examinations, and he took to poetry as a profession. He was given a position at court, where he met Wai Ying-mat and both of them combined to write court poems. When in 755 the emperor who had introduced him to court was dethroned, Do Foo was driven into exile, from which he returned the next year to become Censor. He fell into disgrace with the emperor because of his honesty in fulfilling his duties, and he was appointed governor of a small town; this was almost enforced exile. He resigned and retired to the wilds of Sei Chuen (四川), where he spent a wandering life. Later, however, he was appointed to a more congenial post as President of the Board of Works (工部) which he held for six years before returning to his wandering life. In 770, at the age of 58, he died from over-eating, after being cut off from food for ten days by a flood. Mayers, # 680; Giles, # 2058.

³⁶ Jau Long (周郎) is Jau Yue (周瑜), the critic, from On Hui (安徽 , *On Fai*). In AD 198 he obtained a command in the forces of Suen Kin (孫堅), the father of his best friend, and was popularly known as Jau Long, the name we have in this line. Jau Long was said to have had such a wonderful ear for music that if any one played or sang a wrong note, he would immediately look up even though he might have been drunk. It became almost a proverb to say, 'If there is the slightest thing wrong with the song or the accompaniment, Jau will at once turn his head to look.' Mayers, # 75, 630; Giles, # 428, 1798.

³⁷ The Heaven of Tushita (兜率), Heaven of Satisfaction. The fourth of the six celestial worlds. It is said that *bodhisattvas* are reborn there just before their last re-birth on earth, when they will attain Buddhahood. It is here that Maitreya resides. (See Eighth Preface, Line 8, note.)

³⁸ Baak Sek (白石, literally 'white stone') was so called because he lived on Mount Baak Sek. It is said he boiled white stones for food. Once asked why he did not drink the drug that would bring him to heaven, he replied, 'Those in heaven cannot be as happy as mortal men. In heaven they have to attend and wait on so many beings. That would be worse than serving men on earth.' So he came to be called 'an immortal hidden on earth'. Mayers, # 561; Giles, # 1641.

³⁹ Siu-hung, whose full name was Gwaan Siu-hung (關小紅) was a pipa player during the reign of Emperor Jiu Jung (昭宗, 889–905) of the Tong dynasty (618–907).

It worries him not that in the houses of entertainment he is called a frivolous lover.

Amid red lanterns and green wine [i.e. scenes of debauchery] he sets to music new songs.

He takes his brush and wondrously creates;

Describing fully passion's indifference and passion's allure.

His mastery of the local accent [i.e. Cantonese] makes him an original poet in his own right;

He might well have rivalled the poets at Kei Ting in poetic charm and elegance.[40]

His songs are like the heart-breaking ones of Gong Jau,[41]

And everyone is striving to learn the pipa.

By the banks of the Pearl River is the Jung-yi [i.e. the name of a well-known house of entertainment]

And countless beauties live there,

Who all rely on these songs to dispel their care;

To bring happiness, not to bring sorrow.

The Eleventh Preface

The Deer-park Preface[42]

Formerly I faced the east wind and dared to sing the songs of Canton,

It is almost impossible to forget the accent of your native village.

I thank my master for thoroughly cleansing my ears [i.e. attuning them] to enjoy the pipa's wonderful music,

With a scroll of plum-blossom verses and a fragrant snow-white heart.

My wishes are not fulfilled; my passion is not yet ended,

---

[40] Kei Ting (旗亭, literally: flag-tower) was the place where three equally famous poets of the Tong dynasty: Wong Cheung-ling (黃昌齡, graduated 726), Go Sik (高適, died 765) and Wong Ji-woon (王之渙) met some ten musicians, and held a contest to see whose poems were most popular with these singers.

[41] 'The Songs of Gong Jau' refers to the songs of Baak Gui-yi (白居易, 772–864), one of China's greatest poets. (See Song 12 (Part 4) Line 3, note.) Mayers, # 546; Giles, # 1654.

[42] See Introduction, p. 27, for the allusion possibly intended by the writer of this preface.

Beside the wine, under the candle-light I plainly hear the song.

The reed is newly-made, and its sound is as smooth as the oriole's song,

Would that I could take up the jasper-mounted reed-pipe,[43] and coax its tones!

Your compassionate heart portrays in miniature

Sadness and warning and ridicule.

The bitter heart can only be relieved by heaven's passion,

So I turn and ridicule the Brahmans who mislead the white-robed nuns.

These songs tinged with melancholy urge me to drink,

In comparison, the songs of Chun and Chor are lewd and noisy.[44]

What I regret most is that the strength of spring love has been secretly sapped,

When the willow-branch is snapped,[45] the soul of Siu Suk[46] is wounded.

---

[43] A small musical instrument consisting of a number of pipes of different lengths; it has a spout through which the player sucks in or blows out the air while fingering the keynotes.

[44] See Second Preface.

[45] See Eighth Preface, Line 13, note.

[46] Lei Seung-yan (李商隱, 813–58), the well-known Tong dynasty (618–907) poet and scholar, in his preface to his poem *The Song of the Willow Branch* (柳枝詩) writes that his cousin, Yeung Saan (讓山), got off his horse under a willow-tree near the home of a courtesan called Lau Ji (柳枝), and sang a song of Yin Toi. Lau Ji heard it and immediately asked who had written it. Yeung Saan answered that 'a young cousin of mine (少叔, *Siu Suk*) who lives in my village' had written it. Lau Ji tied a ribbon into a lover's knot and asked Yeung Saan to give it to his 'young cousin' so that he would write a song specially for her. In fact this 'young cousin' was Lei Seung-yan himself and the song he wrote he called: *The Song of the Willow Branch*. Such was the origin of Lei Seung-yan's infatuation for Lau Ji. Mayers, # 364; Giles, # 1188.

The Songs

Song 1 (Part 1)
Dispel Your Sorrows

Everyone has sorrows that weigh on the mind. The first step is you must somehow dispel these sorrows;

Sorrows give you no peace. Dispel these sorrows and then you will have finished with them.

The sea of bitter sorrow is wide, and most of those in it are ill-fated;

But should you be able to draw from this bitter sea of sorrow some happiness you are one of the blessed.

If you are unable to put up with all these sorrows, you have indeed come to a pretty pass;

But even this were better than to enter the hell-gates of a court, where you would be the more to be pitied.

Stand back a little from your sorrows and see the wide expanse of heaven and ocean; you do not need to bemoan your fate.

Dispel all you worries, and you will truly be in a land of endless joy.

If no matter what you do, you cannot completely dispel your worries, then set about doing good secretly.

Oh, you must be circumspect in all your affairs.

There is no danger in storing up for yourself good deeds:

See now, your distant reward is in the life to come; your immediate reward is in the present.

Song 1 (Part 2)
Dispel Your Sorrows

It is hard to dispel sorrows from the heart. But dispel them you must until you are completely free of them.

Looking hard and straight at the word 'dispel' will lighten everything.

I think a thousand sorrows are a thousand sicknesses.

No words can ever express the depth of your sadness.

'Infatuation' is a deep-seated sickness; 'passion' is another.

Unless you eradicate these enslaving thoughts, not even the most potent medicine can cure you.[1]

---

[1] See Songs 12 (Part 1), line 9; 83, line 8.

It is easy to become ensnared among the 'flowers and willows' [i.e. in the houses of entertainment];[2]

Devise some ingenious strategy to quit the 'gentle village' [i.e. the house of entertainment].

You must see through the speciousness of outward appearances[3] [i.e. the phenomenal, the worldly, that which changes and disappears; the desirable, especially feminine attraction] before you can cross the frontier to happiness.

If you are infatuated for long with the 'flowers and willows' you will sink to the depths in the city of sorrow.[4]

Arouse yourself! Realize

This world is inconstant: a willow tree, and men's passions, I tell you,

Veer this way and that before each gust of wind.

Song 2

Choosing a True Heart

In this world you will be hard put to find a single-hearted lover;[5]

If I ever found one, I would follow him even to death.

On the one hand, I would test his sincerity; on the other, I would make certain he did not deceive me.

I would test him until I found his heart was absolutely true; and only then would we begin to talk.

We must beware of all fickle lovers who fritter away our hearts.

Even were a lover to treat me with sincerity, I would still test him several more times.

Out of our million 'guests' [i.e. to the house of entertainment], I would say that not one is true.

---

[2] A similar euphemism is found in the phrase, 尋花問柳, *cham fa man lau*, literally meaning: To seek flowers and ask after willows, and is used to describe a man who consorts with a lot of prostitutes. A woman is called a 'flower' because of her beauty that eventually fades, and a 'willow' because her body is supple and graceful. A woman who no longer retains her virginal freshness is referred to as: a faded willow, a withered flower, 殘花敗柳, *chaan fa baai lau*. (See also Introduction, p. 17.)

[3] See Song 7, line 11.

[4] See Song 12 (Part 1), line 6.

[5] See Song 68, line 9.

The single-hearted lover, like a scattered fragment, is harder to find than a needle in the ocean;

Even if you do find a true-hearted lover, cannot others find him too?

With how many hearts can true love really be shared?[6]

Think carefully about predestined fate which all of us must accept.

Let us be content with our lot:

A previous existence determines our present fate. So envy no one.[7]

Song 3

Do Not Die

Do not lightly spurn life. Our death should be a happy one.

I fear that after death you will say, 'If only I had another chance to die, I would die a timely death.'[8]

Some ought to die; but 'stealing' life they continue to live without a care for their self-esteem.

Some ought not to die, and their death is indeed pitiable.

I believe those who die an untimely death and those who 'steal' life are very different:

The latter suffer from men; the former fill me with sadness.

A glorious death shines more resplendently than any life could ever do.

Loyal ministers and faithful wives are remembered forever.

From the earliest times, girls who made light of life did so because of passion;

When the barriers are broken down, virtue must prevail.

Through the ages, we have seldom seen perfect passion and perfect virtue together;

However, we do have an example of it, not far away:

You have only to read in the '*Dream of the Red Chamber*' about Third Sister and Lau Seung-lin.[9]

---

[6] See Song 61, line 8.
[7] See Songs 9, line 5; 35 (Part 3), line 3; 35 (Part 4), line 8.
[8] See Song 83, line 11.
[9] The famous Chinese novel, *The Dream of the Red Chamber* or *Dream in a Red Chamber* or *Red Chamber Dream* (紅樓夢, *Hung Lau Mung*), more correctly called, *The Story of*

Song 4

Listening to the Oriole in Spring

The broken-hearted dread to hear the oriole's song in spring [i.e. because the oriole, the bird of joy and music, symbolized friendship];

A song that can so easily rend even the soul.

The dawn of spring stirs a man's discontent.

O oriole! Are you and spring together going to crush my heart?

If the oriole's song can, as people say, make me forget my sorrows, then I will listen a while.

Do you think a man cannot compare with a bird, or that a bird cannot compare with a man?

Look how the oriole exults in his own sweet-tongued voice;

It flies to scenes of natural beauty, and there communes with spring.

If only you would speak some round words to that fickle lover for me...

But I am afraid that even though you did not mince your words, he would pretend he had never heard them.

Could I in my dreams be changed into a bird, I would fly away with you to seek him out;

---

a Stone (石頭記) was composed in the later part of AD 17th century by Tso Suet-kan (曹雪芹) (chapters 1–80) and Go Ngoh (高鶚) (chapters 81–120). Third Sister, (尤三姐 , *Yau Saam Je*), is the youngest of three sisters. The eldest was married to Ga Chan (賈珍); and the second sister was the concubine of his brother, Ga Lin (賈璉). Third Sister was unmarried and lived with her two sisters in the Ga household, which had a reputation for debauchery and licentiousness. Third Sister's virtue, however, was unsullied, despite her surroundings.

One day the scholar Lau Seung-lin (柳湘蓮) met Third Sister, and for both of them it was love at first sight. They were betrothed, and Lau Seung-lin gave Third Sister two swords with the characters for mandarin drake and duck# (鴛鴦 , *yuen yeung*) engraved on them.

Some time later, Lau Seung-lin came to hear of the dissolute habits of the Ga family with whom his betrothed was living. Fearing Third Sister had been corrupted by them, he broke off their engagement and demanded back the two swords he had previously given her.

Third Sister handed back one sword to Lau Seung-lin. With the other she stabbed herself to death.

Grief-stricken, Lau Seung-lin became a Buddhist monk.

Obviously Third Sister was a model of both passion and virtue.

\# 'Mandarin drake and duck' (鴛 , *yuen*, the drake; 鴦 , *yeung*, the hen): The Chinese have taken these beautiful waterfowl (Chinese teal) that manifest a unique degree of attachment to each other as a symbol of married love and fidelity; a symbol that appears again and again in these songs.

And speak frankly to him, and make him answer me.

Ah! How helpless I am! Here I am resting on my pillow, dreaming . . .

Had I not been wakened from my dream, I would have flown away with you.

Song 5

Thoughts Arise

Thoughts. Thoughts. My thoughts arise;

And thinking, I stifle my sorrow.

I cannot bear to speak about that fickle lover.

When first we met, he swore his heart would never change;

That our love would be as enduring as the universe; that we would share our destiny.

I was sure I had made no mistake in choosing you, so handsome and talented;

But you thought nothing of casting me aside. And wasted now are those days when I used to cherish you in my heart.

Today I grieve for my lonely life. I dare not complain about your lack of virtue.

You were willing to part with me, 'an exquisite flower in the Laurel Garden'; but why must ne'er-do-wells and wastrels snap my branches?[10]

---

[10] It was believed during the Tong dynasty (618–907) that a laurel tree grew in the moon. During the Sung dynasty (960–1279) it was said that a tree sacred to the memory of the Buddha's birth and death was identical with the laurel tree in the moon: As this 'tree' was especially visible at mid-autumn, the ninth day of the ninth month, when the examination for Provincial Graduate (舉人, *Gui Yan*) was held, getting one's degree was referred to as 'breaking off a branch from the laurel tree'. Successful candidates were readily acceptable and accepted as bridegrooms. In this song, the line suggests: 'If I am as exquisite and precious as the laurel tree, only distinguished men of learning should snap my branch. Not every Tom, Dick and Harry who happens to feel the urge.' (See also Song 11 (Part 2), line 6. Mayers, # 300.)

It is hard to know how best translate the Chinese character 桂, *gwai*. Chinese/English dictionaries give 'cassia'. And in English/Chinese dictionaries 'cassia' is translated as: the gwai tree in the moon. But when you look up, for example, the Oxford English Dictionary under 'cassia', you will find that 'cassia' refers to

You abandoned me for another, abruptly leaving me.

Neither you nor I will ever speak about what fate may hold in store for us, or what doom was predestined for both of us.

With half my life wasted, you now dare to tell me to look for a true friend. Do you think that will be easy?

People call me 'a blighted willow', 'a withered flower'. I have harvested nothing from my life.

The roots of the juniper tree strike deep. Would that our love had been the same.

When we meet in 'The Nine Springs' [i.e. in the next life] everything will be made clear to you.

Our former life did not predestine us to share a present fate; therefore do I find myself brusquely abandoned by you.

Ah, what misery!

Why do I have to stay any longer in this empty world?

It would have been better for me to die; and in heaven, away from all sorrow, wait for you my lord. Even then it would not be too late.

---

the tree *Cinnamomum cassia*, and it also refers to the bark of the *Cinnamomum cassia* from which comes one of the oldest spices (also called Chinese Cinnamon): the aromatic spice used for flavouring in cooking and in particular in liqueurs and chocolate. Senna refers to any of the plants (especially of the species Cassia) whose leaves are known for their cathartic and laxative qualities.

Cinnamon, a genus of the Laurel, is an evergreen tree and is translated in Chinese by 玉桂, *yuk-gwai*. One of its species, the *Cinnamomum camphora*, can grow to 100 feet in height and yields camphor which is used medicinally and for explosives. Cinnamon also refers to the inner bark of an East Indian tree, the species *Cinnamomum zeylanicum*, which having been dried in the sun, is used as a spice. It is from this *Cinnamomum zeylanicum* that we get our 'cinnamon spice'.

Going a step higher on the ladder, we arrive at the Laurel. The Laurel comprises 11 families, 68 genera and more than 2800 species of trees, shrubs and vines, found mostly in the tropics and warmer regions of the world. Most familiar to us, perhaps, is the *Laurus nobilis*, commonly called Bay Tree or Bay Laurel. In ancient Greece a chapelet of leaves and branches from this tree was a symbol of honour presented to victorious athletes and other heroes. One of the 68 genera of the Laurel is the cinnamon tree with its many species of which the *Cinnamomum cassia* is but one.

Given that we have no way of discovering which species of tree from which genus from which family of Laurel, is the 'tree in the moon', I have thought it better to translate *gwai* by the more general term 'Laurel'. In the context of these Cantonese songs, the connotations of *gwai* and laurel are not totally dissimilar.

Song 6

Ungenerous Fate

Too late we came to know each other.[11] So ungenerous is fate![12]

We met for a brief moment; and our parting crushed me.

Why was our meeting so auspicious, yet our time together so short?

The goose which carries my letter to you today laments the distance that separates us.[13]

As a young girl how could I have ever known I would sink this low, here — to be a mere plaything?

Although at night I sleep with another, I feel utterly alone.

I regret that at the outset I did not heed your warnings, my prince [i.e. merely a poetic word for 'you'],

---

[11] See Song 42, line 12.

[12] See Song 81.

[13] Fish and geese were the classical messengers of love or friendship. There is a Chinese phrase, 魚雁往來, *yue ngaan wong loi*, literally meaning: Fish and geese passing to and fro, which refers to correspondence by letter.

The 'fish' element derives from a story about Yan Sin (殷羨) of the 1st century BC who used to throw his letters into the river to be carried to the addressee with the stream or by the fish. A poet relates how he was brought some carp by a boy and on cutting one of them open, found inside it a letter from his beloved, declaring her love for him. The Tong dynasty poet, Lei Seung-yan (李商隱, 813–58) has a line in his poem, *A Message to Secretary Ling-Hu*:

And I send to you a message carried by two carp.

雙鯉沼沼一祇書

The 'geese' element refers to an ingenious method of communication used by So Mo (蘇武). In 100 BC Emperor Hon Mo Dai (漢武帝) sent his envoy So Mo on a mission to the Huns (匈奴). Once there, So Mo set about killing a Chinese renegade, Wai Lut (衛律), whom the Khan of the Huns greatly favoured. Even in prison So Mo refused to forswear allegiance to his emperor. He was later exiled to the desert where for nineteen years he tended the Hun flocks. Legend has it that after many years he tied a note to the leg of a goose which was about to fly southwards. Emperor Hon Mo Dai, out hunting one day, shot down this goose, and learned of the whereabouts of his envoy So Mo. Immediately steps were taken for his release. Mayers, # 628; Giles, # 1792.

The Chinese have taken the goose as a symbol of correspondence by letter. This symbol (of the letter-carrying goose) occurs very frequently in these songs. (See, for example, Songs 16 & 29.) Like the mandarin drake and duck and the phoenix (see Songs 64 & 88), the goose, taking one partner for life and represented in art as flying in pairs, is a symbol of married bliss. As a migratory bird, the goose can also be a symbol of separation. On the other hand it can be regarded as messenger of good tidings from those far away in northern lands. See also Song 28, line 3, note.

Because I wanted to pay my flower-debt [i.e. to ransom herself from the house of entertainment] I went astray with other men.

Now with them I have to be very discerning, and

Choose properly.

Very few in this world pity us flowers [i.e. courtesans].

However, if a man would prop up a flower, he must be extremely careful to fence it about.

Song 7

The World of Flowers

This world of flowers [i.e. this wanton, carnal world] is ugly. But why speak of it?

Ah me! Why did I do so many evil things?

How it chills my heart to see before my very eyes those who have sunk to these depths!

Wantonness. It is the same everywhere.

Better far to fast and pray to the Buddha, and to read the Sutras.[14]

Now, with one stroke of the brush I will blot out the word 'passion', and never more will I dare to have rebellious desires,

And my debt of sin will be cancelled;

Lest I lose my virtue and degrade myself in the 'sell-smile village' [i.e. the place where smiles can be sold].

Morning and evening will I burn joss-sticks,

And clasp my hands,

And in meditation, I will pierce the mask of beauty [i.e. the outwardly manifest].[15]

I am determined to leave this bitter sea of sorrow, and to seek refuge in Gwoon Yam's Boat of Mercy.[16]

---

[14] 'To pray to the Buddha' means to meditate on the Buddha or invoke his name. (See Introduction, pp. 32, 36, 37.)

[15] See Song 1 (Part 2), line 9.

[16] Gwoon Yam (觀音) is treated of in the Introduction, p. 37, et seq. In Chinese tradition, however, she became a historical person, the daughter of King Chong (莊王) of the Chau (周, *Chou*) dynasty. When she refused to marry because she wanted to become a nun, her father ordered her to be beheaded, but the sword

Song 8
The Farewell Banquet

Cheerless is the cup that speeds the parting guest.

When bidding 'farewell' I entreated him a thousand times.

'It will not be long,' he said, 'before you have a letter from me.'

But now, more than half a year has passed — and each single day counted on my fingers — without a letter.

Longing for him I weep; but want no one to know of my secret tears.[17]

How could you be so unkind, you heartless one?

I say no more; except that I have rid myself of you. That never again will I think about you, day or night.

My only regret is that in my dreams we still meet, and with impatient desire I try to embrace you.

Tell me how I may be like a swallow that never flies but in a pair.

The flight of the swallows is not without a purpose: in autumn they fly away, and they fly back in spring,[18]

To whisper sweetly among the flowers.

Song 9
Woe Is Me

My sighs and tears are secret. No one knows my feelings.

Since you went away you have not written a word to me.

---

attempting this shattered, leaving Gwoon Yam unscathed. Not satisfied, her father had her choked. Her soul descended to the underworld, and transformed hell into heaven. The king of the underworld Yim Loh (閻羅) sent her back to life and she was carried on a lotus-flower to the island of Potala (普陀, *Po Toh*) near Ning Boh (寧波), where she lived for nine years healing diseases and rescuing seafarers from shipwreck.

In this song the singer very fittingly calls on Gwoon Yam to rescue her from the 'wide sea of bitter sorrow' and bring her to safety in her Boat of Mercy, her 'Ark of Salvation'.

[17] See Song 56 (Part 3).

[18] The Chinese phrase 秋去春來 , *chau hui chun loi*, meaning going in autumn and coming back in spring, refers to birds of passage, to travellers. The singer is hoping her lover will come back to her.

Because of you, my lord, I am pale and thin;

You have taught me to wanton all night long in dreams of hot passion.

Ah, woe is me! I did not in a former life cultivate virtue, and now in this present life I am scorned and despised.

Fate destines beautiful women to be lonely and sad.[19] How long their sadness will last for, I cannot tell.

You played me false. When I wipe the tears from my cheeks I must turn away from others,

Because these signs of sorrow would betray my yearning for you.

There is no way I can free myself of woe.

Alas, life holds no enjoyment for me.

O Heaven, I want you to decree that in this life there will never be any parting.

Song 10

Infatuation

I have to speak about infatuation.

How can the infatuated person be discerning?

In this world all too many are languishing from love.

If a man nurtures spring-love in his heart but does not reveal it to his beloved,

And is told to be shy and bashful in front of her, how will he ever tie the marriage knot?[20]

Nothing is worse than having something to say and being unable to say it;

It is just like going back to when you were a child.

If you lack steadfastness of purpose,

You will find it hard to overcome the difficulties that would crush you.

---

[19] The Chinese phrase 紅顏薄命, *hung ngaan bok meng*, meaning rosy cheeks, ill-fated destiny, expresses the idea, repeated in these songs, that beauty brings misfortune.

[20] See Song 90, line 9, note.

Song 11 (Part 1)
Lamenting the Ill-fated

Man is lonely; the moon shines brighter than ever.

I have not yet fully paid my lust-debt for wallowing in desire and passion.

Meetings and partings, sorrows and joys — these are decreed by fate.

Why must fate blight famous flowers [i.e. beautiful women], leaving them to wither and die?

Yeung Gwai-fei's jade-like bones are buried under a mountain track;[21]

Over Jiu Gwan's grave the grass is ever green;[22]

---

[21] Yeung Gwai-fei (楊貴妃), whose personal name was Yeung Yuk-waan (楊玉環), one of China's four most celebrated beauties, was the all-powerful, idolized favourite of Emperor Yuen Jung (唐玄宗 713–56), the sixth emperor of the Tong dynasty (618–907). In 735 she became one of the concubines of Prince Shau (壽王), the emperor's eighteenth son. In 738 when the emperor's favourite concubine died, Yeung Yuk-waan was chosen to replace her. She was surpassingly beautiful, and is noted as being the only one of China's historical beauties who was plump. In 745 she was raised to the rank of gwai-fei (貴妃), that is, the highest ranking imperial concubine (a title second only in dignity to that of the empress) and it is as Yeung Gwai-fei that she is most commonly known. In 755, On Luk-saan (安祿山) the adopted son of Yeung Gwai-fei, took advantage of the emperor to acquire power and influence, and mounted a successful rebellion against the throne. The following year, the now ageing emperor, together with Yeung Gwai-fei and his court, fled to Sei Chuen (四川). However, at Ma Ngai (馬嵬), the troops revolted demanding vengeance on the Yeung family, and refusing to go any further unless the emperor put Yeung Gwai-fei and her second cousin Yeung Gwok-jung (楊國忠) to death. The emperor was forced to order a eunuch to strangle his beloved Yeung Gwai-fei before his very eyes. However, some accounts suggest she was hanged on a pear tree and buried by the roadside. Mayers, # 525, 887; Giles, # 11, 2394.

[22] Wong jiu-gwan (王昭君) was said to have been taken into the concubinate of the Hon emperor Yuen Dai (漢元帝), in 48 BC. Although from a poor family, she was surpassingly beautiful. Mo Yin-sau (毛延壽) was commissioned to paint her portrait. But because her father refused to pay him a sum of money by way of bribery, Mo Yin-sau painted her far less beautiful than she was, with the result that the emperor had no wish to see her, and she languished in oblivion for years. One day the emperor chanced to see her and was immediately captivated by her beauty. When Mo Yin-sau's plot was discovered, he fled the imperial court and sought asylum with the Khan of the Huns (匈奴) to whom he showed a painting of the 'real' Jiu-gwan. Smitten by her incomparable beauty and to win her for himself, the Khan invaded China. Only when Jiu-gwan was surrendered to him did he agree to retire beyond the Great Wall. Jiu-gwan went with her captor as far as the banks of the Amur (黑龍江, *Hak Lung Gong*), where she plunged into the river and drowned herself. Her body was interred on the banks of the river, and it is said that the mound above her grave remains covered with green grass. Another version of the same story has it that she was buried alongside the Chinese boundary, close to the Great Wall. The grass on the Hun side of the Great Wall is yellow, whereas on the Chinese side it is green. Mayers, # 45; Giles, # 2148.

Siu Ching, in poverty and bewailing her fate, died looking at her portrait;[23]

Sap-neung drank deeply the waters of misery.[24]

Generally most beautiful women suffer a harsh fate —

Let alone we flowers and powder [i.e. we courtesans] in the houses of entertainment who are dragged down by the extravagant passion of others.

Since we are willow blossoms [i.e. courtesans], and most of us are weak as water,

How can we escape undefiled from the mire, and show ourselves once again constant and faithful?

What I am most afraid of is that we will be like the elm leaves which sad autumn wafts into the Golden Well.[25]

---

[23] An old woman once foretold that Siu Ching (小青) would be precocious, but that her fortune would be fragile. The prophecy came true, for Siu Ching and her lover's wife became bitter enemies. One day Siu Ching said to her maids, 'Send a good portrait painter to me.' The artist came and she told him to paint her portrait. When it was finished, she commented that while the likeness was there, the expression was absent. When a second portrait had been painted, she remarked, 'The expression is there, but it has no life. Perhaps the melancholy of my face deceived you.' So she told him to paint another portrait. During the painting she talked to her maids, looked at them, and plucked at her clothes. When the painting was finished, it was a masterpiece of grace and liveliness. And she said, 'This will do'. When the artist had left, she took her portrait and pouring a libation of wine in front of it said, 'Siu Ching, Siu Ching, was this your fate?' And she fell back on a chair, 'weeping like the rain', and died.

[24] Sap-neung (十娘) was so called because she was the tenth of her brothers and sisters. Her full name was: Do (杜) Sap-neung, and she lived during the reign of Maan Lik (1573–1620), an emperor of the Ming dynasty (1368–1644). She became a courtesan at the age of thirteen, and six years later, already rich with her earnings, she met in Peking Lei Yu-sin (李于先), whose father had sent him there to study for the degree of Provincial Graduate (舉人, Gui Yan). Both of them fell in love with each other. Lei Yu-sin, however, after a year in Peking, had used up all his allowance and his angry father ordered him home. Sap-neung accompanied Lei Yu-sin, and the two of them were travelling on the river Lo Hoh (潞河), making their way to Siu Hing Foo (紹興府) when they met a very wealthy friend of Lei Yu-sin's, called Suen Foo (孫富). Realizing that Lei Yu-sin was almost penniless and in dread of his father's anger, Suen Foo persuaded Lei Yu-sin to sell him his mistress, Sap-neung, for a reasonably large sum of money. The next morning when Sap-neung was being handed over from Lei Yu-sin's boat to that of Suen Foo, she opened a casket she was carrying. Both Lei Yu-sin and Suen Foo were astonished by its jewels of priceless value. Chiding her lover Lei Yu-sin for his cruelty and avarice, and holding the casket of precious jewels in her arms, Sap-neung jumped into the river and drowned herself.

[25] There is a story of a certain Portuguese astronomer, a Yam Tin Gaam (欽天監) at the Imperial Court, who was asked by a rival astronomer Jeung Tin See (張天師),

Rather must we try to be like the plum tree[26] in winter that withstands the rigours of frost and snow.

I think flowers and trees are happy all the year round;

Those weighed down by sorrow will always stifle their grief and keep back their words when talking to others.

We must arouse ourselves!

Everyone is witness to the fickleness of fate.

I will go to the Grave of A Hundred Flowers and there pour out the sum of my life.[27]

Song 11 (Part 2)

Lamenting the Ill-fated

I will lament my ill-fate to the willow tree.

The same pair of entrancing eyes that bids farewell to one guest [i.e. to the house of entertainment] welcomes another.

See how gracefully she bends her willow waist before the wind;

But look, sorrow has knit her brows. Her sorrow must be great.

Young and delicate though she is, spring stirs up her blood;

'On what day does summer change to autumn?' The Portuguese *Yam Tin Gaam* replied: 'In Hok Gung is a well; beside this well grows an elm tree. Before autumn comes, it does not shed its leaves. Take a golden bowl and place it on the rim of the well. On the first day of autumn an elm leaf will fall into the golden bowl. That is the day on which summer changes into autumn.'

Perhaps the epithet 'Golden' (in the expression, 'the Golden Well') refers to the water in the well reflecting the golden leaves on the tree.

However, a Chinese poet of the Tong dynasty (618–907), Wong Cheung-ling (黃昌齡, c. AD 726), has the following line:

In autumn, yellow are the phoenix-leaves over the golden well.

金井梧桐秋葉黃

It may well be to this line the singer is alluding.

[26] See Introduction, pp. 17, 18 and Song 11 (Part 5).

[27] In the time of Sung Jing (崇禎, AD 1628) there was a famous courtesan named Jeung Kiu (張喬). When she died, each of her some hundred lovers planted a flower over her tomb. In time, her tomb, covered with many hued and beautiful flowers, was called: 'The Tomb of Flowers'.

Pitiable it is that like a twig she has been snapped and broken.[28] It grieves my heart.

I am not willing to marry the east wind [i.e. just anybody who comes along]; my love for you will never change.

I know men will resent me because I am leaving my village and my country.

Passion, whether it be short-lived or long, is retribution for evil deeds in a previous life.

I dread the pain of parting; I will not be able to keep my prime for long.

You have flouted my infatuation for you, and you have driven me to the Yeung Gwaan Pass.[29]

My heart can find no place of rest.

After death I cannot imagine who will think of me.

Better for me that I shed my tears for 'The Hundred Flowers',[30] and be changed into a willow leaf tossed on the water's surface.

Song 11 (Part 3)
Lamenting the Ill-fated

I will lament my ill-fate to the lotus-flower.

Oh that we could rise like you, unblemished, from the water.

I remember how talented men and beautiful ladies would come here to bribe the summer [i.e. the time of the lotus flower] to stay for ever.

---

[28] See Song 5, line 9, note.

[29] The Yeung Gwaan Pass (陽關), in the province of Gam Siu (甘肅) on the border of China and Mongolia, is frequently taken in poetry as a symbol of parting. The Tong poet, Wong Wai (王維, 699–759), in his *Farewell to an Envoy on His Mission to Kucha* has the lines:

> I urge thee, friend, another cup of wine to drain,
> Since west of Yang-kwan Pass you'll seek for friends in vain.
>
> 勸君更進一杯酒
> 西山陽關無故人

　　Translation by Tsai Ting-kan in *Gems of Classical Chinese Poetry in Various English Translations*. (See also Song 86, line 8.)
Mayers, # 827; Giles, # 2241.

[30] See Song 11 (Part 1), line 19, note.

You with your jade body stood solitary like the azalea in the abode of the blessed;[31]

Then were you most prized.

How magnificent are the myriad red and green hues of the azalea!

Is the moon's reflection in the water, is the flower's reflection in the mirror real or unsubstantial?

The autumn wind harshly unleaves the trees; and I do not know under whose roof the leaves will fall.

Oh! For how long more will the roots and seeds of passion last?

Ah me, it is indeed terrifying:

Neither fire nor water can devour our passion.

Perhaps the incantation to the lotus-bowl might transform our roots and buds that now lie deep in the murky waters of sin.[32]

Song 11 (Part 4)
Lamenting the Ill-fated

I will lament my ill-fate to the phoenix tree.

---

[31] Yan Chat-chat (殷七七) had the gift of being able to make flowers blossom out of season. Jau Bo (周寶) decided to test Chat-chat's powers. In Hok Lam temple (鶴林寺) was a red azalea (杜鵑, *do guen*), more than ten feet high, and beneath its flowers roamed three flower-spirits. Jau Bo asked Chat-chat, 'Can you make this azalea blossom? We have almost reached the ninth day of the ninth moon. Can you make it blossom in this season?' Two days afterwards, Chat-chat went and slept there. At midnight, the three flower-spirits came and said to him, 'We were commanded by heaven to come down to earth to watch over this flower which has been among men for more than a hundred years. Before long it must return to fairyland. Tonight we will help you to make the flower blossom.' The very next day the azalea began to bud, and by the ninth day of the ninth moon, was in full bloom, as if it were spring-time. Afterwards, the Hok Lam temple was set on fire by rebel soldiers and burnt to the ground. The azalea perished, and is believed to have returned to the abode of the blessed.

[32] Buddhocinga (佛圖登, *Fat To Dang*), who died in AD 384, was a native of India who with the aid of magic spread Buddhism in China (c. 310). The emperor Sek Lak (石勒, 273–332) invited him to his court to test his wisdom. It is related that Buddhocinga took a bowl full of water, burned joss-sticks and recited dharani (咒, *jau*, a formula, often in Sanskrit and forming a part of the Sutra literature in China as early as AD 3rd century, said to protect whoever recites it and to benefit the person by virtue of its mystic power). The water in the bowl immediately produced a green lotus-flower as dazzlingly bright as the sun. Emperor Sek Lak thereupon became a convert to Buddhism. Giles, # 574, 1720.

Once blown off the tree, even a single leaf will murmur against the autumn wind.

The tender green branch knows a thousand sorrows,

But after light rain, it is transformed.

The rustling of its leaves inspires the poet's dream,

And he writes his songs under their green shade.

Were I this poet's patron, I would plant the phoenix tree in his garden,

And tell him not to wait until it had burnt before discovering its worth.[33]

I hate it when autumn spreads sorrow everywhere;

What good is there in making people sad?

Generally, you are the first to pity fragrance and show tenderness to jade [i.e. to be tender and compassionate to young women].[34]

---

[33] The story runs that the renowned musician Choi Yung (蔡邕), whose dates are: 133–92, was sitting beside the fire one day, when he heard the crackle of a burning piece of phoenix wood (桐木, *tung muk*). He said that the tone of the (crackling) sound gave promise of rare excellence. He took the piece of burning phoenix wood from the fire and made it into the body of a lute. Because the handle of the lute showed signs of having been burnt, it gave rise to the name, the Lute with the Scorched Handle (焦尾琴, *jiu mee kam*). Mayers, # 755; Giles, # 1986.

The tree referred to in this Song (line 1) is the 梧桐, *ng tung*, frequently not translated, but simply romanized as 'the wu-tung tree'. (In Cantonese it would be pronounced: 'ng-tung'.) J A Turner in A *Golden Treasury of Chinese Poetry* translates 'wu-tung' as 'Phoenix tree', and I have accepted his translation. This tree is a favourite of Chinese poets. It has a tall, noble stem and great dark leaves, blueish-green-to-grey underneath, with a profusion of flowers whiter than hawthorn in springtime. Writing his *Sketches by the Little Window* (小窗幽記) Chan Mei-gung (陳眉公) describes the phoenix tree:

> For a quiet studio, one should have some green phoenix trees in front and some emerald bamboos behind . . . The beauty of the phoenix tree is that all of its leaves fall off in spring and winter, thus admitting us to the full enjoyment of the sun's warmth, while in summer and autumn its shade protects us from the scorching heat.

(Translation by Lam Yue-tong, in his *Gems from Chinese Literature*.)

凡靜室，須前栽碧梧，後種翠竹···然碧梧之趣，春冬落葉，

以舒負暄融和之樂；夏秋交蔭，以蔽炎爍蒸烈之威。

A Chinese phrase runs: The phoenix roosts in the phoenix tree (鳳棲梧桐, *fung chai ng tung*), and it is said to be the only tree the phoenix deems worthy of its presence. (See also Song 18, line 8, note.)

The lute (琴, *kam*) is a general name for certain musical instruments including the violin, piano and mouth-organ. More precisely it is a seven-stringed plucked instrument similar in some ways to the zither (瑟, *sat*).

[34] See Songs 31 (Part 2), line 4; 33, line 3; 39, line 7; 74 (Part 2), line 12.

I am so delicate and weak that I am afraid the harsh wind will destroy me. Do write to me some words of consolation.

Reflect very carefully on just how many famous flowers [i.e. beautiful women] can endure the weight of frost.

Ah! You have not been true to your heart;

It pains me even to speak of this.

From the beginning of time, the only tree that did not fear old age was the fabled pine tree deep in the valley near where the mountain torrent flowed.[35]

Song 11 (Part 5)
Lamenting the Ill-fated

I will lament my ill-fate to the winter plum.[36]

How can I ever be like you, winter plum, unrivalled among the flowers!

Your ice-like tissue and jade-like form are loved by all.[37]

Although your limbs are proud, you take root anywhere.

I have put you in a tall vase, but I blush to stand beside you.

How many lives of cultivating virtue did you pass through before achieving your present sparkling, crystal-clear, jade-like form?

Alone in the depths of sin I cherish the fragrance of a virtuous life,[38]

---

[35] Three of the last four characters of this Cantonese song are identical to the title of a poem by Baak Gui-yi (白居易, 772–846), in which he speaks of a pine tree, one hundred feet in height and ten feet in girth, that grew bleak and mean in a river glen, deep among mountain precipices, where no man had ever set foot. A Chinese phrase says, 'To live as long as the pine tree or crane' (松鶴延齡, *chung hok yin ling*). The pine was regarded as a symbol of longevity and steadfastness, and its sap was said to turn into amber when the tree was 1000 years old.

[36] See Introduction, p. 17 et seq.; Song 11 (Part 1), line 14.

[37] The literal meaning of these words is: ice-flesh jade-bone (冰肌玉貴, *bing gei yuk gwat*), and they refer to feminine chastity, in obvious contrast to the singer's own life in the house of entertainment. A similar Chinese phrase: 'Clear as ice and pure as jade', (冰清玉潔, *bing ching yuk git*) refers to feminine pure-mindedness. Jade has always been the favourite gem-stone in China. Genuine jade is always cool to the touch and symbolizes the skin of a beautiful woman. It also symbolizes purity. A large number of complimentary phrases (some with erotic overtones) used about a woman have the word 'jade' in them.

[38] See Songs 13 (Part 1), line 16; 42; 68, line 15.

The life of the willow leaves, the lotus flower, and the topaz tree [i.e. three symbols of purity].

I do not think that famous flowers [i.e. beautiful women] have any wish to be ravished by vagrant bees.³⁹

I must be patient,

Preserve the green hills.⁴⁰

My flower- [i.e. sin-] debt fully paid, I hope I will still be able to reach the Isles of the Blest.⁴¹

Song 12 (Part 1)

Passion Is Killing Me

Given my particular character, I reflect on my life,

And find I have a question to ask of heaven:

Why does my lover drift aimlessly like a tuft of soft down from a willow tree?

Why am I, a withered leaf on the water, not made clean and pure?

While men seek happiness in the region of wind and moon [i.e. in the seductive arts of women in the houses of entertainment],

Why do I, amidst groves of mist and flowers [i.e. in the houses of entertainment] build for myself a City of Sorrow?⁴²

I am like Siu Ching who, not seeing her former beauty reflected in her portrait,⁴³

Complained to high heaven, asking for its support.

Truly no medicine can ever cure lovesickness.⁴⁴

---

³⁹ See Songs 35 (Part 6), line 10; 74 (Part 2), line 9.

⁴⁰ The Chinese phrase: 留得青山在 *lau dak ching saan joi* (preserve the green hills) is only the first part of a longer expression, which is completed by: 那怕沒柴燒 *na pa moot chai siu* (and you won't have to worry about having no firewood to burn.) The singer is suggesting that if only she can be patient, perhaps she will find a way out, perhaps her lover . . . perhaps another . . .

⁴¹ During the Chun (秦) dynasty (221–07 BC) it was believed that the Three Isles of the Blest lay in the Eastern Sea, opposite the coast of China. Mayers, # 559, 925.

⁴² See Song 1 (Part 2), line 10.

⁴³ See Song 11 (Part 1), line 7.

⁴⁴ See Songs 1 (Part 2), line 6; 83, line 8.

Can anyone witness to this?

I can. I here own up to and confess my sickness.

Ah yes, it is senseless passion that will kill me.

Song 12 (Part 2)
Passion Is Killing Me

To be pulled and dragged this way and that by passion is killing me.

Overwhelmed by spring sorrow, is there anyone I can talk to?

Although the green willow's nature is to draw tight together the weak tendrils,

Always, as in Jeung Toi, when spring declines, hope fades, and nothing is left but chill poverty.[45]

If there are any distinguished men who appreciate our spring-breeze face [i.e. beaming with smiles, radiant with happiness, with erotic (spring) connotations],

They will certainly sympathize with us, because they suffer from the same sickness.

Tell me, is there anyone who does not resent falling into this world of wind and dust [i.e. of a courtesan]?

There is no gainsaying it, withered red blossoms [i.e. withered women] cannot escape the inexorable decree of heaven.

She is a homeless, forlorn swallow that has left its nest;

Ah! But how the wind is wild!

I have lost my way. I cut a path through the forest [i.e. through this dense jungle of life, eerie, full of dangers].

And so all my life I have been buried. Buried in a field of flowers.[46]

---

[45] Jeung Toi (章臺) is the district where Jeung Toi-lau (章臺柳), a romantic figure of the Tong dynasty, was born. She was said to have been given in marriage to the poor but scholarly Hon Wang (韓翃) by his patron, whose concubine she had been. During the troubled period of AD 756 she became separated from her husband and sought refuge in a convent. Here in her seclusion, she received a note from her husband, who addressed her with reference to her name as, 'Willow-lady of Jeung Toi' (章臺柳). Having forcibly been made the wife of a Tartar chief, she was eventually restored to her husband, Hon Wang. Mayers, # 36; Giles, # 110, 619.

[46] Cf. Song 11 (Part 1), line 19.

Song 12 (Part 3)
Passion Is Killing Me

To be caught in the clutches of passion is killing me.

My great mistake was to swear by the sea and the mountains [i.e. to solemnly pledge her love to him].

After a while, sweet dreams are nothing but paintings,

As unsubstantial as the moon in the stream, the flower in the mirror.[47]

I, pure as the plum blossom, married the east wind.

The day came when you discarded me, just as the poet Lei Seung-yan discarded Ngok Luk-wa.[48]

You made my heart a flag in the wind; and I could not haul it down.

Thinking over it now, it would have been better for me to die in your house, my lord.

I have not dared to speak out plainly to others.

My lord, think about this in your own mind:

Were the promises you made to me true or false?

I hope you will sail on the raft that at autumn tide floats in the moon.[49]

---

[47] See Song 54, line 10.

[48] Ngok Luk-wa (萼綠華) was a lovely nymph, twenty years old, who lived in Naam Saan (南山). In AD 359, she came down from heaven and visited the family of Yeung Kuen (羊權), whom she taught to make magic cures. Then she suddenly disappeared; but afterwards, in the 9th century, became incarnate as a courtesan in So Jau (蘇州), where the poet Lei Seung-yan (李商隱) fell in love with and wrote admiringly of her. In the end, however, he discarded her. Mayers, # 364; Giles, # 1188.

[49] Legend has it that Jeung Hin (張騫), who lived in the 2nd century BC, was sent to discover the sources of the Yellow River (黃河). At that time, people believed the Yellow River was a continuation of the Milky Way (銀河, *Ngan Hoh*). Jeung Hin took a raft and sailed up a stream for many days; until in the autumn he reached a city where he saw a young girl spinning and a young man leading an ox. Jeung Hin asked the girl where he was. The spinning girl gave him her shuttle, telling him to show it, when he had returned to his own country, to the astronomer Yim Guan-ping (嚴君平) who would know where it had come from. When Yim Guan-ping saw the shuttle he made his calculations and found that the very day and the very hour when Jeung Hin received the shuttle from the spinning girl corresponded accurately with the moment when he had observed a wandering star intrude itself between the position of The Spinning Girl (織女, *Jik Nui*), the star Vega in the constellation of Lyra, and The Cowherd (牽牛, *Hin Ngau*), a star in the constellation of Aquila. It was therefore concluded that Jeung Hin had in fact sailed on a raft along the Milky Way. (See also Songs 18, line 10, note; 82, line 11.) Mayers, # 18, 311; Giles, # 29.

Song 12 (Part 4)

Passion Is Killing Me

To live as passion's slave is killing me.

I am spurned as floating duckweed[50]. I am buffeted by the waves.

My lord, after your garments were wet, your lover heard from you no more.[51]

---

[50] Two Chinese phrases, similar to one another, help explain her meaning. One is, duckweed trails, not fixed (萍棕無定, *ping jung mo ding*), and has the sense of wandering aimlessly; the other is, floating like duckweed between north and south (萍浮南北, *ping fau naam bak*), and refers to not having any fixed place to live.

[51] Baak Gui-yi (白居易, 772–846), one of the greatest poets of the Tong dynasty (618–907), was an extremely precocious student. Having graduated at seventeen he immediately began an official career; and under the emperor Hin Jung (獻宗) he rose to high rank. Unexpectedly he was banished to Gong Jau (江州) as Magistrate (司馬). Disgusted with public life, he built a retreat for himself at Heung Saan (香山). Both the name of this retreat and his title, Magistrate of Gong Jau (江州司馬) are synonymous epithets for Baak Gui-yi. (See Tenth Preface, line 11, note.) There with eight other like-minded friends he devoted himself to poetry and speculations about the future life. To remain incognito, no names were used here; the group was generally referred to as, the Nine Gentlemen of Heung Saan (香山九老, *Heung Saan Gau Lo*). One of his poems, *The Pipa*[#] *Song* (琵琶行) tells how when he had been banished to Gong Jau and degraded to the rank of Magistrate, he was sailing one night with a friend down the Cham Yeung River (潯陽江). As they were drinking to forget their sorrows, they heard the plucking of a pipa and immediately went to find out where the music was coming from. It came from a nearby junk where a courtesan was singing and accompanying herself on the pipa. Baak Gui-yi and his friend begged her to join them; and she did. Realizing that she was an excellent musician, he asked her to sing them a song. The courtesan sang of her life: she came from Peking where she was well-known for her musical talents. When she grew old and was no longer in demand she was forced to travel south with a tea-merchant, and give up her life of gaiety. Baak Gui-yi, thinking of his own demotion and banishment, wept as he listened to her song. His poem concludes with the lines:

> Then all her hearers wept
> In sorrow unrestrained; and I the more,
> Weeping until the pale chrysanthemums
> Upon my darkened robe were starred with dew.

> 滿座重聞皆掩泣
>
> 座中泣下誰最多
>
> 江州司馬青衫濕

(Translation by L Cranmer-Byng, in *Gems of Classical Chinese Poetry in Various English Translations*.)

(See also Fourth Preface, line 8, note for another excerpt from this poem.)

\# The pipa is a plucked stringed instrument; a kind of Chinese guitar. More strictly, the pipa is a short-necked Chinese lute (i.e. a plucked, stringed musical instrument belonging to the silk class, because the strings were made of

Although I had a new song to sing, I would blush to sing of the beautiful Nim No.[52]

I grieve that willows on the bank so lightly understand [i.e. so easily fail to appreciate or sympathize with] the seductive arts of women [i.e. in the houses of entertainments].

Tell me, has it ever happened that every night was like the fifteenth night of the first moon?

The moon sinks; the raven croaks; man is troubled and sad;

We are blown apart by the wind and scattered like the clouds, and my happiness ebbs.

Dearly would I love to cease my yearning for you; but when that yearning will cease, I do not know.

Ah, we tacitly understand each other.

Bitterly I call on heaven:

O Heaven! Why did you join two hearts together and then separate them, leaving nothing but loneliness and desolation?

Song 12 (Part 5)

Passion Is Killing Me

To be possessed by the demon of passion is killing me.

I was wrong in the beginning to nurture such deep feeling for you.

Today no one crosses the Lotus River [i.e. frequents the flower-boat houses of entertainment].[53]

---

twisted silk and not of gut or metal) prominent in Chinese-opera orchestras and also as a solo instrument. Of west Asian origin, it was already known in China in AD 2nd century. It has a shallow pear-shaped body with a wooden belly, and sometimes, two crescent-shaped holes. The four silk-strings run from a fastener on the belly to the conical tuning pegs in the sides of the bent-back pegbox. Held vertically on the thigh, the pipa is plucked with a plectrum.

[52] Nim No (念奴), a courtesan who lived during the reign of the Tong dynasty emperor Yuen Jung (唐玄宗 , 713–56), had the most exquisite voice. According to the custom of the time, once a year the emperor would join his people in their celebrations. On one occasion the clamour and din was so great that the emperor could not hear the music. He therefore told his eunuch Go Lik-see (高力士) to shout at the top of his voice that the emperor was going to invite Nim No to sing for them. Immediately there was expectant silence. Everyone was waiting for Nim No to sing. Mayers, # 240; Giles, # 956.

[53] The Lotus River (芙蓉江) refers to the river where the lotus-flower grows. In other words, the flower-boats, houses of entertainment.

Who is there to paint my eyebrows giving them the dainty sweep of a moth's antennae?[54]

Now my lamp is flickering; the moon is waning; little wonder I am sad;

Not even the spirit of sleep could charm away the tears that fill my bright eyes.

So rain veils the Sorceress Mountain; my spring dream is shattered.[55]

Like the partridge I cry out bitterly [i.e. the cooing hen partridge would call seductively to the cock at the time of the spring floods, thus becoming a symbol of disorderly relations].

I carry the burden of lovesickness you gave me.

Ah, I regret my mistake.

Heaven! You should have pity on both of us;

---

[54] The report spread in Cheung On (長安) that Jeung, its governor and an official under the Hon emperor Suen Dai (漢宣帝, 73–48 BC), loved to paint his wife's eyebrows. Angry (perhaps jealous?) officials memorialized the emperor. On being questioned by the emperor, Jeung replied, 'Your servant has heard that of the private dealings between a man and his wife in the boudoir, many are worse than the painting of eyebrows.' The emperor, taken by this retort courteous, did not pursue the matter. Mayers, # 7; Giles, # 21.

[55] 'The Sorceress Mountain' (巫山), the name of a range of mountains forming the well-known Sorceress Gorge (巫山峽) which the Yangtze flows through from Sei Chuen (四川) to Wu Pak (湖北), is one of the marvels of Chinese scenery and a source of supernatural legend. It is so called because of its resemblance to the Chinese character 巫, mo, meaning sorceress, wizard, witch. Sung Yuk (宋玉), a poet of the 4th century BC made this the home of a celestial being, called 'The Immortal of the Sorceress Mountain' (almost a goddess of fertility and moisture), and since then she has figured in all Chinese poetry and romantic allusion. The story runs that when Sung Yuk and Prince Seung (襄王) were visiting the Tower of Cloud-dreams (雲夢臺), Sung Yuk was asked by the prince to explain the meaning of some wonderfully formed clouds. Sung Yuk replied that what he saw were the clouds of morning (朝雲). He went on to explain that a long, long time ago, a prince who had visited the Go Tong Mountain (高唐山), was so tired that he lay down and fell asleep. A beautiful lady appeared in his dream and sang: 'I am the lady of the Sorceress Mountain, a wayfarer from Go Tong. I heard that you had come here, and now with pleasure I will spread for you my mat and pillow.' And so the prince shared the mat and pillow that the beautiful lady of the Sorceress Mountain spread out for them. As she was bidding him farewell, she sang, 'My home is on the sunlit side of the Sorceress Mountain, and I live on the peaks of Go Tong. At the foot of The Bright Tower, every morning I gather the clouds; every night I summon the rain; every morning, every night at the foot of the Bright Tower,' suggesting that her presence was to be felt in the morning clouds and evening rain. When the prince awoke, the lady had vanished. Nothing remained of his dream, except his longing for her. From this legend, the Chinese phrase 'clouds and rain' (雲雨, wan yue) has come to refer to a love encounter, to sexual intercourse. (See Song 51, line 3.) Mayers, # 642, 873; Giles, # 1841.

Why do we have to suffer these agonies because fate brought us together for a time as short-lived as the dew?

Song 12 (Part 6)
Passion Is Killing Me

To have been wounded by passion is killing me.

My lover has gone. Am I pouring out my heart in too many words?

When I say 'farewell', my three souls melt in sorrow,

But the worst heartbreak is thinking about it afterwards.

Today the autumn waters and the tall rushes fill me with hope, because

The man I love is somewhere on the river.

Would that we could meet again, and that this time you would keep your mind on me.

And though in life we might live like butterflies, in death we would be like the mandarin drake and duck [i.e. symbols of fidelity].[56]

Maybe on earth, maybe in heaven I will cancel my lust-debt.

Ah me! I am desperate . . .

Without this yearning I could never live.

In the awesome expanse of sea and sky, one tiny heart is full of tender feeling.

Song 13 (Part 1)
Flowers Are Ever the Same

Flowers are ever the same. How can they know that men's feelings blow now hot, now cold?[57]

In a lover's eyes, flowers are surpassingly beautiful.

It is a pity that flowers have a magical beauty. Can you say that I am unpleasing?

Why are men languid when they look at flowers, but are too busy to look at me?

---

[56] See Song 3, line 13, note. Mayers, # 969.
[57] See Song 89, line 6.

Every year flowers bloom; this is their way,

And their fate is decreed by heaven.

Piteous it is that I am here amid wind and moon [i.e. in a house of entertainment] dragging out my miserable life, and

Not one of those who are fond of me offers love that is as lasting as water.

A loving home filled with tenderness is but an unfulfilled desire.

A flower as if taking pity on a man's loneliness will pair with him.

Some say that I am more beautiful than a flower, but this is indeed excessive praise;

But even were I more beautiful than a flower, as you say, you find it hard to give yourself to me.

This world of flowers [i.e. the carnal, pleasure-craving world] is the root and core of passion;[58]

Flowers are like that.

I have not yet fully paid my lust-debt.

If only I could quickly pay my flower- [i.e. lust-] debt in full, and then with you lead a life of virtue![59]

Song 13 (Part 2)
Flowers Are Ever the Same

Flowers are ever the same. They know not sorrow or joy.

They say that even though a flower has fallen, it will blossom again.

But I am afraid that when my spring has passed, the Lord of the East [i.e. the god of flowers who only visits the world in spring-time] will abandon me,

And once fallen, how can I ever stand straight on my stem again [i.e. blossom again]?

Next spring's rain and dew [i.e. favour] will bring next spring's thoughts.

If you wait until next spring, my blossoming will be too late.

---

[58] See Song 7.
[59] See Songs 11 (Part 5), line 7; 42; 68, line 15.

As a flower I still have bloom and freshness, so perhaps I will not be neglected,

But I had better make sure that when in full bloom no butterflies take advantage of me.

You with your noble heart must be chary when seeking an intimate friend;

No, I am not deceiving you.

Those of you who would pluck a flower, bear this in mind:

Of all the hundreds of flowers, do not by mistake pluck the red cinnamon rose.

Song 14

Ill-fate and Passion

O Heaven! Why was I destined to be born so ill-fated and yet so passionate?

Passion is 'heavy'; all else is light.

If in this world even a single meeting is determined by a previous existence,

How after our years of friendship can I for a moment bear to be separated from you!

When others see how I cherish such lasting love for you, they regret that my life will be short-lived.

I too believe that those who cherish lasting love will be short-lived, and that this is their predestined fate.

Here, I have no worries except one: I fear your love for me will not be steadfast;

I fear that you will wither my whole life and I will become like duckweed floating on the water.[60]

If only I could escape from this region of mist and flowers [i.e. the house of entertainment] and find a place of happiness,

Then, even if you spurned me, I swear I would never speak a word of it.

---

[60] See Songs 12, Part 4, line 2, note; 35 (Part 2), line 14; 52, line 4; 54, line 6; 69, line 24.

I remember I was once a pure young girl. O moon, why will you not take care of me?[61]

I beseech you to unite us this time, lest I become lonely and uncared for.

We were so madly infatuated with each other in our dreams. When I will awaken, I do not know.

Truly passion is burning me up.

In the past I embraced you;

Although I have been hoping against hope, why in so important a matter as our love must we never succeed?

Song 15

It Is Hard to Hold Back My Tears

I find it hard to hold back my tears; they fall and moisten the lotus stalks.

I remember how we talked by the winding balustrade.

You can still see on the whitewashed wall the words you wrote,

And even the lotus-flower song that we sang together leaning against that same balustrade.

---

[61] 'The Old Man in the Moon' (月老, *Yuet Lo*) ties with an invisible red cord the feet of those who are destined to marry. A Chinese saying goes, 'Matches are made in heaven — the bond is from the moon.' The origin of this belief may be the story of Wai Gwoo (韋固), who lived during the Tong dynasty (618–907). He was passing one day through the town of Sung Shing (宋城) when he saw an old man sitting in the moonlight turning over the pages of a book which he told Wai Gwoo contained the marriage destinies of the human race. Then the old man took from his wallet a red cord and said, 'With this cord I tie the feet of husband and wife together. Even though they may come from hostile families or from different countries, their destiny is to marry each other. Your wife,' the old man continued, 'will be the daughter of the old woman who sells vegetables in the shop over there.' The next day Wai Gwoo saw this old woman carrying in her arms a very ugly child of two years of age. He secretly hired a man to murder the child; but the man did not succeed in killing the child. His blow only left a scar on her eyebrow. Fourteen years later, Wai Gwoo became the husband of a beautiful girl, whom he noticed — after their marriage — wearing a patch on her eyebrow. He made inquiries, and found that she was the daughter of the vegetable woman the old man had foretold would one day be his wife, and that she was the same two-year old infant he had tried to have murdered. The 'old man' of the story is identified with 'The Old Man in the Moon'. A Chinese phrase associated with this story is: Feet tied together by the red cord (赤繩繫足, *chek sing hai juk*). (See Song 81, line 2.) Mayers, # 838, 957; Giles, # 2282.

Today the lotus flower is in full bloom, but why are we separated?

I do not know if your journey has been safe, since I have received no letter from you.

The lotus-flower pen tells me to write to you of my lasting sorrow,

But no words can fully describe my grief, endless as the unbroken fibres of the lotus root.

Today grief-stricken I stand at the balustrade,

And remembering the past I sigh.

The withered and faded lotus reminds me how full of suffering human life is.

Song 16

The Geese of the Rivers Siu and Seung

O geese of the Rivers Siu and Seung, you who carry letters,[62]

Is there any news from Hang Yeung?[63]

Your cackling brings on a gloomy, foreboding mood.

You spurned me. Night comes. Evil dreams fill my sleep till the fifth watch [i.e. daybreak];

My spring garments are drenched with my tears, because my lover has left me.

Am I to wait until Hop Foo once again yields up its pearls?[64]

No amount of words can ever do justice to the love I cherish for you.

---

[62] See Song 6, line 4; Song 29.
  The River Seung (湘江) in Hunan (湖南) flows into the Dung Ting Lake (洞庭湖). (See also Song 56 (Part 3), line 6.) The River Siu (瀟江) is a tributary of the River Seung.

[63] See Song 28, line 17. Hang Yeung (衡陽) was a prefectural town in Hunan. The geese fly north in spring-time, and fly south in autumn-time. The singer wonders if the geese have brought her any news.

[64] Used allusively to mean: until the crack of doom. The story is that Maang Seung (孟嘗), a man renowned for his integrity as a magistrate during the reign of the Hon emperor Sun Dai (漢順帝, 126–45) was appointed governor of Hop Foo (合浦), in Gwong Dung. He found the people suffering from the extortions of his predecessor, and also afflicted by the disappearance from their beds of the very lucrative pearl-mussel. No sooner, however, had Maang Seung begun his rule of righteousness than, as if heaven favoured him, the pearl fishery beds again became filled. 'Am I to wait until a similar miracle takes place?' the singer asks. Mayers, # 490; Giles, # 1513.

Ah, my feelings of love will never die.

Where has he gone now, who once held my hand?

My lover has gone! O you geese, carry to him these broken-hearted words of mine.

Song 17

Concord Grass

Concord grass grows near the winding balustrade, but

It hopes to be uprooted and planted near the peony.

Even though flowers will wither and die, who would have thought spring would be so languid?

It is like being separated from you, my lord, by barriers and mountains,

You have cast me off; you have flown away, a goose without its mate.

O geese, in northern lands and southern skies you have grown accustomed to sorrow,[65]

But I am blown about in the houses of entertainment. I alone know how tormented I am.

The day is cold. My sleeves are thin. And I lean on the balustrade longing for you to return;

The west wind blows. The blinds are rolled up. I feel so much alone;

My lord, you enjoying your pleasures are unaware of my excruciating anguish.

It is for you that my eyes are straining. Because of you my heart is broken. Because of you I can neither eat nor sleep.

When you were at home I warned you that your wandering away would only do us harm.

How could I ever have guessed that wandering on the lakes and rivers [i.e. as a wanderer on earth] you would be unwilling to return home?

Other lovers would have heeded their mistress's warning,

But you spurned mine. You did not heed my advice. And here I am left wringing my hands in secret.

---

[65] See Song 16, line 2, note.

Today you are far away, on the edge of the horizon, and I have little hope of seeing you;

Tears forever drench my spring garments.

You brought me so much sorrow, so much lovesickness. I sigh as I clasp the pipa to my breast.[66]

Ah, night is falling,

And my mirror tells me my beauty is fading.

My lord, it is one thing to pluck a flower; it is quite another to plant and tend it.

Song 18

Flowers Are Beautiful

Flowers are so beautiful. Why do they look so sad all the time?

A beautiful flower will be ashamed of you, my lord.

I warn you not to lose your spring radiance [i.e. lose this opportunity].

Before you cast me off, think of the past:

How every day I had to suffer from the deep wound of passion you inflicted on me.

How could I have ever known that my spring dream would end today?

In the past I believed your passion for me was true, but now I know you are nothing but a sham willow [i.e. a humbug].

I hear the chilling words that our phoenix-like [i.e. bridal] union will be rent asunder,[67]

---

[66] See Song 12 (Part 4), line 3, note.

[67] 'Phoenix-like union' refers to the union of husband and wife. In legend, a mythical bird the phoenix (鳳, *fung*) is assisted by the cock (鸞, *luen*) and hen (凰, *wong*) of another phoenix-like species (sometimes referred to as a peacock and peahen, but not the sort we are used to seeing in the zoo). These animals are regarded as good omens; and the phrase, 'The peacock and phoenix sing together' (鸞鳳和鳴, *luen fung woh ming*) is now used to describe a happily married couple. The combination 'phoenix–peahen' (鳳凰) can refer to sexual relations. A Chinese phrase runs: To seek a phoenix without success — meaning to try in vain to get married. The *fung-wong* (鳳凰) is a bird that in Chinese myth watches with the dragon, tortoise and *kei-lun* (麒麟, frequently translated by 'unicorn', although the *kei-lun* can have two or three horns) over the empire and appears in times of prosperity. It is often represented in art as a composite in appearance, and sometimes as a symbol of the empress. (See also Song 11 (Part 4), line 8, note.) Mayers, # 134.

The fragrant and glossy flower parlour [i.e. the house of entertainment] will be ravished by bees [i.e. by those who patronize the houses of entertainment].

When I crossed the Silver River [i.e. the Milky Way] why did you draw up the Crows' Bridge?[68]

---

[68] See Songs 12 (Part 3), line 12, note; 82, lines 9–12.

The Heaven River (天河, *Tin Hoh*), the Milky Way, is also the Silver River (銀河, *Ngan Hoh*). The legend is that the Cowherd (牽牛, *Hin Ngau*) and the Spinning Girl (織女, *Jik Nui*) loved each other so much that they neglected their work. For this they were changed into stars by the Lord of Heaven and stationed at either side of the Milky Way, in Aquila and Lyra respectively. Once a year, on the evening of the seventh day of the seventh moon, crows' wings provide a bridge for the Cowherd and the Spinning Girl to cross the Milky Way (銀河, *Ngan Hoh*) so that they can meet. The story is told that a spirit from Gwai Yeung (桂陽) called Sing Mo-ding (成武丁) told his younger brother that on the seventh day of the seventh month (七夕, *chat jik*), the Spinning Girl must cross the Milky Way to briefly visit the Cowherd. Therefore it is believed she has married him. The emperor Ngai Man Dai's (魏文帝, 220–39) line is remembered by all:

The Cowherd and the Spinning Girl gaze at each other from afar.

牽牛織女遙相望

There are variations of this legend. One is that the daughter of the August Personage of Jade (玉帶, *Yuk Dai*), considered the supreme god in Chinese popular religion, was continually spinning robes for her father. To reward her and taking pity on her loneliness, he married her to the heavenly Cowherd. However, after her marriage, the Spinning Girl was so much absorbed in love that she neglected her work, which greatly displeased her father. In anger he separated the couple by putting one of them to the right and the other to the left of the Heavenly River (Milky Way), allowing them to meet but once a year.

Yet another greatly embellishes these two rather bald accounts. The Cowherd was a mere mortal whose father had given him some land and an ox to plough it. His ox one day said to him, 'If you want a beautiful wife, go on a certain day to the river where you will see all the girls bathing. Their clothes will be on the bank. Pick up a bundle. Come back quick. Hide it somewhere. And I promise you that you'll have a beautiful wife.' The Cowherd was obedient. The bundle of clothes he had picked up at the river bank he threw down an old well behind his house. Very soon, their owner came to look for them. It was none other than the heavenly Spinning Girl who had come down to earth with a few friends and had wanted to bathe; but she could not return to heaven without her clothes. The Cowherd kept her on earth and married her. After some years they had a son, and then a daughter. One day she said to her husband, 'Now that we've been married and have children, tell me where you hid my heavenly clothes.' He showed her the old well behind the house. She retrieved her clothes, put them on, and returned to heaven. The Cowherd, who together with his children were in despair at her disappearance, consulted his ox. 'Master, put each of your children in a basket and tie them to the ends of a pole which you can balance on your shoulder. Then take hold of my tail, shut your eyes, and I'll take you to rejoin your wife.' They reached heaven safely. The Cowherd went straight to her father and demanded his wife. Having called his daughter to her side and discovering that everything

If you act like this I will find it very hard to bear.

Ah yes! In my heart I have seen through you.

Your feelings for me are not what once they were.

My lord, although I have no word from you, I will follow you even to death.

Song 19

How Can I Be Patient?

How can I be patient? The fibres of my heart are rent asunder.

---

the Cowherd had said was true, he made the Cowherd an immortal, appointing him god of a star to the west of the River, and his wife, the Spinning Girl, goddess of a star to the east of the River, with permission to meet once every seven days. Somehow or other, the couple misunderstood the father and took it that they had permission to meet only once a year on the seventh day of the seventh month; and that is what they have been doing ever since. Because they cannot cross the River without a bridge, on that day all the crows fly up to heaven with the twig of a tree and make a foot-bridge for them to cross for their annual re-union. In Northern China, people say that it is bound to rain on the seventh day of the seventh month because the Cowherd and the Spinning Girl weep for joy at seeing each other, and their tears fall down on the earth.

The Spinning Girl and the Cowherd have become the emblem of lovers in separation. Mayers, # 311.

One of the *Nineteen Ancient Poems* (written in the Hon dynasty) relates the legend:

> Far away in the skies is the Cowherd Star:
> Bright on the Milky Way the Maid
> Lightly her snowy fingers raises,
> Jogging her shuttle through its mazes.
> But her stint of work is never-ending,
> And her tears like sobbing showers descending.
> Through clear and shallow the Milky Way,
> Never they'll meet for many a day.
> No word she says, but stares dismayed,
> Alone by that surging River far.

(Translation by J A Turner, in *A Golden Treasure of Chinese Poetry*.)

迢迢牽牛星

迢迢牽牛星　皎皎河漢女
纖纖擢素手　札札弄機杼
終日不成章　泣涕零如雨
河漢清且淺　相去復幾許
盈盈一水間　脈脈不得語

I lament the rose-complexioned [i.e. pretty women]; I also lament my lover.

Love in this world can indeed be long-lasting. But our love? Why does our love end in failure?

You have taken my love of earlier days and flung it into the river [i.e. he has rejected her].

My love for you sprung from the very depths of my heart. But my friend shifted the blame on to me [i.e. thus destroying their union].

Love turned to hate! Too often have I seen this happen.

Try to see how people treat you, my lord. Reflect, my lord, on how you have treated me;

Think over it, right from the beginning ... and then cast me aside.

O Heaven, help me! Bring to ruin whoever is fickle in love.

Yes, it is really true:

I am driven to death; but lest I die suffering a wrong, I undergo this ordeal.

Song 20

This Weary World

I feel weary of this world. Why have you hurt me in this way?

You have squandered the devoted love my heart once cherished for you;

You have practised so many deceits on me; but I was willing to suffer these hardships.

Think of the past. Look into the future. Have I ever slighted you?

Why have you left me for so long? You are no whit less callous than Wong Fooi.[69]

---

[69] Wong Fooi (王魁) was a scholar who failed to pass his examination at Peking. His friend persuaded him to visit the town of Pak Si (北市), where he met a courtesan Yan Gwai-ying (殷桂英) with whom he fell in love. The next year, an imperial decree brought Wong Fooi back to Peking to offer his services to the government. Yan Gwai-ying accompanied him part of the way. In the temple of the sea-god (海神廟), Wong Fooi swore he would be faithful to her forever. They corresponded regularly. When Wong Fooi achieved the highest literary degree of the old system in China, Yan Gwai-ying wrote to congratulate him; but he did not reply. On becoming a magistrate Wong Fooi married a lady by the name of Chui (崔). Yan Gwai-ying sent her lover a letter by a special messenger, but Wong Fooi drove the messenger from his door. When Yan Gwai-ying heard this, she cut her throat, and, after her death, haunted Wong Fooi — so that he too was driven to commit suicide.

I ask you frankly: Who egged you on? Was it of your own doing?

Soldiers tread a cunning path [i.e. in order to ambush]. You were like that. I am indignant with you.

Ah me! Passion weighs heavily.

With one stroke of the brush I will blot out 'friendship' between us. Be rid of you. Never have to concern myself with you again.

Had I given to another the love I gave to you, would I now be suffering because I have no lover?

Song 21

Flowers Are Happy

Flowers are happy. But the moon makes them sorrowful.

O moon! If you pity me in this way [i.e. as a courtesan], you would take my life away.

I think even spring promises may be broken. Things cannot run smoothly all the time.

We agreed that during the second ten days of the month he would wait for me.

O moon! You are so full of tenderness: you fear that we rouge and powder [i.e. courtesans] will never find a protector.

O moon! When you are round and full, we flowers wither. In how many past lives did we fail to cultivate virtue?

O moon! In the year's four seasons, how many are there who really pity us?

What young fresh flower does not wish the moon to steal her fragrance?

Sometimes when the fragrant soul [i.e. the courtesan] awakes from sleep, the moon is bright as noonday.

Whoever pities her shadow, cast by the moon, will more easily feel the sorrow of autumn.

O moon! Would that every night you were always perfectly round! Would that we flowers never lost our bloom![70]

Ah, I do not know if the willow [i.e. her lover] is genuine or an impostor [i.e. whether her expectations are well-founded or illusory];

---

[70] See Introduction, p. 18.

If it is genuine, well and good. And I would willingly be forever a flower planted in the moon.

Song 22

Regrets of Spring

Spring indeed has its regrets. Does not the willow know this?

O willow tree! Every day you are the object of passion. Will there ever be an end to it?

When spring comes, it brings the memory of those who have left us.

Would that the spring-wind, sharp as it is, could sever the bonds of passion!

The cutting spring-wind can slow down the jaded horse at the road stage, so that even the whip will not make it budge;[71]

It can so upset the young maiden sitting in her embroidered boudoir that she is loathe to paint her eyebrows.

Truly, I have handed over my spring dreams to you;

But you waste your time being over-anxious about others.

I fear that as the years go by you will never get accustomed to the autumn wind.

Your face will be pale and wan. Your thin limbs will scarcely support you.

Then you will call on spring [i.e. to return], but spring will not heed you.

Feelings are thinner than paper.[72]

Yearning between lovers is the seed of sorrow.

O willow! Although you have been born and bred in the world of men, never become attached to one who will leave you.

---

[71] Ten *li* (里) make a 'long stage'; five *li* make a 'short stage'. *The Chinese–English Dictionary* (compiled by the Beijing Foreign Languages Institute. 1979) gives 1 *li* = 500 m or 0.3107 miles. Later on in these songs '10 000 *li*' is used to indicate a very great distance. The poet Wong Bo (王褒) has a line which runs:

From the river bridge we watch the travellers;
At the long-stage we speed our departing friend.

河橋望行旅　長亭送故人

(See also Song 51.)

[72] Cf. Song 92, lines 3 and 4.

Song 23
The Tender Moon

The tender moon hangs, as it were, on the side of the painted bower.

O moon! You shine on and at the same time pity our human partings.

My lover is beyond the horizon, but my heart is separated from his by only the breath of a single hair;

Even though our love must stretch ten thousand *li*, we are drawn tightly to one another.

My lord, every day I look for your return; but never see you returning;

The twin fish have no means of bringing your letters to me[73]

Every month brings a full round moon. I have seen this so often.

My love, have you, now far away, ever yearned for my graceful beauty?

I imagine that those who go away and those who stay at home think equally as fondly of each other.

Ah me! I am filled with a secret grief.

I hope that your love for me will never change:

That we can meet,

And then together, among the flowers, see the fullness of the round moon [i.e. as a symbol of the fullness and perfection of their true love].[74]

Song 24
The Heartless Moon

The heartless moon hangs in the inexorable sky.

Lovesick, I do not want the moon to shine on me as I sleep alone.

O moon! you wane, but then you wax again.

---

[73] 'Coming and going like fish and geese' (魚雁往來, *yue ngaan wong loi*) is a phrase used to refer to correspondence by letter. Fish were considered to swim in pairs, thus 'twin fish' became a symbol of marriage. (See Song 58, line 10.) For the 'letter carrying geese', see Song 6, line 4. Mayers, # 932.

[74] See Introduction, p. 14 et seq. (See also Song 26, line 11.)

Why does my lord, once he has gone away, harden his heart against me?

Old man in the moon! I beseech you to make things easier for me.[75]

As you shine on my lord, question him, and see how he answers:

If his heart is perverted and he does not remember me,

Tell him to look inward to his conscience, and upward to heaven.

No man should be so fickle of heart;

Even if you do not remember the present, at least remember our past.

All day long, because of you, I am racked with anxiety;

How can I ever be as gracefully beautiful as that lovely lady in the moon?[76]

If only we could meet, I would be able to see that heartless face as clearly as the moon now does;

The length of the journey would not trouble me.

Certainly I would go and ask him plainly about his intentions,

Lest in this world I carry the burden of mistakenly thinking that happy fate has brought us together as lovers.

---

[75] See Song 14, line 11, note.

[76] 'The lovely lady in the moon' is Seung Ngoh (嫦娥), who is said to have stolen from her husband Hau Ngai (后羿) the elixir of immortality (無死之藥, *mo sei ji yeuk*), which had been given to him by Sai Wong Mo (西王母). She then fled with this drug to the moon, where she was imprisoned forever. She was changed into the frog (蟾蜍, *sim chui*) whose outline the Chinese see on the moon's surface. Mayers, # 94, 178, 572, 957; Giles # 667.

The Tong poet Lei Seung-yan (李商隱, 813–58) has these lines about Seung Ngoh:

> Lady of the Moon
> Now lamplight shades deepen on screens inlaid,
> Whilst stars of morn fall with the Galaxy:
> Her stolen magic draught moans the Moon-maid,
> Stranded by seas of jade in yon blue sky.

嫦娥

雲母屏風燭影深　長河漸落曉星沉

嫦娥應悔偷靈藥　碧海青天夜夜心

(Translation by J A Turner, in *A Golden Treasury of Chinese Poetry*.)
(See also Introduction p. 14, and Songs 34, line 13; 74 (Part 4), line 7.)

Song 25

My Heart

I have but one heart. How can I give it to so many men?

If only all men on seeing me would hate me!

Then, even if I thought of lust, I would have no part in it;

Even were I to have love-thoughts, I would not have sown the seeds of passion.

I grieve most that I do not know why I cannot make men hate me,

And therefore men resent me so much.

And those who have feelings for me will be disappointed.

But this only increases my body's flower- [i.e. lust-] debt. I want to ask my lover:

Do you mean to say Bo-yuk once lived in my body in a previous existence?[77]

Aye! The seed of passion must have a root of passion before it can be firmly planted.

Should I be destined not to marry, then infatuation but injures my ruined life.

You do not believe me? Look at my eyes, more filled with tears than ever Lam Doi-yuk's were, who as a young girl was so infatuated with Bo-yuk.

Truly, I am not indignant.

Although you have given up, your desperation only lasts but a moment.

Lam Doi-yuk's tears may have paid her debt in full, but she was never united with her lover, Bo-yuk; not even in death.

---

[77] Bo-yuk (寶玉) and Lam Doi-yuk (林黛玉) are respectively the hero and heroine of *The Dream of the Red Chamber* (紅樓夢). (See Song 3, line 13.) They were deeply in love with one another, but Bo-yuk was tricked into marrying Bo-jui (寶釵), who impersonated Doi-yuk. The real Doi-yuk was dying from anguish at what she supposed was Bo-yuk's desertion of her. When Bo-yuk found out the deception that had been practised on him, and that Doi-yuk had died, he fell into a death trance. Once his soul left the body, it set off, led by a Buddhist monk, on a journey to the Infinite. At last he was taken to see Doi-yuk. A bamboo screen hanging at the entrance to Doi-yuk's room was raised. Bo-yuk stretched out his hand to greet her. The screen suddenly dropped. The Buddhist monk who had brought him there pushed him backwards and he fell, awaking as though from a dream.

Song 26

The Moon on the Rim of the Sky

The moon, a sickle, hangs on the rim of the sky,

And ripples along the Yangtze waters.

O moon! Men will wait for you to wax round,

But hard it is not to feel sad as we see you waning.

I think life is long and things may not go smoothly.

Even though a man's life be one of virtue, he will still have his share of sorrow:

Man Gwaan, recently widowed, looks for another partner;[78]

Baan Gei inscribes on her fan the lament that one day she would be cast aside like a fan in autumn.[79]

---

[78] Man Gwaan (文君), who lived in the 2nd century BC, was the daughter of the wealthy Cheuk Wong-suen (卓王孫). A certain Si-Ma Seung-yue (司馬相如), in ill-health, and reduced to poverty because of the death of his prince, wandered back to his home in Seng Do (成都), where he was introduced to Cheuk Wong-suen. Later at a banquet, Si-Ma Seung-yue's singing so fascinated Man Gwaan that, although her husband had but recently died, she left her father's house that night and married Seung-yue. The pair then fled to Seng Do but having no resources to live on, returned to Lam Ngon (臨邛) where they set up a small tavern. Man Gwaan served the customers; Seung-yue washed the bowls. His father-in-law, the wealthy Cheuk Wong-suen, shamed by the work Seung-yue had to do, gave them a large sum of money, with which the happy pair returned to Seng Do, to lead an affluent life. Mayers, # 658, 852; Giles, # 1753.

[79] Baan Gei (班姬), whose full name was Baan Jit Yue (班婕妤), was for long the chief favourite of the Hon emperor Sing Dai (漢成帝) who reigned from 32–6 BC, and who conferred on her the title of 婕妤, *jit yue*, in recognition of her literary ability. Later, however, when the more famous Jiu Fei-yin (趙飛燕) — a pet name for a famous Hon beauty, who was so petite that she could dance on the emperor's palm — ousted her from the position of 'favourite', Baan Gei sent the emperor a fan inscribed with a lament that she had been cast aside, 'Thy loving care abruptly broken off', like a fan discarded in autumn. (See also Songs 89, line 4; 92, lines 1–4.) The words 'autumn fan' (秋扇, *chau sin*) now mean 'a deserted wife'. A Chinese phrase recalls this episode: 秋扇見捐, *chau sin kin guen*. It means literally 'laid aside as an autumn fan', and refers to one who is discarded (as a lover, etc.). Mayers, # 538; Giles, # 1599. Baan Gei's Lament contains many of the themes treated of in these Songs, so I give it in full:

> Resentful Song
>
> White silk of Chi, newly torn out,
> Spotlessly pure as the frozen snow,
> Cut to make a fan of conjoined happiness,
> Round as the moon at its brightest.
> It is ever in and out of my master's sleeve

Ah yes! I have turned it over in my mind time and time again.

I will wait until the middle ten days of the eighth moon [i.e. mid-autumn)] are past, and then

O moon! Once again see you grow to perfect roundness.[80]

Song 27

The Moon Over the House

The moon over the house [i.e. of entertainment] seems to hang on the side of the painted balustrade.

O moon! Why do you shine on those who part and at the same time so persistently remain round?

I do not want to be like you who only once a month are perfectly round.

Much more the distance that separates us has added to my sickness at heart.

People say even the very best things are one day cast aside. Do not be too attached to anything.

Re-union after a long separation is better than what went before.

Although I have been cast off, it is hard to sever my love;

It is hard in my nightly dreams to control my soul's mad passion.

I think that parting in life and parting in death are not all that much different.

And its movement makes a gentle breeze.
But oft I fear with the autumn's coming
When cold blasts drive away the torrid heat,
It will be cast aside into a chest,
And love in mid-course will end.

(Translation by Robert Kotewall & Norman L. Smith, in *Gems of Classical Chinese Poetry in Various English Translations*.)

秋扇怨

新製齊紈素　鮮潔如霜雪
裁為合歡扇　團團似明月
出入君懷袖　動搖微風發
常恐秋節至　涼飆奪炎熱
棄捐篋笥中　恩情中道絕

---

[80] See Song 23, line 13.

Had I met you a day earlier, I would have been resigned to having my life shortened by one year.

Heaven! The course of true love never did run smooth. You should leave me some ray of hope.

Ah, if it is not to be, then let it not be!

Better it would have been had we never met,

I would then have been spared the heritage of a life of sorrow. Yet you, O moon, continue to wax round before my very eyes.

Song 28

The Lone-flying Goose

The lone-flying goose startles me as I sleep alone, and

As I gaze at the midnight moon, grief fills my heart.

Then I raise my head and ask the migrant goose:[81]

At this time, in the dead of night, where are you flying to?

The male and the female always fly together; you should closely follow your mate.

Now you cast a lonely shadow; what are you looking for?

We whose lovers are in distant parts find it hard to come close to them;

Even if we had wings it would be hard to swoop down and clasp them to us.

---

[81] See Song 6, line 4, note. The migrant goose (雁, *ngaan*) is referred to by the Tong poet Do Foo (712–70):

> The guest journeys at random ten thousand miles eastwards. How many years will it be before he returns?
> The River City goose that breaks so many hearts [i.e. with disappointment] flies high directly north.

東征萬里客　亂去幾年歸

腸斷江城雁　高高正北飛

The mateless goose flying alone (孤雁單飛, *gwoo ngaan daan fei*) is a Chinese phrase that refers to a widow who has not remarried, and is founded on the belief that geese never mate a second time. It accentuates her almost widow-like state now that her lover is absent from her and has not written even a word to her.

At my wit's end, I can do nothing but resort to my dreams to find this fickle lover of mine.

You woke me up with your plaintive cry, but not even a few words did you bring for me;

Had you brought me a letter from him, I would not resent your coming.

You woke me up, but brought no letter. In wakening me from my dream, you separated me from my lord.

Wishing to relish that sweet dream once more, I fled into my dream-world to find him.

But dreaming gives you nothing to rely on; why, it is like sailing on a boundless and mist-enveloped sea.

Ah me, how frustrated I am!

Who will pity a miserable woman like me?

Now that news from Hang Yeung has stopped[82] [i.e. no more letter-carrying geese], how are you going to rejoin your flock?

Song 29

The Letter-carrying Goose

Did you, O letter-carrying goose, bring me an answer?[83]

If you have no letter for me, do not bother to return.

Today I see you have no reply for me. It must be that his love for me has its limits,

Or perhaps you carelessly lost the letter on your journey,

Or perhaps he is so sorrowful that he is unable to write to me.

If the words were in his head but never put on paper, then bring me blank pages,

So that on seeing the blank pages I can imagine I am reading his outpourings of love.

Our hearts mirror one another, even though no words are exchanged.

Now I see the goose returning, without a letter for me.

Ah, letter-carrying goose! Nothing for me.

---

[82] Cf. Song 16, line 2.
[83] See Songs 6, line 4; 16; 28.

When you come it does not always mean that you bring me a letter.

I will be exactly like him. I will write no letter either. Now, fly back to that fickle creature!

Song 30

The Passionate Geese

The passionate geese fly in pairs to the south.

O geese! Why do you fly so far away on the autumn wind?

On river and lake the goose and gander have always their mate, but

My lover has jilted me. He is now alone, a forlorn shadow living in distant parts.

The wind is fierce; his garments are thin; I have no way of sending more to him;

The winter garments I made for him lie now in my empty room.

Every day I strain my eyes until the sun sets; and my sorrows multiply.

I see nothing but a fence of drooping willows ending in the long dyke.

I have seen a whip-like shadow of a man in the evening there.

Many a time I thought it was my lover coming home to me — but I was wrong.

Ah me! I begin to think . . .

That you have become besotted by the red-dust [i.e. the vanities] of this earthy world.[84]

Perhaps when the clouds are held back, and the winds are stilled, there will be a time for us to meet.

Song 31 (Part 1)

The Region of Mist and Flowers

The region of mist and flowers [i.e. the houses of entertainment] — my heart rebels at the very thought of it.[85]

---

[84] See Song 40, line 2.
[85] See Songs 31 (Part 2); 35 (Part 2), line 2; 35 (Part 3), line 14.

How can I tell the story of my middle-age love to anyone?

If a kindly fate had intended me to be an immortal, I would not have been planted here;

But having been wrongly planted here, I am hoping for some change.

Today I have tasted to the full the flowers and the willows [i.e. life as a courtesan]; the wind and the waves [i.e. the vicissitudes of life].

Moreover, if the pleasure fields dry up, the stem more easily withers.

Since my fate is as frail as a flower, I secretly grieve, because

When age creeps on and flowers die, I must find some support for myself.

Ah me! When flowers wither, I hope someone will bury these flowers. But that does not happen often.[86]

If only when I was in full bloom he had been sympathetic! This is what people say: 'Don't let the wedding day slip by'.

Remember that if a person does not graduate when he is young, he will find it far more difficult to graduate when he is older.

Moreover, when autumn comes, flowers will be utterly different.

Today fate has destined me to be a flower: to blossom and to fade is all my life.[87]

Go and ask the flowers: 'Flowers, who loves you?'

Flowers are unselfish;

If a flower nourishes feelings of love, she will love until death.

Wind, clouds, moon, and dew [i.e. gaiety and sexual dissipation] was the stuff of our mutually infatuate passion.

I do not care whether those men who admire flowers love or hate.

We are a magic seed.

Do not give me up because I am a mere mortal [i.e. only a courtesan];

I am by chance paying my lust-debt, and therefore for a time am cut off from the land of the immortals.

---

[86] See Song 11 (Part 2), line 14.
[87] See Song 40, line 13.

Song 31 (Part 2)
The Region of Mist and Flowers

The region of mist and flowers is indeed a wide and deep sea of bitterness;[88]

Up to now, it has been hard to find a true lover.

Welcoming the new guest and speeding the old one is simply repaying our flower- [i.e. lust-] debt.

Are there any who look kindly on jade and have compassion on fragrance [i.e. on young girls]?

In the war of lust and dissipation, I had thought from the first

That even though my lover wronged me, I would find it hard ever to forget him.

At times I am spurned, but outwardly I betray no sign of my feelings;

But in my inner heart when I think of you, I am desolate.

Tonight, in my loneliness, I vainly turn to the 'region of mist and flowers'.

Ah me! Do not cherish these wild desires.

Even though my heart is one with yours, I find it hard to speak.

I will never be false to your constant love for me.

Song 32
Willow Blossoms

My tears fall copiously for all willow blossoms [i.e. courtesans].

How many sorrows have pierced your heart?

I think when other flowers are blown, they are free from care.

It is you alone [i.e. courtesans] who suffer from fortune's frailty.

They say the land of fragrance [i.e. the house of entertainment] is so magnificent; it is priceless![89]

---

[88] See Songs 31 (Part 1), line 1; 35 (Part 2), line 2; 35 (Part 3), line 14.

[89] The two characters, Land of Fragrance (香國, *Heung Gwok*) are said to be a contraction of 國色天香, *gwok sik tin heung*, national beauty heavenly fragrance, and to be a synonym for the richness and incomparable beauty of the peony (牡丹, *mau daan*). The peony is considered the Queen of Flowers, the symbol of wealth and distinction. 'A peony' is a ravishingly attractive young woman. (See Introduction, p. 17 and Song 62, line 13). Mayers, # 314, 342, 377; Giles, # 1125, 1231.

Can I allow the fierce wind to rend it asunder, making it worse than mud or sand [i.e. of no value]?

Look at the moon. Now it is so fully round; but it will change.

Even if you had a thousand gold, you could not buy ninety years of youth.

If I exhorted you to suppress your feelings, you would certainly hate me.

Even though your spring sorrow were as deep as the sea, your sighs would be in vain.

It is better that I, another ill-fated willow-blossom, weep together with you.

Oh! Let the wind howl!

The fallen catkins [i.e. the patrons of the house of entertainment] have no desire to change.

Let me for ten thousand flowers weep tears that will reach the horizon.

Song 33

Flowers in the Mirror

I do not want to look in the mirror, nor do I envy flowers;

The reflection of flowers in a clear mirror lasts only as long as the twilight mist and cloud.

The mirror pities fragrance [i.e. us courtesans] and it loves us to form our portrait there.

The flowers secretly close their eyes in sleep, and make the mirror their home.

Sometimes the flowers can speak and I ask them to speak to me behind the screen.

If by chance they are adorning themselves, then we can watch them.

If there is a mirror but no flowers, the spring scene loses some of its value;

If there are flowers but no mirror, it will be hard to find spring's promise.

Why is the mirror always fully round, but the flowers are not yet married?[90]

---

[90] 'The mirror is always fully round' refers to the story of Princess Lok Cheung (樂昌公主), the daughter of the last emperor of the Chan (陳) dynasty (557–89).

Alas! Is it a reality or an illusion?

See how the ever-green laurel tree loves to live in the splendour of the moon.⁹¹

Song 34

Flowers Shed Tears

Flowers shed tears, but the moon remains unscathed.

O moon! You see how shrunken our flower-faces are.

Piteous it is that when you, O moon, are perfectly round, we flowers begin to fade.

Though your laurel tree be fragrant⁹² and you be round, you are merely a shadow with no root [i.e. are unsubstantial].

I know the season of blossoming comes but once a year; and how easily it comes to an end.

The mad wind and the driving rain [i.e. love affairs] break my whole body.

Then you in the ninth heaven beyond the clouds and I, we are indeed kindred spirits,

Although we search east and west, who cares for us, layers of fallen petals?

Do not say that the transience of the mist and flowers [i.e. courtesans in the houses of entertainment] is of no importance.

Although married to Chui Dak-yin (徐得言) she was separated from him during the troubles that followed the collapse of the dynasty. Before their separation she broke a mirror in two and gave one half to her husband, keeping the other half for herself. She told him that on a certain day she would put her half of the mirror up for sale in the capital, and this would let him know her whereabouts. Having been captured, Princess Lok Cheung was forced to become the concubine of Yeung So (楊素). She managed to have her half of the mirror put on sale in the market of the capital, where, on the appointed day, her husband came and recognized it, and was able to find out where his wife was being kept. Yeung So returned his concubine to her lawful husband. (See also Song 62, line 9, note.) Mayers, # 423a, 895; Giles # 1383, 2408.

⁹¹ See Song 5, line 9. Legend has it that the magician Ng Gong (吳剛) was banished to the moon because he had offended some of the supernatural powers. He was condemned to cut down the laurel tree which grew there. But this was a Sisyphus-like task, because no sooner had his axe struck the trunk of the tree than the trunk became whole again. Mayers, # 864; Giles, # 2337.

⁹² Cf. Songs 5, line 9; 33, line 11.

Alone I grieve that I suffered men to pluck and snap me. I cannot but think of predestined fate.

Now the cloud-roads [i.e. paths to a certain destiny] are so remote and I know I can entrust myself to no one.

Ah, I am impatient;

I will try asking the beautiful lady in the moon:[93]

'How large is Gwong Hon's palace that it can entomb so many flower-spirits who have had no true lover?'[94]

Song 35 (Part 1)

How Easy It Is

As I play the pipa I feel a hundred sad emotions running though me.

As we grow older, why does our passion not grow weaker?

When youthfulness has passed it is embarrassing to speak of passion;

Indeed you will feel passion's sting at the very mention of the word.

Infatuated up to now I was unwilling to heed it, but

Today when I look at my face in the mirror, I know that I have grown old.

People ask: When wanton pleasures grow old can they still be trusted?

Look at the bruised chrysanthemum. Its stalks still proudly defy the frost.

My fate destines me to fade and fall, why am I still striving for my ambition [i.e. to find a true lover]?

As endlessly as the tide ebbs, so do flowers fade and wither.

Ten thousand seeds of love cease from today.

Nothing is of interest to me now.

How easy it is to sigh!

Let me tearfully and with passion tell of my former days.

---

[93] Cf. Songs 24, line 12; 74 (Part 4), line 7.

[94] According to the legend, Ming Wong (明王), another name for the emperor Tong Yuen Jung (唐玄宗 , 713–56), visited the palace of the moon on the fifteenth day of the eight moon. Over the door of the palace an inscription read: Vast, cold, pure, unsubstantial domain (廣寒清虛之府 , *gwong hon ching hui ji fu*). The first two (廣寒 , *gwong hon*) of the six Chinese characters are used synonymously for the moon's palace.

Song 35 (Part 2)
How Easy It Is

How easy it is to live in the houses of entertainment, but

The place of song and dance is a place without hope.[95]

Heaven has decreed that all beauties be ill-fated.

I lessen my passionate nature and learn to be tender.

Up till now, spring mists have intoxicated the Jeung Toi willow;[96]

[Like the magic willow] daily the willow-lady sleeps three times and rises three times, [i.e. to welcome and speed her 'guests'] and does not feel ashamed;

In the past she welcomed new 'guests', today she speeds the old ones.

Butterflies love to seek the fragrance of flowers by freely skimming over them.

I imagine that if I could buy the green spring[97] and hold it in my hands [i.e. not allow spring to depart],

Not even if the azure clouds gathered thick would I ever know autumn.

Again do not say that willow blossoms [i.e. women] will be pitied after their death.

I have thought about this for a long time.

Luckily the teasing wind carries me along,

And I am a duckweed drifting on the current.[98]

Song 35 (Part 3)
How Easy It Is

How easy it is to get drunk on a thousand bowls of wine,

---

[95] See Song 31 (Part 1), line 1; 31 (Part 2), line 1; 35 (Part 3), line 14.

[96] See Song 12 (Part 2), line 4. The story goes that in the imperial gardens of the Hon dynasty, there was willow-tree that looked very like a man; it was called 'The man-willow'. Every day this man-willow tree rested three times on the ground and three times rose again. Commentators have suggested that in this song 'The man-willow' and the 'Willow-lady of Jeung Toi' have become confused.

[97] See Song 11 (Part 3), line 3.

[98] See Songs 12 (Part 4), line 2, note; 52, line 4; 54, line 6; 69, line 24; 52, line 4; 69, line 24.

When passion is intense and wine is strong.

I think the seeds of enmity were sown in a previous existence.[99]

Whoever firmly plants the root of passion will not easily let it come loose.

Even when drinking, men must respect themselves;

Do not say that when the soul is bewitched and the heart confused that man and woman will blend in perfect harmony.

In fact the pleasure fields are as transient as a chaotic dream,

When the banquet is over and guests have gone, nothing but emptiness remains.

I offer the bowl of wine, but my heart is heavy.

I ask you, for how long more can your cheeks be red as the cherry-blossom?[100]

With whom can I today share the red-brimming wine bowl?

Ah, what is the use?

Before ever I drink, my heart is pained;

To have set foot amiss in the flowery grove [i.e. the house of entertainment] is indeed to have inherited a legacy of sorrow.[101]

Song 35 (Part 4)

How Easy It Is

How easy it is for a ship moored near the willow bank to cast off;

Both oars are of magnolia wood; its crew are immortals.[102]

The east wind blows favourably for me,

Bringing my lover to me.

The mandarin drake and duck that always sleep together are envied by all:[103]

Two shimmering pearls threaded on a single string.

---

[99] See Introduction, p 29; also Songs 35 (Part 4), lines 8–10; 66, line 3; 72, line 6.
[100] See Song 37, line 16, note.
[101] See Songs 31 (Part 1), line 1; 31 (Part 2), line 1; 35 (Part 2), line 2.
[102] Magnolia wood (木蘭, *muk laan*) was used to make oars.
[103] See Songs 3, line 13, note; 12 (Part 6), line 8; 88, line 3.

I would be happy always to look on the face of my lord of the east [i.e. her lover].

This present life is ever bound up with our fate in the next life, just

As the lotus-root fibres and petals of the lily-flower are one and the same body:

One body with a single root remains unchanged.

Never did I think that the shadow of your sail would round the nine windings of the River Seung.[104]

To fulfil one's wishes is indeed hard.

Just as when the string of the kite is taut, it snaps,

So you jilted me; and left me, so far away, to fall to these depths. Pitiful, indeed, it is.

Song 35 (Part 5)

How Easy It Is

How easy it is for the many-coloured clouds to disperse.

The spring sail must leave immediately.[105]

Who would be willing to separate closely intertwined branches [i.e. like those of the trees that sprang up over the graves of Hon Fung and Sik Si]?[106]

---

[104] See Songs 35, line 2; 56, line 3.

[105] 'Spring sail' (春帆, *chun faan*) may refer to Gei Chun-faan (紀春帆), who having been appointed sub-chancellor of Hanlin College (翰林院, *Hon Lam Yuen*), was exiled for revealing certain matters connected with an official enquiry. Giles, # 301.

[106] One day Prince Sung saw a very beautiful lady plucking mulberry leaves. On enquiring who she was, he was told she was Sik Si (息氏), the wife of Hon Fung (韓馮), a government official. Straightaway, he summoned Hon Fung and commanded him to hand over his wife. Unable to do anything to prevent it, Hon Fung saw his wife abducted by the prince's men. Broken-hearted, he committed suicide. Prince Sung then brought Hon Fung's widow to the top of his high tower, and said that, if she were willing, he would make her his princess. The lady replied that she was unwilling and that she thoroughly disliked Prince Sung. Prince Sung made it clear to her she had no choice. So Hon Fung's wife asked the prince if she might retire for a short while to change her clothes and to pay her respects to her late husband's spirit. She went away, and threw herself off the top of the tower. On her skirt were written the words: 'Permit me to be buried in the same grave as my husband.' The prince decided to do just the opposite. He made two graves, completely separated, so that they might look at each other, one from the east, the other from the west, but never be united. One

When things reach such a predicament, what can be done?

A long time ago I found out that love cannot easily be severed.

In the beginning why did you go to the trouble of protecting me so strongly?

Today you have left me. Only my tears — I could speak no words — sped you on your way.

When parting, the lover snaps a thousand willow-twigs;[107]

From time immemorial the long-road stage has been the place of many a broken heart.[108]

Tell me, when will be the appointed time for our meeting again?

Silk fans guard against being thrown aside when autumn has passed.[109]

Woe is me! I am pained because fate is so niggardly.

It is easy to be blown apart by the wind and scattered like the clouds [i.e. to be separated];

Then, even though you are set on leaving, you will find parting hard. It will be too late for regrets.

Song 35 (Part 6)

How Easy It Is

How easy it is for the hair at the temples to silver with age!

---

night twin trees sprang up beside the two graves and within ten days had reached a height of thirty feet. Their branches locked and intertwined; a mandarin drake and duck mated on the branches. The neighbours aptly called the trees with the intertwining branches: 'The tree of love.'

Baak Gui-yi (772–846) of the Tong dynasty (618–907), one of the greatest geniuses of China, in his *The Song of Enduring Woe* (長恨歌) tells the story of Emperor Yuen Jung's love for Yeung Gwai-fei (See Song 11, Part 1, note) and his sorrow after her death. In this poem, the emperor commissions a Taoist priest to find her in the next world. He finds her and the two lines quoted below are part of Yeung Gwai-fei's message for the grieving emperor. She recalls the vows they had made, known only to their own two hearts:

In heaven [we] will fly as two birds with the wings of one (比翼鳥, *bei yik niu*), on earth [we will be] as two trees whose branches intertwine (連理枝, *lin lei ji*).

The three characters 連理枝, *lin lei ji*, are now a phrase referring to marital happiness.

[107] See Eighth Preface.
[108] See Song 22, line 5.
[109] See Song 26, line 8.

Even if a person were very concerned about the Pearl Lady, does he remember his earlier days with her?[110]

The autumn wind forever makes my disappointment more sharply felt:

The prow of the ship is white after one night's frost;

Scarcely any music can be drawn from the four-stringed lute;

Releasing your deepest passion through its strings can only stir up a more lasting sorrow.

How many others have fallen to my depths?

Forget the past, and you will feel no pain.

Good flowers end up being tossed hither and thither by the wind.

Tell me how can I keep in check the wandering butterflies and the mad bees?[111]

From now on I will be utterly forlorn, with nothing to rely on for support.

Ah, woe is me! Softly I sing to myself,

I have paid off my lust-debt,

Yet you have jilted me. Clasping my pipa, desolate, I watch the sunset.

Song 36

The Ebbing Tide

The waters ebb and the waters flow again.

You waters that ebb and flow, are without rest day or night.

From time immemorial people have said a parting is always hard to bear.

Why have you, since our parting, lived elsewhere until now?

Really, in this life the seasons govern the meeting of people:

Spring is the time when flowers bloom; mid-autumn is the time when the moon is full.[112]

---

[110] 'The Pearl Lady' (珠娘 , *Jue Neung*) contains a reference to the Pearl River (珠江 , *Jue Gong*). See Second Preface. The Cantonese considered pearls very precious: A daughter was called 'a pearl maiden', a son was called 'a pearl boy'. Tears may be called 'little pearls'.

[111] See Songs 11 (Part 5), line 9; 74 (Part 2), line 9.

[112] See Song 26, line 10.

At first, I was in deadly fear that passion would not penetrate my heart;

But once I speak of deep passion I have no regard for what it may lead to.

I believe that rare meetings and frequent partings only strengthen passion.

Ah! My lord, think deeply about this:

If we are day in and day out infatuated with one another, how can we ever be like the Cowherd and the Spinning Girl [i.e. in the legend].[113]

Song 37

Flowers Fall Easily

Flowers fall easily; and as easily they bloom again.

How often can you see so magnificent a bloom?

I am afraid that such magnificent flowers will not retain their bloom for long.

When I think of flowers withering, I wish they had never blossomed;

Even the most exquisite of flowers must change.

Look at the bloom fallen from its stem. Can it ever be set on its stem again?

In the end, if you plant passion's root, the bloom will be more lovely;

Yet I fear the twin blossoms of fair flowers will be planted apart.

A fresh flower is so beautiful. But I am afraid the vagrant bees will ravish it.

The fallen flower, without a master [i.e. without a lover, a protector] will feel herself benumbed.

I remember how amid the flowers we swore that our mutual love would be one.

How could I, resting on the flowers and dazed with wine, know that you would be as frivolous a lover as Wong Fooi?[114]

If only we could find and put some questions to the flower-spirit.

Ah, a flower in a mirror . . .

---

[113] See Songs 12 (Part 3), line 12, note; 18, line 10, note.
[114] See Song 20, line 5, note.

After all, is it true passion or false love [i.e. substantial or illusory]?

Why is it peach-blossoms [i.e. beautiful young ladies] are so ill-fated?[115]

Song 38

The Butterfly Dream

When butterflies dream, they dream of circling round flowers.[116]

You butterflies lust to ravish famous flowers [i.e. beautiful women] and so your dreams are a violent frenzy.

I think when mortal man meets the demon of passion then even his pure dreams will be delirious;

---

[115] 'A face like a peach-blossom' (人面桃花 or 桃花面) is a well-known Chinese phrase. The Tong dynasty (618–907) poet Chui Woo (崔護) was something of a recluse. However, on Ching Ming festival he decided to take a walk in the country. After some miles he saw a cottage in the distance, surrounded by the most exquisite peace-blossoms. He wondered who lived there. Pretending he was thirsty he knocked on the door of the cottage and it was opened by the most beautiful and charming lady he had ever seen, who most warmly welcomed him into her home. A chance meeting he would never forget. The next year, on Ching Ming Festival, he decided to visit this enchanting lady who lived in the cottage surrounded by peach-blossoms. When he arrived, he found the door bolted; the place utterly deserted; the beautiful lady gone. The peach-blossoms were as gorgeous as ever. He inscribed four lines on the portals of the door:
> This day last year, just at this door,
> A face and the peach-blossom vied in beauty.
> Today that face has gone to where I do not know,
> The peach-blossom remains swaying in the spring breeze.

去年今日此門中　人面桃花相映紅

人面不知何處去　桃花依舊笑春風

Perhaps of all trees and fruits, the peach is the most 'symbolic'. Peaches of immortality ripened once every thousand (or perhaps only once every nine thousand) years. They are the most common symbol of longevity. (See also Song 57, line 6, note.)

Another Chinese phrase says: Beauty brings misfortune (紅顏薄命 , *hung ngaan bok meng*). Its literal translation means: rosy cheeks, unlucky fate; born under an unlucky star, ill-starred. (See Song 35 (Part 3), line 10.)

[116] Jong Ji (莊子), a philosopher of the Taoist school who lived in the 4th century BC, writes that he once dreamed he was a butterfly. And he was happy to be a butterfly, because he was not aware of himself as Jong Ji. When he woke up, he was sad to find himself Jong Ji again. But he did not know whether he had dreamed himself a butterfly, or whether a butterfly had dreamed itself Jong Ji. He was certain there was a difference between a butterfly and Jong Ji. (See also Song 50, line 11.) Mayers, # 92; Giles, # 509.

Once the soul is possessed and the heart intoxicated, the dream will be both of the sea of sin and the heaven of passion.

Moreover, we love each other and try to be together. How can you imagine our intoxicated dream would vanish so quickly?

It is good for you to seek sweet dreams and in your dreams be perfectly united,

Then by day and by night you will belong to an immortal family.

With my head on my pillow, soul-dreaming, I become a wandering immortal [i.e. her soul can leave her body during dream-time].

See, his extravagant dreams so delude him that even though I call to him, he does not turn round.

In their dreams the mandarin drake and duck are turned into a twin lotus flower;

Never say that dreams are unsubstantial things, or that mortals may change!

Can I believe that my spring-dream is but a fleeting cloud?

Even though the realm of dreams is the realm of pleasure, I warn you not to be too attached to it.

Ah, the dreams of flowers are easily shattered.

Waking from my dream today I find my lover is far apart from me;

What I most regret is that fate joined us together for only the brief moment of a dream.

Song 39

It Is Hard for the Moon to Keep Its Roundness

Flowers fall easily, but the moon with difficulty waxes round.

Flowers and the moon have deep passion resulting in enmity;

In themselves, both flowers and the moon are passionless, but man ever goes on being attached to them.

What I most regret is that flowers and the moon alike age men so quickly, and stir up men's pity.

If flowers have passion, they sadly gaze at the moon.

O moon! You make such efforts to become round; tell me how can I not feel sad and grieved?

If the moon knew how to have compassion on fragrance [i.e. courtesans] why does it allow us to fade?

If the moon shines for a long time on you, then even if the flower fades, still your heart will not be troubled.

There are twelve months in a year. Only twelve times are you fully round.

And although flowers bloom in all four seasons, they blossom for but a brief spell.

Since our fate is as frail as a flower, it is hard for us to look you [i.e. the moon] in the face;

If when I am in full bloom I look at the moon, it seems already waned by half.

Although the moon waxes with such great effort, it seems to be full for only one day.

When flowers fade, men will wait until they bloom again — but only after a whole year has passed.

Our lover is away on the edge of the horizon. We lament our fate to the flowers and the moon.

Ah, woe is me! Distraught am I!

My eyes are strained; my heart will break.

My lord, I fear that before your very eyes flowers now in bloom will wither but the waning moon wax round.

Song 40

On Pre-ordained Fate

I will trouble you for a while to stop and think about pre-ordained fate.

Why do I in this life fall into the red dust [i.e. become a courtesan]?[117]

I think that to be born into this life as a woman is indeed pitiable;

Moreover, young girls in the houses of entertainment have broken stems and they lack roots.

The splendour, the glamour lasts no longer than the drinking of a cup of wine;

---

[117] See Song 30, line 12.

Wait until the guests are gone and the lights are dead, then you will feel broken-hearted.

My 'guest' calls me, 'My lady'; but without a 'guest', I have no standing with anyone;

An instant of coldness makes me vile three times over.

If you meet a 'guest' who has passion, you have someone to rely on for support.

In my heart what I fear most are drunks, they are a deadly plague.

From the day I sank to the depths in houses of entertainment I began to regret it.

Ah! No matter what, I am going to give vent to my anger:

Suffer we must until our tears run dry and we are withered, and this — they say — is 'living'![118]

Song 41

Repentance

I really am very far from being pleased with myself,

For my inconstancy in love has cast a slur on you.

Wait until my heart veers round and it will not be too late to be good to you.

They say that with good wine you have to drink half a bottle before you savour its real taste.

I am so infatuated with you because I eagerly listened to your sweet words.

Today, although the river be deep we must together steer our boat until we come through.

Ah, almost half my life is spent;[119]

It was not my intention to live without you.

When I remember your past love for me, I cannot bear to cause you embarrassment.

---

[118] See Songs 31 (Part 1), line 13; 93, line 6.
[119] See Song 70, line 1.

Song 42

Virtuous Woman and Passionate Man[120]

Why do you get so angry so quickly? Once you see me you become vexed.

We have known each other for so long; each of us has often been angry with the other.

Many times have I been angry with you. But we made it up. Now even the word 'passion' is insipid.

My lord, since you are always angry, I feel I am an embarrassment for you.

I have submitted to you too often, and I fear I have been the plaything of your passion.

I spoke out once in anger lest you became too cruel.

Perhaps after thinking it over you will heed my warning.

Now let us be friends again to avoid having people criticize us.

I realize there is some affinity between us; therefore I am loathe to part from you and to choose someone else.

Granted my face always showed my anger, but my heart never ceased treasuring you;

If only I could lay bare my soul for my lord to see!

I regret that we met each other but too late;[121]

Now we will hold hands and never let go; we must be the virtuous woman and the passionate man.

Song 43

Do Not Be Too Much on Fire

Do not be too much on fire. Excessive heat is followed by wind.[122]

I think the weather and human affairs are very much alike.

You do not believe me? See how when the sun has moved southwards for a number of days, the cold wind follows.

---

[120] See Songs 11 (Part 5), line 11; 13 (Part 1), line 16; 68, line 15.
[121] See Song 6, line 1.
[122] See Song 89, line 11.

Although devoted to your lover you must part; must loosen your hold on each other for a while.

I believe that on this earth meeting times are appointed, which you cannot shy away from;

Year in and year out the seventh night of the seventh moon is the time of meeting.[123]

They say meeting just for one day is of no use;

In only twelve hours how can you tell the sum of your sorrow?

However I must say that meeting for a single day is not useless:

Over a length of time, a single day every year will bring its reward.

Would that men could imitate the Seven Sisters' enduring love, lasting for a thousand years![124]

Here is the seed of true passion:

Parting comes only in life, and not in death — such is the richness of passion.

Song 44

Detain Your Guest

If you must go, then you need not have come in the first place.

I might as well part from you, so that my distress will not be prolonged.

They say that we wild flowers [i.e. courtesans], even though we be exquisite, are not all that precious;

But why then are the young men who lust for flowers bewitched only by wild flowers?

Excellent as my lover is, he is another's husband:

If in the house of entertainment his passion is strong, it will certainly provoke his wife's jealousy.

It were better to sever the bonds of passion, so that my lord will not think of me too much.

When I do not see my lord's face, in sorrow I weep day and night;

---

[123] See Songs 12 (Part 3), line 12, note; 18, line 10, note; 82, line 11.
[124] 'The Seven Sisters' (七姊妹, *Chat Ji Mui*) are the Pleiades, a group of small stars in the constellation of Taurus, commonly spoken of as seven, although only six are visible to the naked eye.

It is hard to control my love for you even though you are away from me.

When after a long separation we meet, I cannot bear to leave you and go home.

Not one in a thousand lives with his beloved; not one in a thousand is completely devoted.

Ah, but this world is tiresome!

As fate would have it, there is one person [i.e. his wife] who constrains you, and another person [i.e. the keeper of this house of entertainment] who constrains me.

Although I cannot share your bed in life, at least in death I shall be buried with you.

Song 45

Reassure Yourself

Reassure yourself. Do not have any doubts,

If I found someone congenial, I would dote on him.

The region of mist and flowers [i.e. the houses of entertainment] is not the place for lasting love;

One day the flowers will wither and then even the butterflies will take advantage of them.

The wild butterflies that ravish flowers will be indeed disappointed.

They do not ravish fresh flowers, but only go to where the wild flowers are.

I do not doubt that if immortal flowers meet immortal butterflies, they will somehow become true lovers.

I am intent on watching where they will fly to,

Sometimes with deep heart and cold eyes they will test me.

Falsely they pretend to ravish the withered flowers, to see if the flowers know or not.

Do not say that we seed of immortal flowers are without root and life [i.e. reckless].

I watch your coming and then I quickly act as the opportunity arises,

Pretending not to know, I go to test you:

Deliberately I sway in the wind, as if I had nothing to rely on.

Ah! We must come to an understanding.

I have suffered many frustrations; perhaps with you my melancholy will be lessened;

My heart is dying for love of you.

Those who are waiting to ravish flowers are standing outside the door.

Butterflies! If you want to ravish me, it will not be too late when my bloom is full blown.

Song 46

I Am Waiting for You

What have you decided? Why are you still doubting?

If you cannot redeem me, you should have told me earlier.

I know waiting for you, my lord, has made me fall into this region of mist and flowers [i.e. this house of entertainment];

So even if I wanted to follow a man to the bank of safety [i.e. be redeemed from this way of life], what chance have I got now?

All I wanted was to talk to you about our joys and sorrows; talk about things past;

How was I to know that you would be disappointed and would give up all thought of returning home?

Someone has incited you to vent your anger on me.

You say my nature is like water, and that like a willow blossom I drift along with the waves.

Now that my words are truly sincere, you still pay me little attention.

Only heaven knows the thousand strands of my sad thoughts;

Moreover, everyone far and near knows I am waiting for you.

Today abruptly you withdrew your hand from mine, leaving me without any support.

The feelings of love I had for you in earlier days were wasted. I now put myself in your hands. You decide what to do.

Can you truthfully say you are deeply grieved? Even in death you could never deceive yourself.

Until I see you face to face and tell you the story of my broken heart, I will never close my eyes in death.

My lord, if you intend to pity [i.e. have tender affection for] me, it were better for you to begin immediately.

If I see you face to face and speak of my heart's bitterness, even death will not worry me.

Do not put more obstacles in your way.

If our meeting is a minute earlier, my lord, then our parting too will be a minute earlier.

Song 47

A Lament for 'Autumn Joy'[125]

I hear people say you are dead. I cannot believe it.

Why did you so foolishly spurn life?

If you died for your 'guest', I do not blame you;

If you died because of your lust-debt, how can I not be grief-stricken and heart-broken?

During your life you looked on me as your lover. Therefore you should have spoken to me about it.

Why did you not during our two or three months of friendship breathe a word of it to me?

You took that passion of earlier days and cast it into the waters.

Even if I had more than enough gold and silver paper to burn, it could not reach the king of hell [i.e. the Chinese Pluto].[126]

What a pity I rejected you, to make you spend the rest of your life wandering around the houses of entertainment;

The regions of mist and flowers [i.e. the houses of entertainment] can bring no satisfaction.

You were called 'Autumn Joy';

I hope when autumn returns there will still be joy.

Now that the winter solstice is past, why am I oppressed by snow and frost?

---

[125] 'Autumn Joy' may have been the mistress of the author of these songs, Jiu Ji-yung, and hence this song would be an expression of his own feelings.

[126] In Buddhist mythology, the king of hell is Yama, whose name in Chinese is 閻羅, *Yim Loh*. Hell is the prison under the earth where he and his assistants deal with culprits. His wife Yami deals with female culprits.

Today I am as weak as a spring breeze and can do nothing to help you.

Fallen flowers without a master [i.e. a protector or lover] are buried in the spring earth.

If in the next life your passions dream, send them to me immediately,

So that perhaps I can do my best — little though it may be — to console my sweetheart.

The path of hell is wide, and your two feet are so dainty;

Hell has no resting place. In whose home will you live?

I do not know whom you trust to honour your white bones on the green hill-side [i.e. to tend the grave which was considered the dwelling-place of the deceased person].

The desolate willow and the waning moon hear only the cry of the cuckoo bird.

Perhaps you have no lover to come and scatter paper money over your grave;

At the Ching Ming Festival you will vainly regret not having the paper money strewn over your grave.[127]

Enough! You should have been a virtuous wife and then I could have set your tablet in the Buddha's shrine,

So that your lonely and masterless spirit could rely on the Buddha's strength.

You should beg Chi Wan to grant you the Buddhist invocations [i.e. the gathas],[128]

Then transformed in the next life, you would never be the wife of any merely passing 'guest'.

If your sin-debts are still unpaid, you will again be doomed to the region of flowers and powder [i.e. the houses of entertainment];[129]

Therefore you should choose a true lover as soon as you can, and do as you see fit.

If our fated passion has not been severed, there would still have been a day for us to meet.

---

[127] The Ching Ming (清明) Festival falls on the 106th day after the winter solstice (roughly corresponding to Easter time), on which day the tombs are visited.

[128] Chi Wan (慈雲) literally means, 'Merciful rain-cloud', and refers to the Buddha's merciful heart which, like a great cloud, saturates the universe. (See also Eighth Preface, line 8, note.)

[129] See Song 9.

Remember this well:

Think of the devotion of our past love,

Had we both been intoxicated with love, I would have found it indeed timely to die together with you.

Song 48
Wounded Spring

Birds cry; flowers fall; spring has a hidden wound;

When looking at withered flowers the older man feels broken in spirit.

Green spring [i.e. the prime of life] is confident there will be someone to look tenderly on it.

But I believe that rouge and powder [i.e. courtesans] will be blown about like leaves from the trees, and be life-long lonely.

I cannot tell who is the devoted, who is the fickle lover.

It is always the same: the rose-complexioned [i.e. beautiful women] will meet heartless men.

Today the butterfly has flown away, deserting the flower in bloom. On whom can I rely for support?

Ah, woe is me! I am choking with grief.

When I think how jade is shattered and fragrance buried [i.e. of the fate of the courtesan], I cannot check the tears that flood my eyes.

Song 49
The Flirting Butterfly

The butterfly settles in the heart of the flower, and you cannot drive him away;

Certainly it lusts after unctuous fragrance, is bewitched by flowers.

Flowers have passion and tenderly regard the butterfly;

But the butterfly is wanton and so becomes infatuated.

When the flower and the butterfly come together, they are two of a kind.

Ah me, I would rather die.

You tell me to sever the bonds of love. You think this will be easy?

Only when the butterfly is dead and the flower withered has the end come.

Song 50

The Lamp Moth

Do not say you have no fear of the fire. Look at that scorched moth;[130]

It flies hither and thither but still it gropes until it falls down the deep chasm [i.e. of the oil lamp].

It wants to know how deep is the chasm and therefore all night it goes groping around,

Completely dazed as if it had met the wind-demon.

How can it know that the square inch[131] of the lamp's chimney-opening lies above a lake ten-thousand *jeung* deep [i.e. of infinite depth]?[132] You cannot fly over it.

Down the waves and tossed on the billows, I do not know how many have perished.

When you feel the fire burning fiercely in your body, you will know your passion was wrong;

Though you want to fly, you cannot soar aloft. I ask you who will then save you?

Even if you were to die — to die ten million deaths — it would not lead anywhere;

Ambitious still you pounce on the oil-lamp.

Would that you could, like the butterfly, awaken from your dream;[133] then flowers too would become awakened.

---

[130] 'A moth caught by the lamp' (撲燈蛾子 , *pok dang ngoh ji*) is a phrase which can refer to a man fascinated by a woman, constantly thinking of her, or it can refer to the lure of fame and gain. (See Songs 58, line 6; 73, line 11; 88, line 7.)
    A Buddhist phrase with a similar sense is: Like a moth flying into the flame is a man after his pleasure (如蛾趣燈火 , *yue ngoh chui dang foh*).

[131] In Cantonese, 'square inch' (方寸 , *fong chuen*) is another way of speaking about the 'heart'. Here the singer is referring to the infinite depth of her love. (See also Song 12 (Part 6), line 12.)

[132] A *jeung* (丈) is a Chinese measurement of length equal to 3.3 m. 10 000 *jeung* = 33 000 m = 20.5 miles.

[133] See Song 38, line 1, note.

Ah, if only I could fly away . . .

Then the world — a world of dissipation and pleasure — could not harm me.

Song 51

Long Dreams

Would that I could dream all day! Dreaming that night and day I was with you;

For a dream can span ten-thousand *li*[134] [i.e. a very great distance].

The loveless rain and clouds have sown passion's seed in me,[135]

And the root of passion once planted in me, I must not let him shake it loose.

Though in your dreams the Sorceress Mountain sends you unrequited away,[136]

In my dreams nevertheless I can say a few words to you and this dispels my sadness a little.

My lord, you should dream when I dream, then it will be good for both of us;

When in my dreams I look for you, make sure you are dreaming at the same time.

My lord, dine early and go to bed early, and do look after yourself.

Ah! My yearning bring me only pain.

When will you think of coming home,

---

[134] See Song 22, line 5, note.

[135] See Song 12 (Part 5), line 7, note. Of Baak Gui-yi (白居易) (772–846), one of China's greatest poets, who at one time was governor of Jung Jau (忠州), it is said that when he had almost crossed the Sorceress Mountain, he inscribed a poem on the walls of the Fairy Maiden's temple, which ran:

> The governor of Jung Jau [i.e. Baak Gui-yi himself], the genius of the day, on coming to the Sorceress Mountain must compose a poem.
>
> Go tell the fairy maiden of Go Tong that I want her to open the rain clouds and to stay a while with me.

> 忠州刺史今才子　行到巫山必有詩
>
> 為報高唐神女道　速排雲雨侯清詞

[136] See Song 12 (Part 2), line 7.

So that I will not wake up separated from you, alone to face the red lamp?[137]

Song 52

Do Not Dream

I advise you not to dream, because I fear we may meet in our dreams,

And once awakened, nothing remains;

The very word 'parting' burns my soul.

My lord, you have travelled to the edge of the horizon, while I am a weed[138] drifting on the water's surface.

Thinking of you I secretly play my pipa;[139]

Oh! How many sorrows pulsate in each finger!

Were you not so constant a lover, my lord, you could not have brought me to such a pass:

See how thin I have grown. Can I still say I am like a flower?

Although today my love-passion is great, it is of no avail.

Woe is me! Sadness has ten thousand roots.

You have wronged me in leaving me lovesick and without a master [i.e. one to protect and support]. I have cried blood-red tears.

Song 53

The Bonds of Love

The bonds of love bind two hearts together.

But your loved one is confined in the tender village [i.e. the house of entertainment].

My lord, either you are unwilling to loose these bonds or I have tied them too tightly.

Your mind is dazed like that of a self-indulgent ruler [i.e. a debauchee, a rake].

---

[137] See Songs 64, line 4; 91.
[138] See Songs 12 (Part 4), line 2, note; 35 (Part 2), line 14; 52, line 4; 54, line 6; 69, line 24.
[139] See Song 12 (Part 4), note.

Although a skilled craftsman says he could unravel these bonds, yet I have no way to ask him.

Even with a sharp knife, you would find it hard to rend asunder this root of passion.[140]

If you are wise, make up your mind to cut yourself loose of this bond, and do not regret it.

How could I ever have thought that in time to come you would grow tired of me, yet still in my dreams would pursue me?

Oh Heaven! You made man. Why did you give him 'passion' to be his guide?

Passion, either long or short, has certainly been pre-ordained.

You cannot deny it, if men did not abuse true passion, we would never suffer distress;

You might be distressed for a brief moment, but there would be a happy end to it.

Truly the best time to possess me is in the moment of delirium.

Ah! Everything is chaotic.

Whether I am clever or stupid is not important.

Passion's gates are hard to break down; even in death I will follow you.

Song 54

The Tree of Love

The tree of love is planted in the city of sorrow;

Without branches, without leaves, it is alone and bleak.

Love is the very life of flowers.

When flowers bow their heads, it is because of you, sir.

When spring is chill, the roots do not strike firm,

And so they are changed into duckweed, and go elsewhere for a re-birth.

I warn the butterflies [i.e. fickle lovers] of this world not to cross the flowers' path.

Ah me, flowers may be fickle,

---

[140] See Song 60, line 5.

But even a butterfly can hardly break free from their spell.

After all, love has no tree; a spring dream has no substance.[141]

Song 55

The Love Knot

No matter what you do you cannot untie the love-knot:

From a former life I am tied to my sin and sorrow.

At first, and for a long time, I was afraid he would not love me;

Today his love is very deep but I fear it will be the womb of many sorrows.

Now he hates; now he loves. Now he loves; now he hates;

Love and hate, inconstant both. I feel in a daze.

I am like a ship on the high seas, driven to the centre of the ocean,

Unable to reach land on either side. How can I be united with him?

Ah! Patience is what I need, for

Frustration will turn to happiness.

See how happy the immortals are. But it is not certain they can, in an instant, reach the Isles of the Blest.[142]

Song 56 (Part 1)

The Tears of Parting

Do not weep when you say 'farewell' to your lover.

Even before I speak of the sorrows of parting, I can hardly control myself.

Everyone knows the difficulties of travelling, and how prudent you have to be.

Two days before he leaves, I will say my farewell words to him on the pillow, enjoining him earnestly . . .

---

[141] The author of these Songs is well aware he is using a type of pathetic fallacy throughout. (See Song 35 (Part 5), line 3, note.)

[142] See Song 11 (Part 5), line 12.

Because if at the actual moment of departing I spoke of such matters it would make him feel angry.

I will force myself to smile so that he may go happily go on his way;

But after he has departed I will want to weep and weep, and perhaps my tears will drown my sorrow;

I will sob till I am almost choking; and I will look for him in my dreams.

If in my dreams I see my lover, I will try to console him;

I will ask him a lot of questions about his journey.

At the beginning it were best not to talk about unhappy things.

Song 56 (Part 2)
The Tears of Parting

No matter what I do I cannot dry my 'farewell' tears.

O tears! Lovers have their affection for each other; you do not have to bother about them.

Love thoughts fill my heart. Can I trust anyone to tell them to?

Even if I unburdened myself completely to others, none will be grief-stricken on my behalf.[143]

The horse and carriage will be here in a moment. Then we must part. He to the north. I to the south.

If only the sparse forest would for my sake try to delay the slanting rays of the sun!

Ah me, I am miserable, as

The bamboo-flute pipes the departure;

My lord, your journey will be difficult, but be sure always to act prudently.

Song 56 (Part 3)
The Tears of Parting

My tears of 'farewell', though I stifle them, surge up again.

---

[143] See Song 96, line 12.

My lord! If only you could come back to me as easily as the tears come back to my eyes, I would not be broken-hearted.

Even though today the time has not yet come to part, I am already looking forward to your return.

When I envisage myself all alone, how can I not be broken-hearted?

I want to dry my tears and be happy for a while talking to you about so many things

You spurn me, and my tears flow endlessly like the River Seung with its nine turnings.[144]

Were my tears able to carry you along like the waters of the river,

Then wherever the waters carried you to, my tears would be with you.

My lord, you can see that my heart, like the river, flows in one single direction.

You must remember how we two on our pillows wept till dawn;

With you I wept until I had no more tears to weep; and you shared my pain;

But even though you shared your tears with me, I felt so miserable.

Ah me, how dejected I am!

When the parting is over, can I easily set my heart at rest?

If only you longed for me as desperately as I long for you, your heart could never alter its course.

Song 57

Unfeeling Words

Words spoken without feeling may warn my lord, but will never make him turn back.

At the moment he is on the edge of the horizon, ten-thousand *li* away.[145]

At my dressing-table I see my spring [i.e. the prime of her life] fading. Who will regard me with tenderness?

Spring has passed and no flower is found in the guest house.

Willow-blossoms at the roadside [i.e. courtesans] stir up men's hearts to pity and to hate, they say.

---

[144] See Song 16, line 1.
[145] See Song 22, line 5, note.

My lord, do not go to the fisherman to ask where the Mo Ling ford is [i.e. the entrance to the Chinese Utopia].[146]

While mist and flowers [i.e. the life of a courtesan] are transient and of no account,

You should be happy with your lot,

And remember that both your parents are always thinking of you, and hoping that you will keep strong and healthy.

Song 58

Unfeeling Eyes

Unfeeling eyes will not be mine as I speed my lord's carriage on its way.

My tear-drops fall like rain; reluctantly I lean against the village gate.

A true heart is like clear water.[147]

I will never finish embroidering my lament,[148] I will never finish writing my letters in blood.

The time for parting has come. I now give you this brief command:

---

[146] The story is told that round AD 376 a fisherman from the district of Mo Ling (武陵) in Yunnan (雲南) province while fishing a river lost his way. He decided to let the boat drift. It drifted along through rows and rows of exquisite peach-blossom trees. Having reached the end of the river, he saw in front of him a mountain which had a cave in it. He entered the cave which eventually led into another world: a large open plain; thousands of houses surrounded by flowers and bamboo and mulberry trees; fields luxuriant with every kind of vegetation; murmuring streams and chirruping birds; the whole scene breathed peace and harmony, security and happiness. The people there rushed to welcome him, and invited him into their houses. They told him that they were the ancestors of those now living, and that they had sought refuge there from the disorders of the Chun dynasty (221–207 BC). None of them had left this 'country' since arriving there. They told him they had neither taxes nor laws. Everybody worked his own piece of land, was happy in his own home. The fisherman returned to the river he had come from, but was never able to find this wonderful place again. 'The ford of Mo Ling' (武陵津) refers to the entrance to the cave. A well-known Chinese phrase comes from this story: 'The world beyond the peach-blossom river (世外桃源, *sai ngoi to yuen*) and refers to Utopia, a 'no-place' of perfection and simplicity.

[147] See Song 90, line 1, note.

[148] So Wai (蘇蕙) was the wife of Dau To (竇滔) who was governor of Chun Jau (秦州) at the end of AD 4th century. Banished by Foo Kin (苻堅) to the desert of Tartary (流沙) he became involved with a concubine, Jiu Yeung-toi (趙陽臺). His wife, bewailing his absence, embroidered a very intricate poetical lament of 840 characters on satin, which she sent to her husband. Mayers, # 141, 619; Giles, # 579, 1781.

'My lord, despite the wonders and glories of Peking, never forget your old home.'

Today my bowl of wine is mixed with tears.

My lord, do not be afraid of getting drunk,

And letting your joyful heart lightly and gaily talk to me for a while.

I want to be born together with you in my next life, where we would be as the twin fish that have but one pair of eyes.[149]

Song 59

Songs Without Feeling

I cannot sing to my lord songs without feeling.

The green waves and the spring tides lead me to inexorable sorrow.

The gentle bird pities me and regards me with affection,

For me it cries: 'I cannot part from my mate'.

Today I cannot prolong my spring [i.e. preserve her youth]. This may not be the fault of my lord.

Inscribe your name in the Goose Pagoda, so that you may more quickly obtain your degree.[150]

I imagine few will be born in the next life as Lei Sin.

Do not neglect your studies.

Today you are alone. Who knows you are another Jeng Yuen-woh [i.e. like the scholar of this name]?[151]

---

[149] A Chinese expression speaks of birds that had only one wing each, and so had to fly in pairs (比翼鳥, *bei yik niu*), and is used to refer to husband and wife. This line refers to fish that always swim together, as if they had only one pair of eyes between them (比目雙魚, *bei muk seung yue*). See Song 23, line 6, note.

[150] A Buddhist monk saw two geese flying overhead. 'If I could catch them, what a meal I'd have!', he said to himself. Suddenly one of them fell to the earth and died. Some other monks who were looking on decided this was a miracle. They buried the goose, and built over its grave what they called 'The Goose Pagoda'. During the Tong dynasty (618–907) the names of the metropolitan graduates were inscribed there; hence the phrase became a synonym for passing this examination.

[151] Lei Sin (李仙) was a courtesan who so captivated the student Jeng Yuen-woh (鄭元和) that he neglected his career. She tore out her eyes. Later Jeng Yuen-woh rose to high office and married Lei Sin. Giles, # 1134.

Song 60

The Debt of Three Lives

I ask you, 'Why were we born at the same time into this flowery [i.e. carnal, pleasure-loving] world,

And since we have been born together in this place, why do we always mutually oppose one another?'

Red powder [i.e. courtesans] and green garments[152] [i.e. loving men] will certainly change,

Therefore I do not wish to plant the root of passion in snow-hardened earth.

How could I think that, like the lotus whose roots may snap but whose fibres remain joined[153] [i.e. apparently severed, but still connected], I should be bound through three lives [i.e. the past, the present and the future] to my love-debts?[154]

Up till now I have been confined to the willow groves [i.e. the houses of entertainment] and flower streets [i.e. the houses of entertainment]), practising my seductive arts.

Although you were like the wild crane and I was like the sea-gull, we were suitably matched.

Ah! The mandarin drake and duck,[155] the clouds and the water are always together.

I had but an insipid relationship with you; passion cast into the ocean.

How could I ever have thought that I would be prompted by a sudden upsurge of emotion. Tell me, how can I free myself of it?

I simply cannot cut myself off from my old and new love.

Alas, there is no end to it all . . .

Enough! It were better that in the world to come you and I lived together in some far-off distant place.

---

[152] See Song 12 (Part 4), line 3, note.
[153] See Song 83, line 2.
[154] See Songs 53, line 6; 9, line 5; 35 (Part 3), line 3; 35 (Part 4), lines 8–10; 66, lines 3–5; 72, line 6.
[155] See Songs 3, line 13, note; 12 (Part 6), line 8.

Song 61

The Single-hearted Palm Tree[156]

I know that you, palm tree, have but a single heart;

You were born with this particular type of heart. Once I saw you, I admired you, and my soul melted with yearning.

You grow up in meagre soil, and without any support;

You are the seed of true passion, therefore you have the root of passion.

If this world of men contained the root of such passion I do not believe men would ever find it.

A tree may have but a single heart; what I sorely regret is the fickleness of my lover.

Recently I have seen that my master's heart is unsettled;

His one heart he would share with many others.[157]

If only he could imitate you in having a single heart, I never would know regret.

Ah, but I am impatient.

I must ask the flower-spirit:

'O spirit of the single-hearted palm tree! Are you willing to help my lover imitate your singleness of heart? If not, I will call you an evil spirit.'

Song 62

Unending

Mutual love is unending.

How can I banish from my heart all thought of the past, all thought of the future?

For my whole life I have been afraid of uttering the word 'parting';

I want to be like the spring silk-worm that spins till it dies [i.e. her affection for him to last till death].

---

[156] The gomuti palm. A Cantonese phrase, 桄榔樹，一條心, *fong long sue, yat tiu sam* (whose literal meaning is: the gomuti palm, a single heart), refers to a single-hearted, devoted lover.

[157] See Songs 2, line 10; 68, line 9.

I do not want to live with you; but I want to die with you,

Lest after today we live separated from one another.

Since the dawn of time, countless are the things that trouble us.

Heaven! You envy my passion, yet you seem so extremely selfish.

Look at the Hung Fat girl who so understood men. My dearest, you are somewhat like her.[158]

Today you should, like another Lei Yeuk-si, pity me because I am tossed about;[159]

This time I have degraded myself and am called dissolute.

Ah me! It is so even today,

You can see my name in the ledger of the fragrant country [i.e. the house of entertainment].[160]

Perhaps some kindred spirit will listen to my broken-hearted words.

Song 63

Facing the Weeping Willow

The broken-hearted fears to face the weeping willow,

Fears to face in the weeping willow [i.e. the courtesan] her pair of charming eyes.[161]

[158 & 159] Hung fat (紅拂) means a red fly-whisk. Hung Fat Nui (紅拂女), meaning the girl with a red fly-whisk, was the beautiful concubine of Yeung So (楊素), a statesman and general during the reigns of Go Jo (高祖, 589–604) and Yeung Dai (煬帝, 605–17) of the Sui dynasty (581–618). One day, when the still unknown military adventurer Lei Yeuk-si (李藥師) was talking to Yeung So, a young girl stood behind him, holding in her hand a red fly-whisk, which was the origin of her name: Hung Fat Nui. The fly-whisk was a symbol of authority and was mainly used by Buddhists. So greatly attracted to Lei Yeuk-si was she that on that very night, dressed as a man, she went secretly to Lei Yeuk-si's room and disclosed her feelings for him: 'Of the many men I have seen, none compares with you. The winding creeper has come to seek an abiding place beside your stately tree.' (See also Song 87, line 13.) The two lovers fled to Shansi (山西) and shared fortunes at the close of the Sui dynasty. Later, for his exploits against the Turkic invaders Lei Yeuk-si was made a duke. For another reference to Yeung So, see Song 33, line 9, note. Mayers, # 6, 196, 374, 895; Giles, # 46, 887, 1112, 2408.

Adriana in *The Comedy of Errors* expresses a thought similar to Hung Fat Nui's:

Thou art an elm, my husband, I a vine,
Whose weakness married to thy stronger state
Makes me with thy strength to communicate . . .

[160] See Song 32, line 5, note.

[161] See Song 76, Part 2, line 1.

I see him knit his brows in sorrow; he is the same as I am.

O willow! Your unending sorrow has also depressed my spirits.

It is a pity that you were not planted in the lady's boudoir, but were planted at the road-stage where people part;[162]

At the sight of a passionate farewell, your heart will be crushed.

I believe that many griefs will never inure you to the lovesickness-debt these songs sing of.

Ah, you must think about yourself;

Look towards Yeung Gwaan.[163]

O willow! Why at the beginning of autumn does your colour change to yellow-green?

Song 64

Hearing the Cry of the Goose

The broken-hearted dreads to hear the cry of the goose;

Is afraid the union accomplished in his dreams will be shattered.

O goose! You are lonely as the peacock, and I am a widowed phoenix;[164]

You complain to the waning moon; solitary, I face the red lamp.[165]

It is a pity that for your whole life you are alone and without a companion;

Although far away on the edge of the horizon, my lover and I can still say we are in touch with one another by letter.

O goose! I pity you. We both suffer from the same sickness. Bring my letter to him, though he is so far away.

Be quick on your journey. Do not delay at the barriers or the rivers.

I watch for the carrier-goose as I watch for my lover, and my heart is all the heavier.

Sorrow has ten thousand shapes.

O goose! Do not let happen to you what happened to my lover: he is now a snapped stalk, a drifting weed.

---

[162] See Song 76, Part 2, line 3, and Eighth Preface, note.
[163] See Song 11, Part 2, line 11, note.
[164] See Songs 18, line 8, note; 88, line 12.
[165] See Song 51, line 12.

Song 65
Born Beautiful

I have been born so beautiful,

Need I fear that no new fish will take my hook?

This morning I held a fish in my hand, as its tail thrashed this way and that.

Now I have put my fishing rod in its case, and need it no more.

If fish and water do not agree, it is because of fate.

I know that in the vast ocean there are many fish.

Stop jumping round everywhere!

An iron net has been spread,

If you once escape my hook, I will leave you to roam the seas.

Song 66
Not All That Beautiful

You are not all that beautiful. Why was I love-smitten when first I saw you?

I believe that even before you were born, it was fated you would win my soul; and so in this life you have made me heartbroken.

A former life planted the root of this life's sin-debt of flowers and powder [i.e. of courtesans];[166]

Because of this, risking death I went in search of flowers, and I happened upon this wondrous fragrance.

Hundreds of thousands of red powders [i.e. courtesans] have I seen, but none was like you.

After I had met you once, I went back and pondered for at least ten days.

If they say that the dead will return to life then I will die with you.

You have treated me harshly. When I am dead and gone, you will say it is no concern of yours.

But not even if someone [i.e. another beautiful person] from heaven came here, would I dare to have lustful desires.

---

[166] See Songs 9, line 5; 35 (Part 3), line 3; 35 (Part 4), lines 8–10; 72, line 6.

You must really forgive me.

Do not, without even speaking a word to me, veer your heart away from mine.

Song 67

Why Are You So Thin?

Why are you so thin? It makes others pity you.

I believe you are grieved because of your passion.

I see you are so thin you can scarcely carry the weight of your clothes; your features have changed.

I advise you to see through the word 'dissipation'[167] for what it is; do not be so spell-bound by it;

Lovesickness will play havoc with your spirit.

See how the madly infatuated butterfly dreams in the flower's boudoir [i.e. the house of entertainment]!

Although your love be extremely deep, do not indulge too much.

You must take thought.

Do not say all you want is dissipation and that you are not afraid your life will be shortened.

Let me ask you, 'In one life how many persons can you tie your destiny to?'[168]

Song 68

My Darling

My darling! Do not be so quarrelsome.

Actually my anger brings on headaches.

When you see a beautiful girl, why do you pay such special attention to her?

I know that you have been callous for a long time; and that you have grown tired of me, because I watch you jealously;

---

[167] See Songs 1 (Part 2), line 9; 7, line 11.
[168] See Song 68, line 9.

I have noticed that recently you have not even one-third of the feeling you once used to have for me.

From the time we first met until now, because of you, all day I suffer distress and anxiety;

The vows you made to me in the beginning were empty; today you have broken your pledge.

I had hoped to have a lover I could rely on;

But it seems to me no man is single-hearted.[169]

I say I will not bother about you; but die and seek a re-birth . . .

But thinking over it, I will not do anything so foolish.

For what would I gain by leaving the world of human pleasures and dying in vain?

I remember — but you do not — the moment of our first meeting;

Why did you deceive me for so long? You only wanted a new plaything.

Now, mend your ways and become a 'new man', and we two will share our marriage destiny.[170]

Ah! How impatient I am!

Do not allow men to call you a fickle lover;

Change your heart and treat me with tenderness. I think I am subservient, my benefactor.

Song 69

No Easy Task

It is no easy task, my dearest! Can you understand my feelings of bitter distress?

More cruel is the wound of lusting with you [i.e. the courtesan] day and night than that of a sharp knife.

Recently I see the number of your familiar 'guests' has declined and no new 'guests' are coming;

On neither side [i.e. with neither old nor new 'guests'] are you successful; water and oil do not mix.

---

[169] Cf. Songs 2, line 1; 61, line 8.
[170] See Song 42.

Early on, I learned that I could not live with you; it would have been better had we never met at all,

And I would not have been day and night so anxious.

I advise you, open up your heart, and find a good partner,

That he may pay off your debts, to avoid being harassed on all sides by your rent-demanding creditors.

The river-side houses of entertainment may be showy and splendid but have you ever known anyone to live well there till old age?[171]

Really, if all you get from him is clear tea and plain rice [i.e. basic sustenance], still you must chose someone who can bring you to safety [i.e. redemption from this way of life].

There have been so many fires recently, and it is no easy task to ply one's trade [i.e. as a courtesan in the houses of entertainment];

The marine magistrate and his police [i.e. collecting taxes] storm in here everyday and shout and scream.

You do not believe me? Then take a look at the ledgers in the flower-boats,

You will see nothing but debts; no settlements. A less than meagre pittance is all.

Although you keep many girls till they are mature [i.e. the courtesan may become a keeper one day], thinking that you will easily make money to pay off your debts,

I believe that in a moment they will slip from your hand, and so you will sink to the depths of hell.

Although recently some keepers have met with good fortune,

Some dozens of young girls have ransomed themselves, but still dozens of others have not yet opened the blankets [i.e. lost their virginity].

As I think about how everything will turn out, there is no certainty, no guarantee of success.

Moreover, not one in a hundred can avoid this misfortune.

Please repress your desires, and seek a place of refuge.

Do not be afraid that you will not be able to find some way out.

You must put this sort of life behind you as soon as you can, [172]

---

[171] See Song 31 (Part 1), line 1.
[172] See Song 1 (Part 2), line 8.

So as not to be like duckweed which shows its face for all to see [i.e. like common prostitutes (as opposed to courtesans) exposing themselves for sale].[173]

Song 70
Half a Life's Bitterness[174]

Half a life's bitterness — both of us know well what this means.

Why after all this bitterness have we no happiness? Tell me how will it all end.

Since I first became aware of myself I knew that life was not easy.

I hope when I have carried my burden through this world I will have heart's delight.

Could I have ever thought that before I paid my debt I would sink to the region of flower and powder [i.e. to the houses of entertainment]?

We drift on the rivers and lakes in all directions;

Fate has decreed my poignant bitterness, and I am indignant.

Ah! Woe is me! I cannot put up with it.

Do not talk about the past;

I do not want to spend the rest of my life sunk in this sea of bitterness from which there is almost no escape.[175]

Song 71
It Is Hard to Conduct Oneself

It is hard to conduct oneself. Never a day free from care.

Though I love you sincerely, you are not aware of it.

For you I weep and sigh the whole day long.

I have thought about what it would mean to spend the rest of my days like this. Do you think such a life means anything for me?

---

[173] See Songs 12 (Part 4), line 2, note; 35 (Part 2), line 14; 52, line 4; 54, line 6.
[174] See Song 41, line 9.
[175] See Song 1 (Part 1), line 3.

You have told me that with a true heart I should treat all men; but this is not easy.

When once I see you my lord, O my lord, I do not want to miss our wedding day.

Never say that the Pearl River[176] [i.e. by metonymy, those of the Pearl River flower-boats] is an unfeeling place.

Today for 'passion's' sake I am entangled and therefore am so infatuated;

When you speak, why do you treat us so callously?

I blame you because even when you are face to face with me your thoughts are far away;

If you will keep me in your mind, I will keep you in mine.

Ah, do not hate me;

Be constant from beginning to end.

When in the flower and powder groves [i.e. in the house of entertainment] you can understand us women.

Song 72

Utterly Helpless

I am utterly helpless. I have driven myself mad by thinking about it.

Middle-age quickly silvers our hair.

Since the beginning of time, the rose-complexioned [i.e. beautiful women] have found it very hard to change their ill-fate.

There is no denying that the passion of red-powder [i.e. of a courtesan] is the womb of her sorrow.

I have been reflecting on this 'dusty' [i.e. earthy, mortal] world;[177] tell me how I can escape its sea of bitterness.

Had we in our past life cultivated virtue, then perhaps we might have escaped this sorrow,

I know I did not in my past life cultivate myself, therefore I have fallen this low. And for so long.[178]

---

[176] See Second Preface, note.
[177] See Fifth Preface.
[178] See Songs 9, line 5; 33 (Part 3), line 3; 35 (Part 4), lines 8–10; 72, line 6.

Ah, it is hard to sever the bonds of love;

The lover goes. The root of love remains.

I cannot bear to look back. I must put one question to Tathagata [i.e. the highest epithet of the Buddha].[179]

Song 73
Sent Far Away

Do not be too inflamed with passion. Passion that is too inflamed will be hard to cast aside.

Even one single day's separation leaves me truly desolate.

Though I may be beautiful I have not yet come safely through; our predestined union has not yet been completed.

Moreover, dry wood near a flame can easily catch fire:

You tell me to wait three years for you. But I am still young, and

I fear that when I am grown to maturity, I will have no one to rely on. Today my mistake will begin [i.e. if she decides to wait three years for him].

From now on, I will disclose my feelings only in the company of orioles and swallows;[180]

Alone I grieve that since I must continue to offer the goblets and wine cups, my sin is not yet forgiven.

What I regret is that my fate is as frail as a flower and that men are so worthless;

Had fate been kind, would I today have to live in this hut [i.e. this house of entertainment]?

I hope one day, covered with honours, you will return home dressed in your academic robes.[181]

When you have paid your book-debt [i.e. fulfilled his duty of studying], my flower-debt too will be cancelled.

But now alone in your lodgings you are wrapped in your soul's dream.

Ah! No news from you.

---

[179] See Introduction p. 27.
[180] See Song 4.
[181] See Song 50; 58, line 6; 88, line 8.

When will the good omen of red snuff appear on my oil lamp?[182]

See, glorious Peking is ten-thousand *li* across the water.

Song 74 (Part 1)

Spring

Spring, do not go away just yet, I have something to talk to you about.

Year after year we part and each time my feelings are wounded.

When I see how frightful is the plight of flowers, my soul is delirious.

I think life is uncertain, so that meetings and partings are irregular.

Were my fate not wedded to yours, I would not be so insistent;

Why having been so close for three months are we now separated in two different places?

See, my prince has gone home; my disappointment increases;

I had no means of keeping you here; it seems I have flouted the sights and sounds of spring [i.e. wasted time].

I think the glorious hopes of spring are but empty and hollow.

Ah, I have nothing more to say!

I accompany my lord down the Naam Po river.[183]

Now I have something to say but I find it hard to write; unfortunately there is not enough paper on which to express the depth of my passion.

---

[182] When Chinese lamp-oil is very pure, no snuff forms. But if impure, a red-hot snuff appears which is considered a sign that the lover will quickly return. When a husband who has been away for some time writes saying that he is soon coming home, his wife and concubines gather round the oil lamp and watch for the omen of the red-hot snuff. (See also Song 91, line 14.)

[183] The Naam Po (南浦) is a river of Hupeh (湖北) which flows into the Yangtze. A poem by Gong Yim (江淹) has the lines,

> The spring grass is emerald green, the spring tide flows green.
>
> I accompany my lord down the Naam-po (river), my heart is sorely wounded.

春草碧色　春水綠波

送君南浦　傷如之何

Since the time of the Warring States (475–221 BC), poets have referred to the Naam Po river as the place of bidding farewell to those starting out on a long journey.

Song 74 (Part 2)
Flowers

O flowers, do not fade just yet; let me admire your fragrant beauty a little longer;

In dejected sorrow and the darkening rain, we gaze at each other.

Is there a single heart not filled with pain when we sing of the ill-fate of the rose-complexioned [i.e. young beauties]?

Men in this human world are wandering adrift like you.

O flowers, sometimes when the night is still you waft your fragrance to me.

It is really burdensome if you [i.e. flowers] are deep-red or but lightly tinted [i.e. attractive].

Were you flowers not fragrant, you could never excite my true passion.

Pitiable it is that I have no strength to protect flowers; I hate the east wind;

Nor against the frenzy of the bee or the wandering of the butterfly can I do anything to help.[184]

Ah me, my sorrow has ten thousand shapes; and

The past is mostly like a dream.

You should compose a song on the silk-stringed pipa of phoenix-tree wood[185] to whoever pities fragrance [i.e. has tender affection for us women].

Song 74 (Part 3)
Autumn

Autumn, do not grow old just yet. You must still bind up the year;

Sorrow entangles my heart as I face the rushes and reeds.

They say the soughing of the autumn wind makes men afraid.

I love to watch the clear autumn waters reflect the rosy clouds.

Seeing that you, autumn, have no feelings, you will not tug for long at my heart-strings.

---

[184] See Song 11 (Part 5), line 9; 35 (Part 6), line 10.
[185] See Song 11 (Part 4), line 7, note.

You always keep the bright moon shining on my gauze-covered windows.

Generally speaking, men find delight in those who are natural and graceful.

Do not say the wind has made you haggard from grief and now you are thinner than the chrysanthemum;

I think Sung Yuk's elegy for autumn is nothing but empty words;[186]

Who does not want in autumn to float on the raft of the immortals?[187]

Now since I have shown compassion for autumn, autumn should show some compassion for me.

Ah, I am choking with grief, as

I pluck the chrysanthemum under the eastern hedge.[188]

See the Cham Yeung river, where tears are shed to the music of the pipa.[189]

Song 74 (Part 4)

Moon

O moon! Do not decline just yet. You have to shine on me throughout the night.

When at night I think of my lover, I am all the more desolate.

Men only know that you are perfectly round, and therefore they beam with smiles,

How can they understand that when you have reached perfect roundness, you little by little begin to wane?

O moon! Once a month you are perfectly round. But your roundness I see too seldom.

Would that I could meet you for thirty nights and every night you would invite me to come to you!

---

[186] Sung Yuk (宋玉), who lived about 300 BC, was both a statesman and a poet like his uncle, the famous Wat Yuen (屈原). This poet is referred to in Song 12 (Part 5), line 7, note, as being the source of the legends associated with the Sorceress Mountain. Mayers, # 326, 642; Giles, # 503, 1841.

[187] See Song 12 (Part 3), line 12, note.

[188] Autumn is the season of chrysanthemums.

[189] The Cham Yeung river (潯陽江) is in the district of Anhui (安徽, *On Fai*). (See Song 12 (Part 4), line 3, note.)

Ask Seung Ngoh about 'meetings' and 'farewells'. She should understand something of this.[190]

Why does happy fate that brings lovers together not open a path for me? And why has the Blue Bridge been pulled asunder?[191]

I have too many things weighing on my mind. I wish that you, O moon, would take care of them for me.

Ah me, my sorrow is endless;

No one can express my feeling and emotion.

Would that I could meet my lord every night, and that our meetings would be as recurrent as the tide!

Song 75

The One Word 'Passion'

The one word 'passion' is more baneful than arsenic.

But why without a reason can it [i.e. passion] break my heart?

I scratch my head and say to heaven: 'Heaven! Do not be like this.

---

[190] Seung Ngoh (嫦娥), already mentioned in Songs 24, line 12, note and 34, line 13, has become the generic name for all immortals in the moon. It is reported that the emperor Tong Yuen Jung (See Song 34, line 14, note) travelled to a palace in the moon where he saw ten Seung Ngohs, dressed in shining clothes, seated on white phoenixes, dancing under the laurel tree.

[191] 'The Blue Bridge'(藍橋 , *Laam Kiu*) is in Cheung On (長安), an ancient capital of China. It is the bridge under which Mei Sang-go (微生高), a model of devotion and constancy, lost his life. He had a rendezvous with a woman under this Blue Bridge. While waiting for her to come, the waters suddenly rose, and rather than break his appointment with her, he stood clasping the wooden support until he was drowned in the flooding waters.

The Blue Bridge is also famous as the scene of the amorous adventure of Pooi Hong (裴航), a scholar of the Tong dynasty (618–907). He was told in a dream that his future bride would be the beautiful Wan Ying (雲英). The next day Pooi Hong on his way home crossed this Blue Bridge, the hiding place of spirits, and being very thirsty he went into a hut to ask for a drink. An old lady called to her daughter to bring the visitor a drink. Her exceptionally beautiful daughter obeyed, and in answer to Pooi Hong's question replied that her name was Wan Ying. Immediately Pooi Hong asked the old lady for permission to marry her daughter. She would give her permission, she said, provided that Pooi Hong could bring her a pestle and mortar of jade for making certain magic drugs. It took Pooi Hong one month to find this pestle and mortar of jade, which he then exchanged for his bride, Wan Ying. Both Pooi Hong and Wan Ying were later admitted to the rank of 'spirits'.

In Chinese, The Blue Bridge has become a symbol for the meeting place of lovers, and of betrothals. Mayers, # 332.

My fate is as frail as a flower, and you do not protect me.'

What I regret most is that I have erred in love, and hence have so many love-debts.

Why was I not in the beginning given a heart of stone?

See the wife changed into a block of stone, forever watching her husband depart.[192]

I must reconsider it.

You can shatter my soul and break my spirit, if you like.

It is ever the same: those who are passionate must pay the debt [i.e. must suffer].

Song 76 (Part 1)

The Passionate Willow

The passionate willow I give as a present to my fickle lover.

My lover! Is not 'parting' pitiable?

With all my heart I hope you will never reject me;

May we both preserve our love as wide as the ocean, as high as the mountains.

How could I think that I was not destined for you? How could I think I would be abruptly parted from you?

Now mists and water, clouds and mountains obstruct the path [i.e. that would bring us together].

As a young girl could I ever have known that parting would be so bitter?

Woe is me; I am truly frustrated.

Now, I rely on the willow to tell the story of my feelings;

Therefore, although it is so far to this parting-stage, I am not afraid of the trouble.

---

[192] It is said that on the North Mountain (北山) in the Mo Cheung (武昌) district of Hupeh (湖北) there is a rock called 'Mong Foo Sek' (望夫石), which looks exactly like a woman standing upright. Legend has it that a wife whose husband was sent by the government on an extremely dangerous mission accompanied him to the North Mountain where she stood and watched his departure so intently that she was transformed into stone; thus giving the rock its name, which literally means: 'gazing into the distance-husband-rock'.

Song 76 (Part 2)
The Passionate Willow

Both eyes of the passionate willow are weeping.[193]

O willow tree! When you see others you are happy; why is it when you see me you are sad?

You grow at Pa Bridge[194], therefore I know you are paying a sin-debt;

You speed people on their way home; but filled with loneliness you watch the mandarin drake and duck sleeping on the waters.[195]

O willow! You find it hard to support your delicate frame, just like me;

You are not afraid of the spring breeze, but you dread having to face the autumn frost.

Today, you are withered and you seem to have nothing to rely on;

Ah me, I had better not change my mind.

When troubles come to a head, there is always hope:

It has always been true that before we can hope for new life, new sprouts must burgeon from the dry willow.

Song 77
The Sorrow I Cannot Dispel

I cannot dispel my sorrow.[196] I grieve that I am ill-fated and that I have suffered many a set-back during my life.

O Heaven! You made me like this. Tell me how I can be united with my lover in this life.

Do you think I do not like to wear fresh flowers?

I must be fated not to enjoy any romance; my passion is wasted.

I shoulder all the burden of my love-thoughts and look for someone to buy them [i.e. for someone who will love her].

Whoever I meet tells me to turn to the willow groves and flower streets [i.e. the houses of entertainment],

---

[193] See Song 63, lines 1–2.
[194] See Eighth Preface (notes); Song 63, line 5.
[195] See Song 12, Part 6.
[196] See Song 1 (Parts 1 & 2).

And that if someone offers a price, I should sell; and even if no price be offered, I should still sell,

To repay my past debts.

Far better than hawking myself in the street.[197]

Lest despite all my yearning I remain without a protector, never knowing a single day of peace and content.

Song 78

In the Depths of Sorrow

I am so deep in sorrow that I do not bother to spruce myself up.

The embroidered blinds have not been rolled up, because I am afraid of the cold wind;

My waist is only half the size it used to be; my heart, because of you, is sick.

Where are you now, unwilling to leave your pleasure and return home?

Though you never think about me here in the house of entertainment, at least you should think of your family at home;

Though you do not think of your wife and children, you should remember your father and mother.

When you are living so far away on the edge of the horizon, why have you veered your heart's course away from me?

Ah, woe is me! Why do I have to suffer in this way?

My lord! Do not listen to those who would try to make you change the direction of your heart.

Song 79 (Part 1)

What Is the Best Thing to Do?

What is the best thing to do? I fear our mutual friendship will not last till old age;

Sincere though our passion may be, unfortunately it will never climax.

---

[197] See Song 69, line 4.

In this life I have wedded my destiny to yours, but we must wait till the next life to consummate our union.

You are now a monk! I am now a nun!

If you do not believe me, read in *The Dream of the Red Chamber* the story of the mandarin drake and duck; and how

Because Bo-yuk's fate was not to marry his beloved Doi-yuk, therefore she was so lonely;

And when Doi-yuk was dying, she sobbed, 'Ah! Bo-yuk, you are so very....'[198]

I can find no outlet for my grief.

Can even heaven lessen the pain of parting?

Enough! I think I had better be cool in my dealings with you so that you will not accuse me of being a fickle woman.

Song 79 (Part 2)

What Is the Best Thing to Do?

What is the best thing to do? My lord, your family is poor and your parents are old;

And of eight thousand paths before you, none can bring you credit [i.e. bring him to her].

You have spurned me and left me fallen here at the edge of the horizon, where I never receive a letter from home.

My lord has returned to Naam Leng and I live bitterly sorrowful in the capital.[199]

Your sword may indeed flash brightly, but its brightness no one has yet seen;

The young leafless bamboo may one day reach the sky;

But if your name comes after Suen Saan's[200], the colour will drain from your cheeks.

---

[198] See Songs 3, line 13, note; 25, line 9, note.

[199] Naam Leng (南嶺) is a mountain range in the extreme north of Canton, on the frontiers of Gwong Dung (廣東) and Gong Sai (江西).

[200] Suen Saan (孫山) was the last name on the list of successful candidates. When Suen Saan was asked whether a friend of his has passed or not, he replied that his friend's name came after his own. In other words, his friend had failed.

The green willow provokes my passion more than a sharp knife.

The gold I kept beneath my pillow is all spent, I am reluctant to make excellent wine [i.e. she is reduced to great poverty],

I have nothing to requite you with,

Except my tears strung together like pearls.

My lord, when you go home will you, for my sake, carry my tears with you?

Song 80

Only One Body

I have only one body; just tell me how I can I accommodate two lovers.

I am happy to have two lovers, but at the same time I feel frustrated.

Both of them come here night after night; and invariably they choose me.

Were there only one man one night, it would be less harassing.

Despite myself I am accommodating with one until he goes looking for someone else.

I fear if this pestilent fellow brings me to no good end, I will bitterly regret the very first step.

I am also afraid that the other fickle lover will not tolerate me much longer;

For the bystanders have carried too many tales.

Ah, if only I could split my heart in two, then I could become two persons;

They would have no need to flare up [i.e. out of jealousy].

It would be more pleasant to me than preserved pineapple were I able to prevent my two lovers from taking vinegar [i.e. from becoming jealous].[201]

---

[201] 'A woman drinking vinegar' (喫醋娘子 , hek cho neung ji) alludes to the story of the wife of Fong Yuen-ling (房玄齡) who lived during the Tong dynasty (618–907). It is said she drank a bowl of vinegar, given to her as poison, rather than allow a concubine into the house. 'A woman drinking vinegar' simply means, a jealous woman. Today the expression, to drink / take vinegar (呷醋 , haap cho) means to be jealous (as in a love affair).

Song 81

Do Not Be Afraid of Ungenerous Fate[202]

Do not be afraid that your fate is against you; you must be steadfast.

If you are steadfast, there will be no need to grieve that 'the old man in the moon'[203] does not pity you.

To say that fate is against you and that the time is out of joint is to take a short-sighted view.

In half your life-time, you have never had one day of real enjoyment, and I fear that even after death you will feel you have been wronged.

If you say the 'eight characters' [i.e. indicating one's horoscope] were already determined at your birth, what need is there to think about the future?[204]

We do not know if what has been predetermined will 'come true' or not. There probably was never an immortal who could tell us about our future.

In a word, you must do what is humanly possible; and perhaps your luck will change.

Stop blaming yourself!

Do not say good things are as hard to come by as we expect.

Be steadfast and patient, and the broken mirror will be made round once again [i.e. lovers will be re-united].[205]

Song 82

Lamenting the Shortness of Life

I lament the shortness of life and that I can only have one life;

Men drive me to death, but tell me how can I bear to throw my life away.

Had I one life to give to each man, I would not care.

---

[202] See Song 6.

[203] See Song 14, line 11, note.

[204] The 'eight characters' (八字 , *baat ji*), in four pairs, indicating the year, month, day and hour of a person's birth, were formerly used in fortune-telling. Mayers (Part 2) # 257.

[205] See Song 33, line 9, note.

There is no alternative to this broken life; only with the greatest pains have I kept the remnants of my life till this day.

I can never requite the passionate lovers who gave their life for me;

They died with a peaceful heart, and I consider it was my fate that led them to this.

I believe it is a mark of youth to lose one's life because of a lust for flowers;

In reality, only love that lasts to the very end can rival the red-beet that age makes more beautiful.[206]

See how the Cowherd every year meets the Spinning Girl, and they are not young;[207]

Their hearts truly mirror one another.

On the Seventh day of the Seventh moon, they rejoice together.

Only after a long life of lasting love can you cross the Crows' Bridge.[208]

Song 83

Unhurt by the Wind

The wind cannot snap the fibres of passion;

The fibres of passion are drawn up so tightly that even if you cut them it is hard to sever them completely.[209]

When they are entwined about the heart we are no longer in control;

The soul is not longer itself; nothing remains but frenzied passion.

If the mutual passion of lovers is frenzied, they could die of infatuation;

They would die in peace, for it was not in vain they had known each other for so long.

But I greatly fear if one of them is infatuated, the other may not be;

Unrequited love brings a sickness no medicine can cure;[210]

---

[206] The red beet (老來嬌, *lo loi giu*, literally: age-come-beauty) is so called because it grows more beautiful with age.
[207] See Songs 12 (Part 3), line 12, note; 43, line 6.
[208] See Song 18, line 10, note.
[209] See Song 60, line 5.
[210] See Song 1 (Part 1), line 6; 12 (Part 1), line 9.

Then, even though you were willing to die for his sake, he will give you small thanks for it.

Ah woe is me! Life means nothing to me.

I tell you in all honesty, if his love for you were true, your death would be a timely one.[211]

Song 84

The Cable of Love

I call on you, cable of love, to bring my lover to me.

If you can bring him to me, then for my sake, do not ever loose him from me.

It is true the bonds that bind are the fibres of our heart, therefore they are long lasting;

If I meet a man who severs these bonds, I feel so benumbed.

Cable of love! I hate you when you separate us; I love you when you bring us together.

We are tugged at from all directions. I do not know when we can come together again.

I have put my heart in your hands.

It grieves me that you always wish to sever the bonds, driving me almost insane.

I think there is no need to swear by the mountains and the seas,[212]

The most important thing is that you do not change your heart.

For if our hearts are not one, no cable can bind you to me.

Song 85

Lovesickness

Why are you so sick? You look pale and wan;

I never thought lovesickness could penetrate to the vitals [i.e. be beyond cure].

---

[211] See Song 3, line 2.
[212] See Song 12 (Part 3), line 2.

I believe heaven and earth [i.e. fate] has allotted me a love-fraught destiny and has drawn up the symptoms of my sickness.

Since my sickness is like yours, my lord, I must take the same medicine as you.

Oh my lover, the medicine is so hard to take! When you took it, what effect did it have?

Today bitterness has filled my heart; we two are cruelly wounded;

Right from the beginning our love was doomed. Is there now anything we can hope for?

No road opens up before us. The sea of bitterness is wide.

If after death our fates could be wedded, I would worship Buddhist idols,[213]

But I fear my six roots[214] are not purified, and I cannot reach the Western Paradise.[215]

When dealing with worldly affairs, you are indulging in idle fancy to talk about the world to come.

I have nothing to rely on.

The houses of entertainment are simply hellish. What is the sense in talking about 'enduring as the heavens and earth?'

Song 86

Soul-dissolving Willow

The willow that overwhelms with sorrow gloomily pulls at my garments.

O willow! Since you evoke passion, how can you tolerate partings?

---

[213] *Bodhisattva*, translated into Chinese as 菩薩, *po saat*, refers to those who have to pass only once more through human life before becoming Buddhas, and includes also those Buddhas who are not yet perfected by entering Nirvana. (See also Introduction p. 32.) In recent Chinese, however, *po saat* (菩薩) simply means 'an idol'.

[214] Purification of the 'six roots' refers to the eradication of earthly desires caused by the workings of the six organs of perception: the eyes, ears, nose, tongue, body and mind. What is called in Buddhist terminology 'the six dusts' (六塵, *luk chan*) refers to the qualities produced by these organs of perception. 'Dust' means dirt, whatever defiles the pure mind, and these six qualities are the cause of all impurity.

[215] The Western Paradise (西方, *Sai Fong*) is where souls live until they achieve Nirvana. (See Introduction p. 36.)

The east wind blows for only one night, my lover is already a thousand *li*²¹⁶ away,

Clouds at dusk and trees in spring excite my yearning.²¹⁷

How can my letters reach you across the barriers and mountains?

Your passion must be as gold or rock, [i.e. symbols of hardness and strength] — forever unchanging.

Do not say that because we are now holding hands our passion will last forever. In a while when our hands are unclasped, you will flout my favours.

Remember how at Yeung Gwaan I gave you a willow twig.²¹⁸

I lost my virginity because of you when I was a very young girl,

Ah me! The very word 'passion' . . .

My lord! You may not think about the present; but the past you must remember.

Song 87

The Region of Mist and Flowers

Diabolical indeed is the region of mist and flowers [i.e. the houses of entertainment],²¹⁹

You suffer as many torments as you enjoy sensuous pleasures.

Snow, moon, wind and flowers [i.e. the vicissitudes of life] I have seen them all;

How many unlimited pleasures can you buy, I ask you.

They are transient as mist. You would be very wrong to be infatuated by them.

Not all the mountains in the world could ever fill up a bottomless river.

If you speak about genuine virtue and genuine passion — who has ever died for you?

---

²¹⁶ See Song 22, line 5, note.
²¹⁷ 'Evening clouds and spring trees' (暮雲春樹 , *mo wan chun sue*) refers to longing for a dear one's return.
²¹⁸ See Eighth Preface, line 13, note; Songs 11 (Part 2), line 11, note; 63, line 5; 76 (Part 2), line 3.
²¹⁹ See Songs 35 (Part 2), line 2; 35 (Part 3), line 14; 40, line 13; 6.9.

I fear that when all savings are spent, no matter how intimate our friendship has been, we will be parted.

Flowers and willows [i.e. courtesans] hurt more than one person.

You must really think about this:

Quench the fire in your heart.

Everywhere I warn young men of the world not to become entangled amiss with water creepers.[220]

Song 88

The Mandarin Drake and Duck[221]

The mandarin drake and duck are inseparable in this life;

It is ever the same, men on the edge of the horizon [i.e. separated from their loved one by a very great distance] become the more disconsolate when they see the mandarin drake and duck,

That eat and sleep together and cannot bear to be separated.[222] Tell me, how do you expect me to be content?

I have one request, mandarin drake and duck, to make of you: I want to be reincarnated as you, and not as a human being.

My lover is remiss about love's duty, and there is nothing more important for him than fame and wealth.[223]

I know it is hard to buy 'green spring' [i.e. retain one's youthful beauty], you will waste your fortune for nothing.

---

[220] See Song 62, line 9, note: Hung Fat Nui's words to Lei Yeuk-si. 'Creepers relying on a tree' is frequently a symbol of marriage.

[221] See Songs 3, line 13, note; 12 (Part 6), line 8; 35 (Part 4), line 5; 38, line 10; 60, line 8; 76 (Part 2), line 4; 79 (Part 1), line 5.

[222] The great Chinese poet Do Foo has the line:
  The mandarin drake and duck do not sleep alone.

鴛鴦不獨宿

  A line expressing similar sentiments is found in Number 2 of *The Nineteen Ancient Poems*:
  It is hard to sleep in an empty bed alone.

空牀難獨守

[223] See Songs 50, line, note; 58, line 6; 73, line 11.

With his vulgar eyes he wants his share of the empty fame he esteems so much.

He says he is ambitious only for my sake; but is willing to sever passion's root.

From a great distance, we watch you enjoying yourself; while helplessly we look on.

Ah me! How foolish it is.

Even if you attain the rank you have set your heart on, I will regret it.

I am thinking of the widowed phoenix and the companionless peacock, and I feel utterly inconsolable.[224]

Song 89

The Fan

I hold in my hand a Chai [i.e. today's Shandung] silk fan,

And I recall that I have not held one for a year.

When the hot weather returns I always think of you, my fan,

But why when autumn comes are you discarded?[225]

Generally speaking, as fans are discarded, so men weary of us.

Think carefully how men's passions blow now hot, now cold,[226] I cannot bear to speak about it.

The way of the world is the same: hot and cold. Do not grieve over yourself.

Who has not first of all been hot before being cold?[227]

When you are in a warm place you must reckon with the cold that will follow.

When you meet a person for the first time, do not let the heat of your passion run away with you;

You may say, 'Well, that is the way things are', but in the frenzy of heat all you have is infatuation. Will you be able to foresee that later on things will change?

---

[224] See Songs 18, line 8, note; 64, line 3.
[225] See Song 26, line 8, note.
[226] See Song 43, line 3.
[227] See Song 13 (Part 1), line 1.

Alas! You are so deeply bound up with one another.

Put the affairs of your heart to one side.

Enough! Now that you are cast out in the cold, you do not remember the earlier warmth.

Song 90

Knitting a Silken Fabric

Boil pure water, hart's tongue [i.e. a plant, a type of rush] and gingko [i.e. a Chinese tree cultivated for its rich foliage].[228]

Since I am pure and white why should I be afraid of your lightness of love?

Wrap the passion-flower and the peppermint in tissue paper[229] and give them to me.

Although your passion be as thin as tissue-paper, tell me, who can it hurt?

Wrap up a few lungans and [Chinese] sand pears,[230]

Symbols that we shall separate and be parted for some time.

How can silk thread pass through the eye of the fine embroidery needle?

It is all wrong:

The thread must fit the needle before the silken fabric can be knit.[231]

---

[228] In this first line there is an untranslatable play on words in Chinese. In the Chinese text we have the words: *'pure* water' (清水 , *ching shui*) and *'gingko'* (白菓 , *baak gwok*) literally *white* fruit. In the second line, the singer applies to herself the adjectives 'pure' and 'white', both of which refer to her goodness and integrity.

[229] If a woman felt that her lover has been unfaithful to her, she would send him an iris and some peppermint leaves. In Chinese the iris is: 白芷 , *baak ji*, which two characters are pronounced in Cantonese similarly to words which mean *'white paper'*: 白紙 , *baak ji*. When a lover received an iris, he would immediately think of 'white paper' and realize he was being told his feelings were as thin as paper. The Cantonese pronunciation of the words for peppermint (薄荷, *bok hoh*) suggests by collocation the words frequently used in these songs: fickle lover (薄倖 , *bok hang*).

[230] In Cantonese, the second character of the word for 'sand pear' (梨 , *lei*) is phonetically identical with the Cantonese word for 'separation' (離 , *lei*). The symbolism of the pear is mentioned in the following line.

[231] 'Knitting a silken fabric' is frequently a metaphor for marriage. The Chinese words: 絲蘿 , *si loh*, refer to creepers and also to a type of fabric. (See also Songs 10, line 5; 62, line 9, note.)

Song 91

Facing the Lonely Lamp

The broken-hearted dreads to face the lonely lamp.[232]

Lonely and cold with my own thoughts I watch my shadow, and my heart breaks within me.

Now with none to share my pillow and sheets, who have I to rely on?

O silent shadow! To whom can I pour out my sorrow?

Although you, my shadow, and I make two, this comforts me little in my grief.

I will take a cup, and together with you, we shall be three.[233]

Oh, my shadow! I love you, I love you. Because neither in life nor in death do you part from me; you are always close to me;

Even at the ends of the earth you and I would never part.

My lord, forlorn I watch the silver lamp, yet we have kindred hearts.

If only I could send my shadow to talk to you,

If only you could meet my shadow and see in it my soul.

Ah, woe is me! How miserable I am!

Even in my dreams it is hard to come near to you.

I will imagine I see the red-hot lamp-snuff : the happy omen that we shall see each other for a long time.[234] I must not turn to my shadow as if I were wounded in spirit.

---

[232] See Song 51, line 12.

[233] The Chinese poet Lei Baak (李白, 699–762) has a very well-known poem about himself and his shadow and the moon, in which he says:
> I drank alone. There was no one with me —
> Till, raising my cup, I asked the bright moon
> To bring me my shadow and make us three.

(Translation by Witter Bynner, in *Three Hundred Poems of the T'ang Dynasty*.)

獨酌無相親

齊杯邀明月

對影成三人

[234] Song 73, line 15, note.

Song 92

The Peach-blossom Fan

The peach-blossom fan has a heart-rending verse written on it;

With deep passion written in this way, why even the fan itself will feel sorrowful.

Fate is as frail as the peach-blossom; passion as weak as paper;[235]

Peach-blossoms painted on paper are the most fragile of all.

My lord, since you write about flowers, you must first of all understand what it means to be a flower.

It is hard to keep 'green spring' [i.e. the prime of life]; do not spoil the flower-season.

I believe that even consummate pleasure is not to be trusted.

The round fans of autumn are pining in the inner boudoirs,[236]

Where young girls paint ten thousand leaves and a thousand flowers — all for the sake of 'passion'.

You do not believe me? Then think of the mutual love and fidelity of the poet Hau Chiu-jung and the courtesan, Lei Heung-gwan. Had their passion been less deep, could they ever have been so happily united?[237]

Song 93

The Waves at the Prow

At the prow of the ship, the waves meet and part.

The billows of yearning surge within me.

My lord, you were born in the sky of passion; I grew up in the sea of lust.

I should think when the sky meets the water, the water will rely on the sky.

---

[235] See Songs 22, line 12; 26, line 8, note.
[236] See Song 26, line 8, note.
[237] Hau Chiu-jung (侯朝宗 , 1618–54) was a poet who lived just before the collapse of the Ming dynasty (1368–1644). Lei Heung-gwan (李香君) fell in love with him, and although powerful officials tried to court her, she remained faithful to the vows she had sworn to Hau Chiu-jung. Giles, # 666.

How can we rouge and powder [i.e. courtesans] be as unchanging as the green hills?

Look at the withered flowers on the water — such is our pitiable lot.[238]

The years flow on like a river. For how long more will they flow?

You must love yourself.

Even if you were to be canonized after your death as a Buddha or an immortal, you will not necessarily be at peace.

Enough! It were better to make the most of the present moment and together with you live in the Hall of the Moon and the Tower of the Winds [i.e. the place of the heavens].

Song 94

Hearing the Cawing of the Crow

The broken-hearted dread to hear the cawing of the crow.

I think it caws so painfully because it is looking for a branch to settle on.[239]

Who does not hope to fly high? But after all it is not that easy;

Moreover, you are not yet fully fledged.

Why do you, O my crow, make a bridge only for others to cross, and yet you do not understand your own dejected plight?[240]

---

[238] See Songs 31 (Part 1), line 13; 40, line 13.

[239] Crows caw at night when they miss their mate. *The Crows That Caw By Night* (烏夜啼), a poem by the famous Tong dynasty (618–907) poet, Lei Baak (李白, 699–762) has these lines:

> Through dusty clouds beside the [city] wall, the crows come home so late.
>
> And cawing fly from bough to bough as each one seeks her mate.

(Translation by W J B Fletcher in *Gems of Chinese Verse*.)

黃雲城邊烏欲棲

歸飛啞啞枝上啼

> A Chinese phrase says that 'Good birds choose their trees to roost in' (良禽擇木而棲, *leung kam jaak muk yi chai*). (See also Song 11 (Part 4), line 8, note.)

[240] See Song 18, line 10, note.

On both sides there is a rushing and fluttering against one another; but you must find some resting place to support yourself.

Today, the wind is fresh and the dew is cold, and the dense forest blocks your path,

So you must think well ahead:

Do not wait till the crow's head turns white before you realize that the world is a place of troubles.

Song 95

Dressing the Hair

I part my hair and do up my coiffure,

Hoping that he may part the way and return home.[241]

In the heart [i.e. the centre] of the bun I must braid in the wig.

If my heart is steadfast, need I fear slanders?

I bind tight my hair near the roots and plait ringlets at the end,

Because I must follow my lord to the end before I attain my desire.

The flower-tube with the flowers must go through the bottom of the coiffure.

I will completely pay off my flower-debt and urge you to take me home.

It is very important that the flowers match the head-dress, and the moon-laurel be fastened in the curls on either side.[242]

Then will 'the old man in the moon' and 'the flower-spirit' protect both of us; and as our hair silvers with age they will keep us as close together as eyebrows [i.e. they will remain a devoted couple to the end of their lives].[243]

---

[241] In lines 1 and 2 there is a play on the Chinese word 'to open' (開, *hoi*), which means to 'part the hair' and 'open the way'; in line 3, a play on the Chinese word 'heart' (心, *sam*) which also means 'centre'; in lines 5 and 6, a play on the word '*end*' (尾, *mei*) in: 'ringlets at the end' and 'follow to the end'.

[242] See Song 5, line 9, note.

[243] See Song 14, line 11, note.

Song 96

Paying the Flower-debt

I think my destiny is fulfilled, or perhaps my flower-debt is paid off;

'Debts paid off and destiny fulfilled' stirs up in me the sorrow of parting and the anguish of farewell.

When we two were so infatuated with each other, could I have ever dreamt our love would not last?

As I recall the past pleasure of wind and moon [i.e. her romance and erotic activity] it is as if my dream was shattered, my soul bewitched.

When first we met, I was still very young;

Pouring out to you the secrets of my innermost heart, I dreaded to hear the cock crowing over the water.

I only thought that our time was so long, we should plan together;

Little did I know that because of the deep love between you and your wife you could never bring the lowly me to your home.

You have broken my stem; I am left drifting; and I trust no one to bind it up again.[244]

I am thinking about myself: how aimlessly I am drifting; I must find a resting place.

Today men say we are callous; even if this is not true, it seems to be true;

Even among my very many sisters [i.e. other courtesans] is there one who can understand how troubled my heart is?[245]

This green garment I am wearing is drenched with my tears.

I should reconsider it.

My lord, you have most certainly hardened your heart against me, and you have no desire to see me —

Because from the very day I heard you say, 'I am going', never, never have you returned.

---

[244] See Song 11 (Part 2), line 6.
[245] See Song 56 (Part 2), line 4.

Song 97

Burn Pure Oil

How many hearts [i.e. wicks] will half a lamp-bowl of oil light?[246]

My lord, your heart changes so often. Tell me how I can go after it.

I see your heart is so aflame there is not enough oil for it;

See how much pure oil there is in that other lamp-bowl.

The deeper the wick goes, the drier it becomes; and the oil gets less and less;

If only some oil could be poured drop by drop on the almost dry heart [i.e. wick]!

You do not fear my nagging.

Do not be like a person that nobody regrets.

You must brace up your heart and become a proper man.[247]

---

[246] Throughout this song there is a play on the Chinese word 'heart' (心 , *sam*). A different word pronounced in exactly the same way (芯 , *sam*) means 'wick'.

[247] The play on the word 'heart/wick' is repeated. You must brace up your heart, bestir yourself, 'pull up your socks', make up your mind, is one sense of the phrase, 剔起心頭 , *tik hei sam tau*, while the phrase can also refer to trimming the wick of a lamp, adjusting it to the proper position to absorb the oil and so maintain the flame. A Cantonese expression is: 索油 , *sok yau*, which literally means, 'to soak up oil'. Its transferred and 'real' meaning is, to tease, take liberties with, play around with a woman for one's own amusement and delectation. In this song, 'wick' and 'oil' obviously have an erotic symbolism. It is interesting to note that the Cantonese connotations for the word oil (油 , *yau*) are very similar to those of the English word lubricious (oily), which derives from the Latin *lubricus* meaning slippery; near synonyms of lubricious are lascivious, lewd, wanton.

Appendices

Appendix I: The Original Prefaces in Chinese

Author's Preface

粵謳篤摯履道士願樂欲聞。請以此一卷書普渡世間一切沈迷慾海者。

道光戊子九月題於綠天書幌

Second Preface

戊子之秋，八月既望，蟋蟀在户，涼風振蕚，明珊居士惠然詣我，悄然不樂曰，此秋聲也，增人忉怛，請為吾子解之。余曰，唯唯。居士曰，子不覽夫珠江乎，素馨為田，紫檀作屋，香海十里，珠户千家，每當白日西逝，紅燈夕張，衣聲綷䌨雜以珮環，花氣氤氲蕩為煙霧，襛纖異致，儀態萬方，珠女珠兒雅善趙瑟，酒酣耳熱遂變秦聲，於子樂乎。余曰，豪則豪矣，非余所願聞也。居士曰，龍户潮落，罣更夜午，游舫漸疎，涼月已靜，於是雛鬟雪藕纖手分橙，蕩滌滯懷，抒發妍唱，吳歌甫奏，明燈轉華，楚竹乍吹，人聲忽定，於子樂乎。余曰，麗則麗矣，非余所心許也。居士曰，三星在天，萬籟如水，靚妝已解，薌澤微聞，撫冉冉之流年，惜厭厭之長夜，事往追昔，情來感今，乃復舒彼南音，寫伊孤緒，引吭按節，欲往仍迴，幽咽含怨，將斷復續，時則海月欲墮，江雲不流，輒喚奈何，誰能遣此。余曰，南謳感人，聲則然矣，詞可得而徵乎。居士乃出所錄，曼聲長哦，其意悲以柔，其詞婉而摯，此繁絃所謂悽入肝脾，哀感頑艷者，不待何滿一聲固已青衫盡濕矣。

石道人序

Third Preface

生長蠻鄉操土音
琵琶斷續聲咿啞
多少離愁多少情
當筵誰是心如鐵

俚詞率口幾關心
漫作竹枝長短吟
前因若夢未分明
忽聽低頭唱一聲

柳絮如郎妾似絲
癡懷恨緒真無賴
青州大尹筆花飄
更費搜羅成艷體

名閨猶有蘇臺詞
譜出新聲君莫疑
姊妹心情待曲描
任教頑鈍亦魂消

題粵謳四截句
梅花老農

Fourth Preface

抱起琵琶放下酒杯
　　聽此清謳
想重重綺障最難分手
　　茫茫慾海未易回頭
相惜相憐似嘲似勸
　　怕說歡娛愛說愁
憑參透
　　任空空色色總付東流
土音曲譜誰修
　　倘早遇漁洋定見收
算崑腔近雅已成習熟
　　秦聲雖壯究欠溫柔
鳴咽悲涼激昂頓挫
　　水底魚龍也出遊
還知否
　　把人情世略付歌喉

沁園春
紅蓼灘邊漁者

Fifth Preface

俯拾即是　著手成春
薄無情悟　時見美人
歡樂苦短　風日水濱
盡得風流　妙契同塵
如有佳語　識之愈真
超以象外　花草精神
其曰可讀　與古為新

集司空詩品
九天仙客

Sixth Preface

載酒徵歌紀勝遊
兩行紅袖燒銀燭
東船西舫鬧清歌
一擲纏頭三百萬
一串歌珠一縷情
驚鴻淒絕無留影
應是前身杜牧之
十年不作揚州夢

是真名士自風流
倚醉樽前數粵謳
每到聞歌喚柰何
泥人無那是橫波
舊時南部最知名
莫更當筵唱渭城
慣將新恨寫新詞
容易秋霜點鬢絲

前村漁隱

Seventh Preface

一點楊花一寸心
為君續灑千行淚

萬花飛處恨難禁
譜入雍門再鼓琴

自題楊花一闋
即以題弁粵謳
耕烟散人

Eight Preface

鐵板銅琶屬女郎
錦囊謄譜當時曲
第一歌喉占綺筵
如何自厭麻姑爪
別派新聲數莫愁
桂梁蘭室誰家婦
莫上銷魂舊板橋
無人解唱煙花地

珠江沸耳聽鶯簧
檢點前塵鬢有霜
蘇娘遺韻散春烟
合掌慈雲繡佛前
蕭郎陌路碧雲收
繡襪瑤環弄阿侯
橋頭秋柳半飄蕭
苦海茫茫日夜潮

邃江居士題

Ninth Preface

遏雲新調擅風流
今夜珠江江上月
水珮風裳落舞筵
多情譜出烟花記
繁華消息竟如何
怪底此歌能解恨
清歌一曲杜韋娘
為問幾人能顧曲

曾憶蘇臺舊日遊
簫聲吹徹海天秋
黃金難買薛濤箋
慧即才人俠即仙
妙響低徊不厭多
有人偷付雪兒歌
醉拂春風滿袖香
至今猶艷說周郎

瓣香居士

Tenth Preface

兜率生天色界空，何妨身入綺羅叢。
風流白石無多讓，豈獨吹簫伴小紅。
不厭青樓薄倖名，燈紅酒綠譜新聲。
拈來一管生花筆，寫盡閒情與艷情。
土音新操自成家，也向旗亭鬬麗華。
似唱江洲腸斷句，人人爭學抱琵琶。
珠江江畔總宜樓，名樓無限名姝住上頭。
都仗此歌態解事，多生歡喜莫生愁。

瑤仙題

Eleventh Preface

曾向東風擅越吟，最難忘是故鄉音。
多君洗盡箏琵耳，一卷梅花香雪心。
未了心願未了情，酒邊燭底聽分明。
新簧初炙鶯喉滑，欲把瑤笙媚此聲。
一段婆心解說微，如悲如勸復如譏。
苦心要向情天解，翻笑波羅誤雪衣。
贏得清謳侑酒尊，秦聲楚調總蛙喧。
祇憐有力春偷負，折柳重傷少叔魂。

鹿野題詞

Appendix II: The Original Songs in Chinese

Song 1 (Part 1)
解心事（一）

心各有事。總要解脫為先，
心事唔安。解得就了然。
苦海茫茫多半是命蹇。
但向苦中尋樂。便是神仙。
若係愁苦到不堪。真係惡算。
總好過官門地獄。更重哀憐。
退一步海闊天空。就唔使自怨。
心能自解。真正係樂境無邊。
若係解到唔解得通。就講過陰隲個便。
唉。凡事檢點。
積善心唔險。
你睇遠報在來生。近報在目前。

Song 1 (Part 2)
解心事（二）

心事惡解。都要解到佢分明。
解字看得圓通。萬事都盡輕。
我想心事千條就有一千樣病證。
總係心中煩極。講不得過人聽。
大抵癡字入得症深。都係情字染病。
唔除癡念。就係妙藥都唔靈。
花柳場中最易迷卻本性。
溫柔鄉裏總要自出奇兵。
悟破色空方正是樂境。
長迷花柳就噲墮落愁城。
唉。須要自醒。
世間無定是楊花性。
總係邊一便風來。就向邊一便有情。

Song 2
揀心

世間難揾一條心。
得佢一條心事。我死亦要追尋。
一面試佢真心。一面妨到佢噤。
試到果實真情。正好共佢酌斟。
喋喋吓喋到我哋心虛。箇箇都妨到薄倖。
就俾佢真心來待我。我都要試過佢兩三勻。

我想人客萬千。真吓都有一分。
箇的真情撒散。重慘過大海撈針。
況且你噲揾真心。人哋亦都噲揾。
真心人客真話夠幾箇人分。
細想緣分各自相投。唔到你著緊。
安一吓本分。
各有來因。你都莫羨人。

Song 3
唔好死

唔好死得咁易。死要死得心甜。
恐怕死錯番來。你話點死得遍添。
有的應死佢又偷生。真正生不顧面。
有的理唔該死。實在死得哀憐。
我想錯死與及偷生。真正爭得好遠。
一則被人辱罵。一則惹我心酸。
大抵死得磊落光明。就係生亦有咁顯。
你睇忠臣烈女都在萬古留傳。
自古女子輕生。都係情字引線。
關頭打破。又要義字為先。
情義兩全千古罕見。
唔在幾遠。
你睇紅樓夢上三姊與及柳湘蓮。

Song 4
聽春鶯

斷腸人怕聽春鶯。
鶯語撩人更易斷魂。
春光一到已自撩人恨。
鳥呀。你重有意和春共碎我心。
人哋話鳥語可以忘憂。我正聽佢一陣。
你估人難如鳥。定是鳥不如人。
見佢恃在能言。就言到妙品。
但逢好境就語向春明。
點得鳥呀。你替我講句真言。言過個薄倖。
又怕你言詞關切。佢又當作唔聞。
又點得我魂夢化作鳥飛。同你去揾。
揾著薄情詳講。重要佢回音。
唉。真欲緊。做夢還依枕。
但得我夢中唔叫醒我。我就附著你同行。

Song 5
思想起

思想起。
想起就含悲。
不堪提起箇箇薄倖男兒。
起首相交。就話無乜變志。
估話天長地久咯。共你兩兩相依。
我想才貌揀到如君。亦都唔識錯你。
枉費我往日待你箇副心腸。你就捨得把我別離。
今日祇怨我命孤。唔敢怨。君呀你冇義。
捨得我係桂苑名花。梗乜俾的浪子折枝。
累得我半站中途。丟妹自己。
若問起後果前因。你我都切勿再提。
呢陣半世叫我再揀過箇知心。都唔係乜易。
開口就話我係敗柳殘花。有乜正果歸。
點曉得檜樹根深。重要跟到底。
九泉相會。正表白過郎知。
一定前世共君你無緣。故此今日中道見棄。
唉。真正冇味。
浮生何苦重寄。
不若我死。在離恨天堂等君你再世。都未遲。

Song 6
緣慳

相識恨晚。自見緣慳。
呢吓相逢就別。我實見心煩。
做乜相見咁好時。相處都有限。
今日征鴻兩地怨孤單。
做女個陣。點知流落呢處受風流難。
夜夜雖則成雙。我實見單。
當初悔不聽王孫諫。
欲還花債。誤到人間。
既落到人間。須要帶眼。
還要噲揀。
世上惜花人亦有限。
但係好花扶持起。就要曲意關闗。

Song 7
花花世界

花花世界嚤。有乜相干。
唉。我何苦做埋咁多冤孽事斡。
睇見眼前個的折墮咯。你話幾咁心寒。
我想到處風流都是一樣。
不若持齋念佛去把經看。
呢回把情字一筆勾消。我亦唔敢亂想。
消此孽賬。
免至失身流落呢處賣笑村場。
呢吓朝夕我去拈香。
重要頻合掌。
參透色相。
定要脫離呢處苦海。直渡慈航。

Song 8
離筵

無情酒錢別離筵。
臨行致囑有萬千千。
佢話。分離有幾耐。就有書回轉。
做乜屈指如今。都有大半年。
我相思流淚。又怕人偷偷睇見。
你個無情何苦得咁心偏。
我祇話日夜丟開唔掛念。
獨惜夢魂相會。又試苦苦相纏。
叫我點能學得個隻雙飛燕。
唉。佢唔飛亂。秋去春回轉。
呢喃相對細語花前。

Song 9
訴恨

偷偷嘆氣。此恨誰知。
自從別後都有信歸期。
呢番憔悴都係因君你。
教奴終夜夢魂癡。
唉。前世想必唔修。至噲今日命鄙。
注定紅顏係咁孤苦。唔知苦到何時。
虧我背人偷抹腮邊淚。
恐憂形跡露出相思。
總係無計丟開愁一個字。
唉。真正有味。
天呀。我想你呢噲生人總有別離。

Song 10
辯癡

難為我辯。是癡情。
情到癡迷。有邊一個醒。
世間多少相思症。
但有懷春。不敢露形。
叫佢含羞對面點把絲蘿訂。
真正有口難言苦不勝。
大抵都係少年兒女性。
心唔定。
所以咁多磨滅事咁難成。

Song 11 (Part 1)
嗟怨薄命（一）

人寂靜。月更光明。
慾海情天個的孽債未清。
離合悲歡雖則係有定。
做乜名花遭際總是凋零。
你睇楊妃玉骨埋山徑。
昭君留墓草青青。
淪落小青愁弔影。
十娘飲恨一水盈盈。
大抵生長紅顏多半是薄命。
何況我哋青樓花粉。更累在癡情。
既係做到楊花。多半是水性。
點學得出泥不染。都重表自己堅貞。
怕祇怕悲秋桐葉飄金井。
重要學寒梅偏捱得雪霜凌。
我想花木四時都係樂境。
總係愁人相對就噲飲恨吞聲。
唉。須要自醒。
命薄誰堪證。
不若向百花墳上訴吓生平。

Song 11 (Part 2)
嗟怨薄命（二）

嗟怨薄命。對住垂楊。
送舊迎新。都係個對媚眼一雙。
見佢迎風嬝娜。個的纖腰樣。
又見佢雙眉愁鎖恨偏長。
青青弱質都是憑春釀。
獨惜被人攀折。你話怎不心傷。
捨得我唔肯嫁東風。我心都有異向。
偏要替人擔恨在去國離鄉。
若問情短情長。都是冤孽賬。
恐怕離愁。唔捱得幾耐風光。
虧我癡心一點付在陽關上。
輕蕩漾。
身後唔禁想。
不若替百花垂淚。化作水面飄楊。

Song 11 (Part 3)
嗟怨薄命（三）

嗟怨薄命。對住荷花。
點能學得你出水無瑕。
記得才子佳人來買夏。
亭亭玉質。好似閬苑仙葩。
當時得令高聲價。
千紅萬綠幾咁繁華。
水月鏡花唔知真定假。
秋風殘葉唔知落在誰家。
情種情根唔知何日罷。
唉。真可怕。
水火難消化。
或者蓮花咒鉢。正化得我哋孽海根芽。

Song 11 (Part 4)
嗟怨薄命（四）

嗟怨薄命。對住梧桐。
飄零一葉怨秋風。
嫩綠新枝愁萬種。
曾經疎雨分外唔同。
蕭疏偏惹騷人夢。
詩人題詠在綠陰中。
若係知音。便早帶佢去亭邊種。
漫到焦時始辨桐。
恨祇恨佢一到秋來。隨處播弄。
惹人愁悶。問你有乜甚功。
大抵憐香惜玉。你心先動。
恐怕吹殘弱質。你早把信音通。
細想名花有幾朵捱得霜花重。
唉。你心錯用。
提起心腸痛。
自古經秋唔怕老。祇有澗底蒼松。

Song 11 (Part 5)
嗟怨薄命（五）

嗟怨薄命。對住寒梅。
點能學得你獨占花魁。
冰肌玉骨堪人愛。
雖然傲骨到處能栽。
高插你在膽瓶。我羞作對。
晶瑩玉質。問你幾世修來。
獨抱芳心沈在孽海。
亦都係柳絲。蓮性。碧梧胎。
我想名花未必終肯被遊蜂採。
須忍耐。
留得青山在。
還清花債。依舊可以到得蓬萊。

Song 12 (Part 1)
真正攞命（一）

將我品性。想吓生平。
對住皇天我要問佢一聲。
做乜佢風中弱絮飛無定。
做乜我水上殘花又洗不清。
人在風月場中尋出樂境。
做乜我在煙花叢裏築起愁城。
好似小青照不出前生影。
就把彌天幽怨一力擔承。
實在無藥可醫心裏病。
誰肯做證。
我自招還自認。
係喇。攞人條命都係箇一點癡情。

Song 12 (Part 2)
真正攞命（二）

真正攞命。卻被情牽。
一縷春恨唔知向乜誰言。
雖乃係綠柳多情牽緊弱線。
總係章臺春老望絕寒烟。
縱有才人賞識我的春風面。
皆因同病故此相憐。
你話淪落在呢處風塵誰不厭。
總係殘紅飛不出奈何天。
噉就飄零一樣好似離巢燕。
唉。風又亂扇。

失路在林間蔫。
噉就一生埋沒葬在花田。

Song 12 (Part 3)
真正攞命（三）

真正攞命。卻被情拿。
共你海誓山盟箇一念差。
回頭好夢都如畫。
好似水中明月鏡中花。
我梅魂虛把東風嫁。
到底孤負多情夢綠華。
累我不定心旌難以放下。
料應條命死在君家。
人前我亦未敢分明話。
唉。君你偷偷想吓。
底事真和假。
我望你早乘秋水泛月中槎。

Song 12 (Part 4)
真正攞命（四）

真正攞命。卻被情招。
虧我浮萍無定。係咁浪飄搖。
君你青衫濕後。我就知音渺。
縱有新詞羞唱到念奴嬌。
恨只恨楊柳岸邊風易曉。
你話何曾夜夜是元宵。
月落烏啼人悄悄。
真正雲散風流。好似落潮。
共你相思欲了唔知何時了。
唉。心共照。
若把皇天叫。
天呀。做乜個一個纏綿。就向個一個寂寥。

Song 12 (Part 5)
真正攞命（五）

真正攞命。卻被情魔。
共你私情太重都係錯在當初。
今日芙蓉江上無人過。
我玉鏡憑誰畫翠蛾。
呢回殘燈斜月愁無那。

縱有睡魔迷不住我帶淚秋波。
睞就雨暗巫山春夢破。
好似鷓鴣啼切苦叫哥哥。
你一擔相思交畀過我。
唉。真正恨錯。
天呀。你亦該憐憫吓我哋兩個。
做乜露水姻緣偏嚐受此折磨。

Song 12 (Part 6)
真正攞命（六）

真正攞命。卻被情傷。
做乜知音人去話偏長。
話起別離兩字我就三魂蕩。
第一傷心還在過後思量。
今日秋水蒹葭勞妹盼望。
所謂伊人在水一方。
點得再會共哥有期你心有異向。
等我生為蝴蝶。死作鴛鴦。
或者在地在天消此孽帳。
唉。心欲喪。
不能無此想。
你睇海天無際只賸一寸柔腸。

Song 13 (Part 1)
花本一樣（一）

花本一樣。點曉得世態炎涼。
對住情人分外香。
可惜花有妙容。難道奴就薄相。
做乜看花人懶。看妾人忙。
花開歲歲都是花模樣。
花亦憑天為佢主張。
可惜我在花月場中捱盡的苦況。
就有一個惜花人似得水咁情長。
溫香美滿都是成虛想。
花亦似憐人孤寂伴佢成雙。
人話奴貌勝花都是過獎。
就俾你如花美眷願亦難償。
花花世界都是情根強。
花噉樣。
重還不了風流帳。
點得我早日還完花債共你從良。

Song 13 (Part 2)
花本一樣（二）

花本一樣。憂樂佢都唔知。
佢話落花還有再開時。
恐防春老東君棄。
落後焉能再上枝。
來春雨露自有來春意。
若再等到青春。放也遲。
雖係鮮花咁好未必無人理。
須防開透被蝶蜂欺。
你芳心檢點去尋知已。
唔係噤你。
探花人緊記。
總係百花頭上莫錯折薔薇。

Song 14
薄命多情

天呀。你生得我咁薄命。乜事又生得我
　　咁多情。
情字重起番來。萬事都盡輕。
我想人世但得一面相逢。都係前世鑄定。
況且幾年共你相好。點舍一吓就分清。
人哋見我待得你咁長情。都重愁我嚟短
　　命。
我想情長就係命短。亦分所當應。
呢吓萬事可以放心。單怕郎冇定性。
怕你累我終身零落。好似水面浮萍。
點得撇卻呢處煙花尋一個樂境。
個陣你縱然把我虧負。我都誓願唔聲。
想我女子有咁貞心。做乜月你唔共我照
　　應。
重要多煩你撮合呢變。免得哽我咁零丁。
我兩個癡夢癡得咁交關。未知何日正醒。
唉。真正樊。
在過共你同交頸。
做乜望長望短大事總唔成。

Song 15
難忍淚

難忍淚。瀝濕蓮枝。
記得與君聯句在曲欄時。
你睇粉牆尚有郎君字。

就係共你倚欄相和個首藕花詩。
今日花又復開。做乜人隔兩地。
未曉你路途安否。總有信歸期。
蓮筆叫我點書呢段長恨句。
愁懷寫不盡。好似未斷荷絲。
今日遺恨在呢處曲欄。提起往事。
唉。想起就氣。
睇住殘荷凋謝咯。我就想到世事難為。

Song 16
瀟湘雁

瀟湘雁。寄盡有情書。
衡陽消息俾做何如。
雁呀。你聲聲觸起奴愁緒。
虧我夜來殘夢捱到五更餘。
春衫濕透離人淚。
叫我點能等得合浦還珠。
為郎寫不盡相思句。
唉。情又不死。
握手人何處。
雁呀。我個知心人去。你為我帶呢首斷
　　腸詞。

Song 17
同心草

同心草。種在迴欄。
祇望移根伴住牡丹。
點想花事係咁闌珊。春事又咁懶慢。
好似我共郎兩地隔斷關山。
丟奴一去可似孤零雁。
雁囉雁。你在地北天南重辛苦慣。
我在青樓飄泊自見心煩。
天寒袖薄倚凭欄杆盼。
西風簾捲自見孤單。
君呀。你在歡處不知奴咁切慘。
我為你眼穿腸斷。又廢寢忘餐。
往日勸你在家唔好拆散。
點估你江湖飄蕩不肯歸還。
想起人哋嘅情哥咁聽妹諫。
虧我諫哥唔聽。咁就十指偷彈。
今日人遠在天涯。相見有限。
時常珠淚濕透春衫。
累得我多愁多病抱住琵琶嘆。

唉。天欲晚。
夕照花容減。
君呀。你摘花係咁容易。要想吓種花難。

Song 18
花貌好

花貌咁好。做乜日日咁含愁。
人如花面卻為郎羞。
咁好春光勸你唔好洩漏。
把人虧負。要想起吓前頭。
情字個種深傷。你妹平日捱夠。
一場春夢點估至今休。
往日估你一個真情。今日知到係假柳。
聽人冷語拆散我鸞儔。
花房香膩卻被蜂侵透。
做乜銀河得渡就把鵲橋收。
如果你噉樣子做人。你妹真正惡受。
唉。我偷睇透。
你心腸唔似舊。
君呀。你若係有厘聲氣。我死都要追求。

Song 19
心點忿

心心點忿。拆散絲羅。
怨一句紅顏。怨一句我哥。
世界做得咁情長。做乜偏偏冇結果。
就把舊時個種恩愛付落江河。
共你相好到入心。又被朋友嫁禍。
因愛成仇你妹見盡許多。
試睇人哋點樣子待君。君呀。你就回想
　　吓我。
從頭想過。正好共我丟疎。
天呀。保佑邊一個薄情。就好邊一個折
　　墮。
唉。真正冇錯。
免使枉死含寃受此折磨。

Song 20
累世

真真正累世。也得你咁收人。
枉費你妹從前個一片心。
多端扭計。你妹情願受困。

思前想後。試睇待薄過你唔曾。
做乜分離咁耐啫。就學王魁咁薄倖。
我定要問明邊一個唆攪你。定係自己生心。
兵行詭道。你妹心唔忿。
唉。情可恨。
一刀斬斬斷兩橛丟開。你妹唔喉掛恨。
啋。捨得我待郎嘅樣子心事。愁有個至愛情人。

Song 21
花本快活

花本快活。為月正添愁。
月呀。你嘅樣子憐香。就嚇把我命收。
我想春信尚有愆期。唔得咁就手。
共佢約定月月中旬都肯為我留。
月呀。你嘅樣子多情。又怕我哋紅粉不偶。
得你月圓我哋花又謝咯。你話幾世唔修。
月呀。一年四季多少憐香友。
邊一朵鮮花唔愛月你把佢香偷。
有陣香魂睡醒月重明如畫。
總係對影憐香倍易感秋。
點得月你夜夜都嚇長圓。花又開箇不透。
唉。唔知真定假柳啫。
但得係就好咯。自願世世為花種在月裏頭。

Song 22
春果有恨

春果有恨。柳豈唔知。
柳呀。你日日係咁牽情。到底有乜了期。
春來偏惹離人意。
可恨春風如翦。又翦不斷情絲。
累得長亭病馬鞭唔起。
又累得繡閣臨妝懶去畫眉。
正係春夢一場都交畀過你。
替人憔悴枉費你心機。
恐怕年年捱不慣個的秋風氣。
青黃滿面瘦骨難支。
箇陣意欲尋春春又不理。
情薄過紙。
愁種在相思地。

柳呀。你生長在人間。切莫去綰箇種別離。

Song 23
多情月

多情月。掛在畫樓邊。
月呀。你照人離別又似可人憐。
人在天涯你妹心隔一綫。
萬里情思兩地掛牽。
我日日望君。君呀。唔見你轉。
雙魚無路把書傳。
月月係咁月圓。你妹經看過幾遍。
你在他鄉曾否盼妹嬋娟。
我想出路與及在家都係同一樣掛念。
唉。偷偷自怨。
願郎你心事莫變。
到底能相見。
箇陣花底同君再看過月圓。

Song 24
無情月

無情月掛在奈何天。
相思嫌月照住孤眠。
月呀。你有缺時。還有復轉。
做乜我郎一去得咁心堅。
哀求月老為我行方便。
照見我郎試問一句。睇佢點樣子回言。
若是佢心歪唔記念。
叫佢手按住良心睇一吓天。
做人唔好做得咁心肝變。
你唔記如今都要記吓在前。
為郎終日腸牽斷。
叫我點能學得個個月裏嬋娟。
捨得相逢學月咁易見個無情面。
我唔怕路遠。
定要去問明佢心事見點。
免使虛擔人世呢段假意姻緣。

Song 25
心

心祗一個。點俾得過咁多人。
點得人人見我都把我來憎。

個陣我想著風流都無我分。
縱有相思無路去種情根。
恨祇恨我唔知邊一樣唔得人憎。
故此人哋將我咁恨。
個一個共我交情。就個一個死心。
累得我一身花債。欲把情人問。
唔通寶玉係我前身。
唉。我話情種都要佢有情根方種得穩。
若係無緣癡極亦悞了殘生。
唔信你睇眼淚重有多得過林黛玉姑娘。
　自小就癡得個寶玉咁緊。
真正係有念。
就俾你係死心。亦不過乾熱一陣。
佢還清個的眼淚。就死亦不得共佢埋羣。

Song 26
天邊月

天邊月。似簾鈎。
泛在長江任去流。
月呀。你有團圓人嚆等候。
總係眼前虧缺恨難收。
我想人世咁長。唔得咁就手。
大抵好極人生都有一樣愁。
你睇文君新寡重去尋佳偶。
班姬團扇尚悲秋。
唉。心想透。
待等八月中旬候。
月呀。總有一個團圓在後頭。

Song 27
樓頭月

樓頭月。掛在畫欄邊。
月呀。做乜照人離別。偏要自己團圓。
學你一月一遍團圓。你妹重唔係乜願。
何況天涯遙隔愈見心酸。
人話好極都要丟開。唔好咁綣戀。
大抵久別相逢。重好過在前。
雖則我心事係咁丟開。總係情實在惡斷。
第一夜來重唔禁得夢魂顛。
我想死別共生離。亦唔差得幾遠。
但得早一日逢君。自願命短一年。
天呀。雖乃係好事多磨。亦該留我一線。

唉。做乜唔得就算。
不若當初唔見面。
免得我一生遺恨月呀。你對住我長圓。

Song 28
孤飛雁

孤飛雁。驚醒獨眠人。
起來愁對月三更。
擔頭細把征鴻問。
你欲往何方得咁夜深。
雌雄有伴你便跟應緊。
呢陣影隻形單。問你點樣子去尋。
我地天涯人遠難親近。
有翼都難飛去爪得佢親。
無計夢中尋箇薄倖。
又俾你哀聲撩醒。未講得幾句時文。
捨得帶佢一紙書來。我亦唔捨得把你怨恨。
累得我醒後無書。夢裡又別君。
意欲話好夢可以再尋。我還向夢搵。
又怕茫茫烟水渺渺無憑。
唉。真正肉緊。
淒涼誰見憫。
呢陣衡陽聲斷。問你點覓同羣。

Song 29
傳書雁

傳書雁。共我帶紙書還。
唔見佢書還。你便莫箇番。
今日不見回書。大抵佢心事都有限。
抑或你帶書唔子細失落鄉關。
縱使佢愁極寫書心事懶。
有書唔寄。你便達一紙空函。
等我一張白紙當佢言千萬。
二人心照盡在不言間。
呢陣不見書回空見雁返。
唉。雁囉雁。
你亦不必傳書柬。
等我照樣不回書信。你便去見個個薄情男。

Song 30
多情雁

多情雁。一對向南飛。
雁呀。秋風何苦重咁遠飄離。
你在江湖留落尚有雌雄侶。
虧我影隻形單異地棲。
風急衣單無路寄。
寒衣做起誤落空閨。
日日望到夕陽。我就愁倍起。
只見一圍哀柳鎖住長堤。
又見人影一鞭殘照裡。
幾回錯認是我郎歸。
唉。我思想起。
想必紅塵耽誤了你。
點得雲斂風晴共你際會期。

Song 31 (Part 1)
烟花地（一）

烟花地。想起就心辭。
中年情事點講得過人知。
好命注定仙花。亦都唔種在此地。
縱誤種。亦望有的更移。
今日花柳風波。我都嘗到透味。
況且歡場逝水更易老花枝。
既係命薄如花。亦都偷怨吓自己。
想到老來花謝。總要搵的挨依。
唉。我想花謝正望到人哋葬花。亦都係
　希罕事。
總要花開佢憐憫我。正叫做不負佳期。
細想年少未得登科。到老難以及第。
況且秋來花事總總全非。
今日我命注定為花。就算開落過世。
你試問花。花呀。誰愛你。
佢都冇的偏私。
花若有情。就要情到底
風雲月露正係我哋情癡。
至到人哋賞花憎愛我都不理。
仙種子。
休為凡心死。
我為偶還花債。故此暫別吓瑤池。

Song 31 (Part 2)
烟花地（二）

烟花地。苦海茫茫。
從來難搵箇有情郎。
迎新送舊不過還花帳。
有誰惜玉與及憐香。
我在風流陣上係咁從頭想。
有個知心人仔害我。縱死難忘。
有陣丟疎外面似極無心向。
獨係心中懷念你。我暗哋悽涼。
今晚寂寥空對住烟花上。
唉。休要亂想。
共你有心都是惡講。
我斷唔孤負你個一點情長。

Song 32
楊花

紛紛灑淚。淚盡楊花。
你有幾多愁恨記在心懷。
我想別樣花飛無乜掛帶。
單係你替人承受呢一段薄命寃家。
佢話香國係咁繁華。真係有價。
點忿俾狂風吹散。嗽就賤過泥沙。
你睇月呀係咁樣團圓。都會變卦。
縱有千金難買九十韶華。
我若勸你勘破春心。唔恨亦假。
你縱春愁如海。亦都柱自嗟呀。
不若我苦命楊花同你哭罷。
唉。風任擺。
墮絮無心化。
等我替你萬花垂淚灑偏天涯。

Song 33
鏡花

我唔願點鏡。又不想貪花。
鏡光花影都係過眼烟霞。
鏡會憐香就愛花作畫。
花容偷睡就在鏡裡為家。
有陣花能解語請入屏間話。
幸得花愛臨妝又向住他。
若係有鏡無花。春色就減價。
若係有花無鏡。又怕春信難查。

點得鏡係咁長圓。花又不嫁。
唉。真定假。
你睇桂影長春愛住月華。

Song 34
花有淚

花有淚。月本無痕。
月呀。你照見我哋花容瘦有幾分。
可惜。月呀。你有圓時。我哋花總係噲褪。
就俾你桂香輪滿。都係有影無根。
我想花信不過二十四番容乜易盡。
遇著風狂雨驟。哪就斷送了我終身。
個陣你在九霄雲外縱有心相印。
總係東西尋逐。點顧得我哋墮溷飄茵。
莫話過眼烟花無乜要緊。
獨惜被人攀折未免想起吓來因。
呢陣雲路係咁迢遙。我亦知相託都冇分。
唉。心不忍。
試把嬋娟問。
問你廣寒宮有幾闊咯。點葬得咁多冇主花魂。

Song 35 (Part 1)
容乜易（一）

手抱琵琶百感悲。
做乜老來情事總不相宜。
青春一去難提起。
提起番來苦自知。
一向癡迷唔肯料理。
今日鏡中顏色自見嫌疑。
人話風流老大還堪恃。
試睇菊殘猶有傲霜枝。
身世係咁飄蓬。重爭乜硬氣。
好似水流花謝渺渺無期。
相思萬種從今止。
無的味。
嘆聲容乜易。
等我帶淚和情訴吓舊時。

Song 35 (Part 2)
容乜易（二）

容乜易過在青樓。
歌舞歡場事事休。
薄命紅顏天注就。
減低情性學吓溫柔。
至此春烟迷住章臺柳。
任佢三眠三起總不愧羞。
往日迎新。今日送舊。
蝶愛尋香點自由。
只估買斷青春挐住手。
綠雲深鎖不知秋。
再有話楊花重曉得去憐身後。
心想透。
恰被風拖逗。
哪就化作浮萍逐水流。

Song 35 (Part 3)
容乜易（三）

容乜易醉。酒千盅。
情有咁深時。味有咁濃。
我想寃家必定前生種。
種穩情根不肯放鬆。
酒邊都要人珍重。
莫話魂迷心亂兩下交融。
大抵歡場過眼渾如夢。
席散人歸萬事空。
遞盞傳盃心事重。
問你面上桃花有幾耐紅。
今日霞觴滿酌唔知憑誰共。
唉。中乜用。
未飲心先痛。
一生遺恨誤入花叢。

Song 35 (Part 4)
容乜易（四）

容乜易放。柳邊船。
木蘭雙槳載住神仙。
東風為我行方便。
吹得情哥到我面前。
鴛鴦共宿人人羨。
好似兩顆明珠一線穿。

滿意東君常見面。
今生還結再生緣。
正係藕絲縛住荷花片。
一體同根有乜變遷。
唔想帆影就隨湘水轉。
難遂願。
線緊風箏斷。
虧我流落在呢處天涯。實在可憐。

Song 35 (Part 5)
容乜易（五）

容乜易散。彩雲飛。
春帆頃刻就要分離。
誰人肯願分連理。
事到其間點樣子設施。
早知割愛唔輕易。
何苦當初一力護持。
今日送別無言惟有淚。
離人折盡柳千枝。
長亭自古傷心地。
你話後會何曾有定期。
紈扇預防秋後棄。
唉。嗟命鄙。
風流雲散易。
箇陣欲捨難分。恨亦已遲。

Song 35 (Part 6)
容乜易（六）

容乜易老。鬢蒼蒼。
關心誰記往日珠娘。
秋風陣陣添惆悵。
白滿船頭一夜霜。
四條絃澀難成響。
總係彈到情深怕惹恨長。
淪落幾人同我一樣。
不記從前就不嚐慘傷。
好花畢竟成飄蕩。
叫我怎能禁得個的蝶浪蜂狂。
此後我孤零無乜倚向。
唉。低自唱。
還了風流帳。
虧我手抱琵琶悶對夕陽。

Song 36
水噲退

水噲退。又噲番流。
水呀。你既退又試番流。見你日夜不休。
臨行自古話難分手。
做乜分手到如今。又在別處逗遛。
大抵人世相逢都憑個氣候。
花行春令月到中秋。
當初慌死情唔透。
一講到情深。總不顧後頭。
在我都話會少離多情重更厚。
唉。君你想透。
若係日日癡埋。你話點做得女牛。

Song 37
花易落

花易落。花又易開。
咁好花顏問你看得幾回。
好花慌久開唔耐。
想到花殘我都願佢莫開。
好極花容終噲變改。
你睇枝頭花落點得再上枝來。
大抵種得情根花就可愛。
總怕並頭花好又要分栽。
鮮花咁好又怕遊蜂採。
落花無主自見癡呆。
記得花前發誓都話同恩愛。
點想倚花沈醉有個薄倖王魁。
點得尋著箇箇花神拉住佢問句。
唉。花在鏡內。
究竟真情還是假愛。
到底桃花箇種薄命。問佢點樣子生來。

Song 38
蝴蝶夢

蝴蝶夢。夢繞在花前。
蝶呀。你為貪採名花。故此夢得咁倒顛。
我想人世遇著情魔。就係清夢都噲亂。
一吓魂迷心醉。就夢到孽海情天。
況且相愛又試相連。點信癡夢噲短。
定要追尋香夢。向夢裡團圓。
箇陣朝朝暮暮夢作神仙眷。

離魂一枕夢當遊仙。
睇佢綺夢係咁沈迷。就呼喚都不轉。
重要鴛鴦同夢化作並頭蓮。
勢有話夢幻本屬無憑。人事嚟改變。
點想一場春夢都是過眼雲煙。
大抵夢境即是歡場。勸你休要眷戀。
唉。花夢易斷。
今日夢醒人去遠。
恨只恨意中人祇結一段夢中緣。

Song 39
月難圓

花易落。月又難圓。
花月深情就結下呢段冤枉。
花月本係無情。總係人哋去眷戀。
恨只恨催促人容易老咯。重去惹人憐。
花若係有情。就愁把月見。
月你團圓得咁辛苦喇。你話怎不心酸。
月若係曉得憐香。又點肯把花作賤。
但得月輪長照住你。就係花謝亦見心甜。
總係共計十二箇月一年。月呀。你亦不過圓十二遍。
就係四時花信到咯。亦不過向一時鮮。
總係我哋命薄如花。難得月你見面。
得到我對月開時。又怕你缺了半邊。
雖則月係咁難圓。重有圓個一日可算。
花謝等到重開。要隔一歲添。
總係人遠在天涯。就嚟對住花月自怨。
唉。心緒亂。
眼穿腸欲斷。
君呀重怕花開長對住你落咯。月缺對住你長圓。

Song 40
想前因

煩過一陣。想起吓前因。
此生何事墮落紅塵。
我想託世做到女流。原係可憫。
況且青樓女子。又試斷梗無根。
好極繁華不過係陪酒箇陣。
等到客散燈寒。又試自己斷魂。
有客就叫做姑娘。無客就下等。
一時冷淡把我作賤三分。

或者遇著人客有情。都重還有的倚憑。
鬼怕個的無情醉漢。就係攞命災瘟。
大抵箇日落到青樓。就從箇日種恨。
唉。總係由得我著緊啫。
總要捱到淚盡花殘。就算做過一世人。

Song 41
自悔

實在我都唔過得意。
算我薄情虧負曬你。
等我掉轉呢副心腸。共你好過都未遲。
人哋話好酒飲落半樽。正知到吓味。
因為從前耳軟。所以正得咁迷癡。
今日河水雖則係咁深。都要共你撐到底。
唉。將近半世。
唔共你住埋唔係計。
細想你從前箇一點心事待我。叫我點捨得把你難為。

Song 42
義女情男

乜你惱得咁快。一見我就心煩。
相逢有咁耐咯。惱過亦有咁多番。
共你惱過正好番。箇情字都帶淡。
君呀。你時常係咁樣子惱法。我實在見為難。
我減頸就得你多。又怕把你情性弄慣。
削性開喉共你嗌過一變。免使你惡得咁交關。
或者你過後思量。重聽我勸諫。
呢回從新相好過。免俾別人彈。
我都係見你共我有的合心。故此唔捨得丟你另揀。
就係時常共你惱出面。都係掛你在心間。
點得心事擺開從君你過眼。
箇陣相見恨晚。
呢回二家唔放手。重要做箇義女情男。

Song 43
唔好熱

唔好咁熱。熱極嚟生風。
我想天時人事大抵相同。

The Original Songs in Chinese 183

唔信你睇回南日久就有涼風送。
共佢好極都要離開。暫且放鬆。
我想人世會合都有期。唔到你放縱。
年年七夕都係一日相逢。
人哋話相逢一日都係唔中用。
一日十二箇時辰。點盡訴得苦衷。
我話相逢一日莫話唔中用。
年年一日。日久就嚇成功。
點得人學得七姐咁情長千載共。
真情種。
只有生離無死別。分外見情濃。

Song 44
留客

你如果要去。呢回唔哽你開嚟。
索性共你分離。免得耐耐又試慘悽。
人話我哋野花好極唔多矜貴。
做乜貪花人仔。偏向箇的野花迷。
我郎好極都係人哋夫婿。
青樓情重是必怨恨在深閨。
不若割斷情絲免使郎你掛繫。
但得我郎唔見面。任得我日夜悲啼。
相思兩地實在難禁抵。
久別相逢我叫點捨得你去歸。
千一箇唔係住埋。千一箇唔得到底。
唉。真正累世。
湊著你我都有人拘制。
生不得共你同衾。死都要共埋。

Song 45
心把定

心要把定。切莫思疑。
但得意合情投我就一味去癡。
煙花到底不是長情地。
有日花殘就嚇被蝶欺。
箇的野蝶採花都係無乜氣味。
咁好鮮花唔採。偏向箇的野花棲。
總係仙花遇著仙蝶就嚇成知己。
死命留心睇佢向邊一處飛。
有陣深心冷眼重嚇將人試。
假意採吓箇的殘花。睇佢知到未知。
莫話我哋仙花種子無根氣。
睇住你來頭我就早早見機。

我知到都詐作唔知。還去試你。
偏向風前擺曳。好似冇的挨依。
唉。須要會意。
多受的折磨。或者共我消滅的晦氣。
我心都為你死。
箇的貪花都是在門外企。
蝶呀。你有心來探我。等我開透都唔遲。

Song 46
奴等你

打乜主意。重哽乜思疑。
你唔帶得奴奴。你便早日話過妹知。
我只估話等郎至此落在呢處煙花地。
捨得我肯跟人去上岸乜天時。
只望共你叙吓悲歡。談吓往事。
點想你失意還鄉事盡非。
一定嘅攪有人將我出氣。
話我好似水性楊花逐浪飛。
呢陣講極冰清。你亦唔多在意。
萬般愁緒只有天知。
況且遠近盡知奴係等你。
今日半途丟手。嗽就冇的挨依。
枉費我往日待你箇副心腸。今日憑在你
　　處置。
漫道你問心難過。死亦難欺。
唔見面講透苦心。死亦唔得眼閉。
君呀。你有心憐我。你便早日開嚟。
見面講透苦心死亦無乜掛意。
唉。休阻滯。
但得早一刻逢君。我就算早一刻別離。

Song 47
弔秋喜

聽見你話死。實在見思疑。
何苦輕生得咁癡。
你係為人客死心。唔怪得你。
死因錢債。叫我怎不傷悲。
你平日當我係知心。亦該同我講句。
做乜交情三兩個月。都冇句言詞。
往日個種恩情丟了落水。
縱有金銀燒盡。帶不到陰司。
可惜飄泊在青樓孤負你一世。
煙花塲上冇日開眉。

你名叫做秋喜。
只望等到秋來還有喜意。
做乜纔過冬至後就被雪霜欺。
今日無力春風唔共你爭得啖氣。
落花無主敝就葬在春泥。
此後情思有夢你便頻須寄。
或者盡我呢點窮心慰吓故知。
泉路茫茫你雙腳又咁細。
黃泉無客店問你向乜誰棲。
青山白骨唔知憑誰祭。
袁楊殘月空聽個隻杜鵑啼。
未必有個知心來共你擲紙。
清明空恨個頁紙錢飛。
罷咯。不若當作你係義妻。來送你入寺。
等你孤魂無主仗吓佛力扶持。
你便哀懇個位慈雲施吓佛偈。
等你轉過來生誓不做客妻。
若係冤債未償再罰你落花粉地。
你便揀過一個多情早早見機。
我苦共你未斷情緣重有相會日子。
須緊記。
念吓前恩義。
講到銷魂個兩個字。共你死過都唔遲。

Song 48
傷春

鳥啼花落暗傷春。
人老對住花殘想起就斷魂。
青春自信都有人憐憫。
恐怕脂粉飄零寂寞一生。
唔知邊一箇多情。邊一箇薄倖。
總係紅顏偏遇個的喪心人。
今日蝶去剩朵花開。叫我何所倚憑。
唉。喉帶咽哽。
想到玉碎香埋。阻不住兩淚淋。

Song 49
花心蝶

花心蝶。捍極佢都唔飛。
一定貪圖香膩卻被花迷。
花為有情憐憫蝶使。
蝶為風流。所以正得咁癡。
大抵花蝶相交。同一樣氣味。

唉。情願死。
叫我割愛實在唔輕易。
除是蝶死花殘正得了期。

Song 50
燈蛾

莫話唔怕火。試睇吓個隻烘火燈蛾。
飛來飛去總要摸落個盞深窩。
深淺本係唔知。故此成夜去摸。
迷頭迷腦如似著了風魔。
佢點曉得方寸好似萬丈深潭。任你飛亦
　不過。
逐浪隨波唔知喪盡幾多。
待等熱到轆身。情亦知到係錯。
總係愛飛唔得起。問你叫乜誰拖。
雖則係死咯。任你死盡萬千佢重唔肯結
　果。
心頭咁猛。依舊向住個的猛將張羅。
點得你學蝴蝶夢醒。個陣花亦悟破。
唉。飛去任我。
就俾你花花世界。都奈我唔何。

Song 51
長發夢

點得長日發夢。等我日夜共你相逢。
萬里程途都係一夢通。
個的無情雲雨把情根種。
種落呢段情根莫俾佢打鬆。
雖則夢裡巫山空把你送。
就係夢中同你講幾句。亦可以解得吓愁
　容。
君呀。你發夢便約定共我一齊方正有用。
切莫我夢裡去尋君你又不在夢中。
君呀。你早食早眠把身體保重。
心想痛。
問你歸心何日動。
免至我醒來離別獨對住燈紅。

Song 52
唔好發夢

勸你唔好發夢。恐怕夢裡相逢。
夢後醒來事事都化空。

分離兩個字豈有心唔痛。
君呀。你在天涯流落。你妹在水面飄蓬。
懷人偷抱琵琶弄。
多少淒涼盡在指中。
捨得你唔係噉樣子死心。君呀。你又唔
　　累得我咁重。
睇我瘦成噉樣子重講乜花容。
今日恩情好極都係唔中用。
唉。愁萬種。
累得我相思無主淚啼紅。

Song 53
相思索

相思索。綁住兩頭心。
溫柔鄉裡困住情人。
君呀。抑或你唔肯放鬆。定是奴鄉你緊。
迷頭迷腦好似昏君。
縱有妙手話解得呢個結開。亦無路可問。
就俾你利刀亦難割得呢段情根。
你有本事削性丟開唔掛恨。
點想日來丟淡。夢裡又要追尋。
天呀。你既係生人做乜把情字做引。
但係情長情短未必有的來因。
總係唔錯用個點真情。就唔使受困。
縱使一時困住。到底有日開心。
真正最噌收人。都係瘟緊個陣。
唉。都係噉混。
唔怕精乖。唔怕你混沌。
總係情關難破。就係死亦要追尋。

Song 54
相思樹

相思樹。種在愁城。
無枝無葉冷清清。
相思本是花為命。
每到低頭只為卿。
總係春寒根強生唔定。
啵就化作浮萍又往別處生。
我勸世間蝴蝶莫去穿花徑。
唉。花有定性。
就係蝶亦終難醒。
究竟相思無樹。春夢亦無憑。

Song 55
相思結

相思結。解極都唔開。
一定冤孽前生結下來。
當初慌久唔恩愛。
今日恩愛深時反惹禍胎。
愛了又憎。憎了又愛。
愛憎無定。自見心呆。
好似大海撐船撐到半海。
兩頭唔到岸點得埋堆。
唉。須忍耐。
折磨終有福在。
你睇神仙咁安樂。未必一吓就到得蓬萊。

Song 56 (Part 1)
分別淚（一）

分別淚。莫灑向離人。
離愁未講已自難禁。
邊一箇唔知到行路咁艱難。須要謹慎。
總係臨行箇一種說話。要先兩日向枕畔
　　囑咐殷懃。
若係臨時提起就噲撩人恨。
不若強為歡笑。等佢去得安心。
自願去後大大哭過一場。或者消吓怨恨。
器到箇一點氣難番。又向夢裡尋。
夢裡見著箇箇多情。就要安慰佢一陣。
細把行蹤問。
首先唔好向佢講到半句苦楚時文。

Song 56 (Part 2)
分別淚（二）

分別淚。搞極都唔乾。
淚呀。人有人哋牽情噲乜你咁著忙。
相思滿腹唔知憑誰講。
講極過人知。都有箇為我慘傷。
頃刻車馬就要分開南北二向。
點得疎林將就吓。為我掛住斜陽。
唉。心想愴。
風笛吹離況。
君呀。你前途辛苦都要謹慎吓行藏。

Song 56 (Part 3)
分別淚（三）

分別淚。轉眼又番場。
君呀。捨得你學我眼淚咁易回頭。哽乜我咁慘傷。
今日別期未了就把歸期望。
想想到一自自孤寒。叫我怎不斷腸。
意欲忍淚暫歡。同你細講。
虧我淚流不斷好似九曲湘江。
點得眼淚送君好似河水一樣。
水送得到箇方時。我淚亦得到箇方。
君呀。你見水好似見奴心莫異向。
須念吓我哋枕邊流淚到天光。
我雙淚盡哋落到君前。你便為我分吓苦況。
就俾你共我分開流淚。都係見淒涼。
唉。心想愴。
別後心難放。
總係你學我望郎咁心事望我。就不嚕掉轉心腸。

Song 57
無情語

無情語。勸不轉君身。
眼底天涯萬里人。
妝臺春老重有誰憐憫。
客邸無花又算一春。
人話路頭花柳最惹得人憐恨。
君呀。你莫尋漁父去問武陵津。
雖則過眼煙花無乜要緊。
你便安吓本分。
乃念雙親長念你。都係箇一點精神。

Song 58
無情眼

無情眼。送不得君車。
淚花如雨懶倚門閭。
一片真心如似白水。
織不盡迴文。寫不盡血書。
臨行致囑無多語。
君呀。好極京華都要念吓故居。
今日水酒一杯和共眼淚。

君你拚醉。
你便放歡心共我談笑兩句。
重要轉生來世共你做對比目雙魚。

Song 59
無情曲

無情曲。對不住君歌。
綠波春水奈愁何。
好鳥有心憐憫我。
替我聲聲啼喚。捨不得哥哥。
今日留春不住。未必係王孫錯。
雁塔題名你便趁早一科。
我想再世李仙無乜幾個。
休要放過。
今日孤單誰識你係鄭元和。

Song 60
三生債

花花世界。問你點樣子生埋。
既係生埋在呢一處咯。做乜又總總相乖。
大抵紅粉與及青衫終嚕變改。
所以情根唔肯向雪泥栽。
點估話絲連藕斷結下三生債。
致此牽纏風月在呢處柳巷花街。
雖則你似野鶴我似閒鷗。無乜俗態。
總係鴛鴦雲水兩相唉。
我只話淡淡啫共你相交。把情付與大海。
點想心血一陣陣來潮。叫我點樣子放開。
到底舊愛與及新歡我都唔嚕自解。
唉。真冇了賴。
罷咯。不若轉生來世共你海角天涯。

Song 61
桄榔樹

桄榔樹。我知到你係單心。
你生來有箇種心事。我一見就銷魂。
你在瘦地長成。又無乜倚凭。
是真情種。故此有噉樣情根。
我想人世有噉樣情根。你真正惡搵。
樹猶如此。我怨只怨句情人。
我近日見郎心帶不穩。

一條心事。要共幾箇人分。
捨得佢學你噉樣子單心。我就長日有恨。
唉。真真正不忿。
要把花神問。
樹呀。你唔肯保佑我郎學你噉樣心事。
　　我就話你係邪神。

Song 62
無了賴

無了賴。是相思。
思前想後你話點得心辭。
一世怕提離別兩字。
好似到死春蠶尚吐絲。
不願共你同生。情願共死。
免令日後兩地參差。
古來多少傷心事。
天呀。你噉妒忌我呢多情。似極有私。
你睇紅拂女係咁識人。嬌你略似。
今日飄泊應憐我李藥師。
呢會降格任人呼我做浪子。
唉。今若此。
香國傳名字。
或者有箇知音來聽我呢首斷腸詞。

Song 63
對垂楊

斷腸人。怕對住垂楊。
怕對垂楊箇對媚眼一雙。
見佢愁鎖住眉尖。同我一樣。
柳呀。做乜你愁唔了又試惹起我愁腸。
可惜咁好深閨唔種。種你在離亭上。
見一遍離情。就嗱碎一遍瞻肝。
恐怕愁多捱不慣呢首相思帳。
唉。須要自想。
試睇。睇吓陽關上。
柳呀。做乜初秋顏色你就變了青黃。

Song 64
聽哀鴻

斷腸人。怕聽哀鴻。
驚散姻緣在夢中。

雁呀。你係孤鶯奴係寡鳳。
你哀殘月。我獨對燈紅。
可惜你一世孤單無侶可共。
我哋天涯人遠。重話有信息相通。
雁呀。我共你同病相憐。你便將我書信
　　遠送。
你莫向江關留戀阻滯行踪。
我望雁可比望郎。心事更重。
愁有萬種。
雁呀。你莫學我情郎身世只係斷梗飄蓬。

Song 65
生得咁俏

我生得咁俏。
怕有鮮魚來上我釣。
今朝拿在手重係咁尾搖搖。
呢回釣竿收起都唔要。
縱不是魚水和諧。都係命裡所招。
我想大海茫茫魚亦不少。
休要亂跳。
鐵網都來了。
總係一時唔上我釣啫。我就任得你海上
　　逍遙。

Song 66
唔係乜靚

你唔係乜靚啫。做乜你一見我就心傷。
想必你未出世就整定銷魂。今世惹我斷
　　腸。
亦係前世種落呢段根苗。今世正有花粉
　　草帳。
故此我拼死去尋花。正碰著此異香。
紅粉見盡萬千唔似得你噉樣。
相逢過一面。番去至少有十日思量。
捨得死咯噉話死去噲番生。我又同你死
　　帳。
難為我真正死咯。箇陣你話有乜相干。
呢會俾佢天上跌箇落嚟。我亦唔敢去亂
　　想。
真真要見諒。
莫話粒聲唔出就掉轉心腸。

Song 67
乜得咁瘦

乜得你咁瘦。實在可人憐。
想必你為著多情。惹起恨牽。
見你弱不勝衣。容貌漸變。
勸你把風流兩箇字睇破吓。切勿咁癡纏。
相思最噲把精神損。
你睇癡蝶在花房。夢得咁倒顛。
就係恩愛到十分亦唔好咁縊戀。
須要打算。
莫話只顧風流唔怕命短。
問你一身能結得幾多箇人緣。

Song 68
心肝

心肝呀。你唔好咁鬥劣。
竟自氣到我頭瘟。
做乜見親人好樣你就分外留神。
知你日久生心。呢回嫌妹眼緊。
見你近來待我都冇往日三分。
我係相識到至今為你長日受困。
枉你當初同誓。今日背了前盟。
我只估話有箇情哥為做倚凭。
算來男子冇箇真心。
只話唔掛你死去投生。
想過唔做得咁笨。
點好讓人快活我自己做了枉死冤魂。
記得起首相交。今日你就唔記得箇陣。
做乜你騙人咁耐。你又試貪新。
呢回你改過自新。我共你緣正有分。
唉。心不忍。
免招人話薄倖。
你便修心憐憫我。算我怕你咯。恩人。

Song 69
真正惡做

真正惡做。嬌呀。汝曉得我苦心無。
日夜共汝轆埋重慘過利刀。
近日見汝熟客推完。新客又不到。
兩頭唔到岸。好似水共油撈。
早知到唔共汝住得埋。不若唔相與重好。
免使掛腸掛肚日夕咁心操。
勸汝揚起心肝尋過箇好佬。
共汝還通錢債免使到處受上期租。
河底下雖則係繁華。汝見邊一箇長好得到老。
究竟清茶淡飯都要揀箇上岸正為高。
況且近日火燭咁多。寮口又咁惡做。
河廳差役終日係咁嗌嘈嘈。
唔信汝睇各間寮口部。
總係見睇唔見結。白白把手皮搏。
就俾汝有幾箇女都養齊。好似話錢債易造。
恐怕一時唔就手。就墮落鄭都。
雖則鴇母近日亦算有幾家係時運好。
贖身成幾十箇女。重有幾十箇未開鋪。
想到結局收場未必真係可保。
況且百中無一箇的境遇實在難遭。
汝好心撥埋尋着地步。
唔怕冇路。
回頭須及早。
好過露面拋頭在水上蒲。

Song 70
辛苦半世

辛苦半世。都係兩箇人知。
做乜苦盡總不見甘來。汝話有乜期。
我自係識性就知到做人唔係乜易。
只望捱通世界正有的心機。
點想冤債未償。墮落花粉地。
江湖飄泊各東西。
我苦極都係命招。埋怨吓自己。
唉。唔忿得氣。
往事休提起。
點肯話終身淪落在呢處苦海難離。

Song 71
人實首惡做

人實首惡做。都冇日開眉。
俾極真情待汝。汝都未知。
我為汝淚流長日咻氣。
我想過做人咁樣子。汝話有乜心機。
汝叫我箇箇待到咁真心。唔得咁易。
總係見君。君呀。我就唔肯負卻箇段佳期。
莫話珠江盡是無情地。

今日為情字牽纏。所以正得咁癡。
做乜開口就把薄情看待我地。
怪得汝時常相聚都係貌合神離。
呢會你唔念奴。奴亦唔念你。
唉。唔好咁厭氣。
做箇存終始。
等汝花粉叢中識吓我哋女兒。

Song 72
無可奈

無可奈。想到癡呆。
人到中年白髮又催。
自古紅顏薄命真難改。
總係紅粉多情都是惹禍胎。
我想塵世汝話點能逃得苦海。
總要前生修得到。或者早脫離災。
一定前世唔修。故此淪落得咁耐。
唉。難割愛。
人去情根在。
不堪回首咯。我要問一句如來。

Song 73
寄遠

唔可咁熱。熱極就唔難丟。
一旦離開實在見寂寥。
好極未得上街緣分未了。
況且乾柴凭火也會燒。
叫我等你三年。我年尚少。
總怕長成無倚。我就錯在今朝。
此後鴛儔燕侶心堪表。
獨惜執盞傳杯。罪未肯饒。
自怨我命薄如花。人又不肖。
捨得我好命。如今重隻乜住寮。
保知汝一朝衣錦還鄉耀。
汝書債還完。我花債亦消。
總係呢陣旅舍孤寒魂夢繞。
唉。音信渺。
燈花何日兆。
汝睇京華萬里一水迢迢。

Song 74 (Part 1)
春花秋月 ── 春

春呀。你唔好去自。重有一句商量。
共你年年離別實係情傷。
睇見花事係咁飄零。我就魂魄蕩。
大抵人生難定都是聚散無常。
捨得真正係共你有緣。我亦唔敢咁勉強。
做乜綢繆三個月。又試兩地分張。
睇吓王孫歸去我就添惆悵。
挽留無計算我負卻春光。
我想繁華春望亦都成虛況。
唉。無乜別講。
送君南浦上。
呢回有書難寫。可惜紙短情長。

Song 74 (Part 2)
花

花呀。你唔好謝自。重要賞吓芳容。
無聊愁對住雨陰中。
講到紅顏薄命邊箇話心唔痛。
算來人世共你一樣飄蓬。
花你有時夜靜重把香來送。
真正累人。如果係箇的淺深紅。
若係花你無香。未必惹得我真情動。
獨惜我護花無力。怨恨東風。
呢回蜂狂蝶浪亦都唔中用。
唉。你妹愁有萬種。
往事多如夢。
邊箇有憐香心事。你便譜入絲桐。

Song 74 (Part 3)
秋

秋呀。你唔好老自。重要繫住吓年華。
滿懷愁緒對住蒹葭。
人話秋風蕭瑟堪人怕。
我愛盈盈秋水浸住紅霞。
既係秋你有情。未必把我長牽掛。
睇見你常留明月照我窗紗。
大抵可人盡在箇的豐瀟灑。
莫話因風憔悴。敢就瘦比黃花。
我想悲秋宋玉都是成虛話。
邊一箇對秋唔想去泛仙槎。

呢回我亦憐秋。秋亦要憐我一吓。
唉。你妹喉帶咽啞。
採菊東籬下。
你睇潯陽江上淚滴琵琶。

Song 74 (Part 4)
月

月呀。你唔好落自。重要照到我通宵。
夜裡懷人更重寂寥。
人哋只曉得月你團圓。心就喜笑。
點曉得月到圓時一自自減消。
月呀。你一箇月一遍團圓。我見你圓得
　　太少。
點得相逢三十夜。夜夜都把我相邀。
試把聚散問下嫦娥。應亦略曉。
點解我姻緣無路。啲就拆斷藍橋。
更有心事許多。重想月呀你同我照料。
唉。你妹愁都未了。
衷情誰為表。
點得夜夜逢君學箇的有信海潮。

Song 75
情一箇字

情一箇字。重慘過砒霜。
做乜無情白事斷人腸。
搔首問天。天呀。你又唔好啲樣。
命薄如花。總不為我主張。
怨只怨我生錯作有情。故此多呢種孽帳。
當初何不俾我鐵石心腸。
你睇頑石尚有望夫留在世上。
須要自想。
任你魄散魂飄蕩。
總係邊一箇多情。就向邊一箇抵償。

Song 76 (Part 1)
多情柳（一）

多情柳。贈俾薄情夫。
夫呀。分離二字問你可憐無。
一心只望你唔虧負。
兩存恩愛水遠山高。
點想共你無緣。啲就分拆在半路。
呢陣煙水雲山阻隔路途。

做女箇陣點知離別得咁苦。
唉。真正可惱。
呢會衷情都係憑柳你代訴。
故此咁遠至到得呢處離亭。我亦不憚勞。

Song 76 (Part 2)
多情柳（二）

多情柳。淚眼雙雙。
柳呀。做乜見人快活見我就淒涼。
你種在灞橋就知到你係冤孽帳。
送人歸去淨對住個對宿水鴛鴦。
柳呀。你弱質咁難扶。同我一樣。
春風唔怕。怕捱到秋霜。
今日形容枯槁。似極無倚傍。
唉。唔好異向。
到頭終有望。
自古新萊還只望佢再發枯楊。

Song 77
愁到冇解

愁到冇解。怨一句命蹇時乖。
天呀。你啲樣子生奴。你話點得一世埋。
鮮花豈有話唔思戴。
總係命裡帶不得風流。都係白白哦。
相思擔起尋人買。
逢人都叫我轉過柳巷花街。
重勸我有價可沽。無價亦可賣。
還了舊債。
好過隨街擺。
免得相思無主冇日開懷。

Song 78
愁到極吔

愁到極吔。懶整殘妝。
繡簾唔捲為怯風寒。
你妹半減腰圍。心都為你愴。
你在何處貪戀風流總不返故鄉。
就係唔念你妹呢處青樓。亦該思憶吓府
　　上。
就係妻兒唔掛。都要記念吓爹娘。
做乜身在天涯。你心就異向。
唉。何苦啲樣。
君呀。切莫聽人唆攪你掉轉心腸。

Song 79 (Part 1)
點算好（一）

點算好。共你相交又怕唔得到老。
真情雖有。可惜實事全無。
今世共你結下呢段姻緣。等到來世正做。
你為和尚。我做齋姑。
唔信你睇紅樓夢上有段鴛鴦譜。
個個寶玉共佢無緣。所以黛玉得咁孤。
佢臨死哭叫四個字一聲。唉。寶玉你好。
真正無路可訴。
離恨天難補。
罷咯。不若共你淡交如水。免至話我係
　　薄情奴。

Song 79 (Part 2)
點算好（二）

點算好。君呀。你家貧親又咁老。
八千條路噉就有一點功勞。
虧我留落在呢處天涯。家信又不到。
君歸南嶺我苦住京都。
長劍雖則有靈。今日光氣未吐。
新篁落籜。或者有日插天高。
孫山名落朱顏槁。
綠柳撩人重慘過利刀。
金盡牀頭清酒懶做。
無物可報。
珠淚穿成素。
君呀。去歸條路替我帶得到家無。

Song 80
身只一箇

身只一箇。叫我點順得兩箇情哥。
一頭歡喜。一便把我消磨。
佢兩箇晚晚開來。偏偏要叫我。
捨得一人一晚都免使我咁囉唆。
削性共佢一箇好埋。等佢尋過別箇。
又怕箇瘟屍唔好得到底咧。我就苦怨當
　　初。
又怕箇薄情唔愈得我。
箇的傍人唆攪是非多。
唉。點叫我心破得做兩邊。人變得做兩
　　箇。

呢會唔使動火。
但得佢二家唔食醋咯。重好過蜜餞菠蘿。

Song 81
唔怕命寒

唔怕命寒。總要你心堅。
捨得心堅愁有一箇月老哀憐。
莫話命寒時乖你就尋箇短見。
半世有一日開懷。恐怕你做鬼亦冤。
若係話刊定板八箇字生成。唔到你算。
又未知到後來真定假。未必有箇食飯神
　　仙。
大抵人事都要盡番。或者時運嗰轉。
唉。休要自怨。
莫話好事難如願。
若係堅心寧耐等。就係破鏡都嗰重圓。

Song 82
嗟怨命少

嗟怨命少。恨我帶不得幾多條。
人人都係咁攞命。叫我點捨得把佢來丟。
捨得我有命每箇俾佢一條。無乜緊要。
無奈呢一條爛命。好費事正剩到今朝。
箇的多情為我喪命。我亦填唔了。
佢死亦見心甜。都算得我命裡所招。
我想貪花喪命都係因年少。
究竟風流到底正算得老來嬌。
你睇牛女歲歲都有相逢。大抵佢年紀亦
　　不小。
唉。心共照。
七夕同歡笑。
總係長命又要長情。正可以渡得鵲橋。

Song 83
吹不斷

吹不斷。是情絲。
情絲牽住割亦難離。
牽到入心箇陣就無乜主意。
魂魄唔全只剩一點癡。
若係兩箇情癡。就俾佢癡到死。
死亦心甜不枉做故知。

鬼怕一個情癡。一個唔多在意。
單思成病。藥亦難醫。
個陣你肯為佢捨生。佢亦唔多謝到你。
唉。真正冇味。
實在話過你聽咯。你要死亦訪到情真死
　　都未遲。

Song 84
相思纜

相思纜。帶我郎來。
帶得郎來莫個又替我攪開。
是必纜你係心緒絞成。故此牽得咁耐。
逢人解纜我就自見癡呆。
纜呀。你送別個陣可憎。回轉個陣可愛。
總係兩頭牽扯。唔知幾時正得埋堆。
我心事一條交你手內。
可恨你時時要斬纜。噉樣就亂我心懷。
我想誓嚊也定要對住個山。盟嚊也定要
　　對住個海。
總要心莫改。
若係唔同心事。纜都絞你唔埋。

Song 85
相思病

也你咁病。見你面帶青黃。
相思唔估噲入到膏肓。
我想天地俾我一段情緣。就係同我寫一
　　幅病狀。
既係與君同病藥亦同嘗。
郎呀。藥咁難嘗到底你嘗見點樣。
今日苦上心頭淨我共你兩個慘傷。
我兩個大早就死心病重還有乜指望。
眼前無路苦海茫茫。
如果死後共我結得再世姻緣。我就把菩
　　薩供養。
又怕我六根唔淨到不得西方。
世事講到來生。亦都全係妄想。
無乜倚向。
青樓就係地獄咯。重講乜地久天長。

Song 86
銷魂柳

銷魂柳。黯牽衣。
柳呀。既曉得牽情。又點捨得別離。
東風一夜人千里。
暮雲春樹惹妹相思。
關山迢遞你妹書難寄。
總要情同金石。永不更移。
莫話呢陣握手長情。歇下分手就負義。
須記陽關贈君一枝。
你妹自小失身原是為你。
唉。情一個字。
君呀。你唔念如今。都要念吓舊時。

Song 87
煙花地

煙花地。是邪魔。
有咁多風流。就要受咁多折磨。
雪月風花我亦曾見過。
無限風流問你買得幾多。
只可當佢係過眼煙雲。若係癡就噲錯。
恐怕鑿山難補個有底深河。
若講到真義真情邊個共你死過。
總怕全盡牀頭。好極都要疎。
大抵花柳害人非獨一個。
唉。須想過。
好熄心頭火。
普勸世間人仔莫誤結個段水上絲蘿。

Song 88
鴛鴦

鴛鴦一對。世上難分。
總係人在天涯見佢倍愴神。
佢眠食都捨不得離開。叫我心事點念。
問一句鴛鴦呀。我願托生為你不願為人。
都係佢情義體得咁鬆。至此佢名利看得
　　咁緊。
想到青春難買。就枉費你千金。
都係俗眼重箇的虛名。故此想分佢一份。
又想話為奴爭啖氣。正捨得割斷情根。
我哋相隔睇住你相歡。如果係肉緊。
唉。真正係笨。

就被你覓到封侯。你妹都要悔恨。
想想到呢陣鳳寡鶯孤。叫我怎不斷魂。

Song 89
扇

手拈一把齊紈扇。
提起共你分攜隔別一年。
熱起番來常記念。
做乜但到秋來就噲棄捐。
大抵扇有丟抛人有厭賤。
細想人情冷暖總不堪言。
世態炎涼休要自怨。
冷時邊一箇唔在熱時先。
總係熱處須從涼到打算。
莫箇逢人就熱得咁癡纏。
雖則話係嘅啫。熱極箇陣只曉得癡迷。
　　點想到後來人事改變。
唉。瘟咁縈戀。
撥埋心事一便。
係囉。呢會丟埋箇的冷處。總不記得熱
　　在從前。

Song 90
結絲蘿

清水燈心煲白果。
果然清白怕乜你心多。
白芷共薄荷包畀過我。
薄情如紙。你話奈乜誰何。
圓眼。沙梨。包幾箇。
眼底共你離開暫且放疎。
絲線共花針。你話點穿得眼過。
真正係錯。
總要同針合線正結得絲蘿。

Song 91
對孤燈

斷腸人。怕對孤燈。
對影孤寒想吓就斷魂。
呢陣衾枕咁孤單無乜倚凭。
影呀。你無言無語叫我苦對誰伸。
雖則共你成雙亦難慰得我恨。
不若把杯同影共作三人。
愛則愛你生死不離咁跟得我緊。
就係天涯海角你我都難分。
君呀。呢陣銀燈獨對心相印。
恨只恨我隻影難隨共你酌斟。
願你對影暫將魂魄認。
唉。心不忿。
夢寐難親近。
當作挑燈長見我切勿對影傷神。

Song 92
桃花扇

桃花扇。寫首斷腸詞。
寫到情深扇都噲慘悽。
命有薄得過桃花。情有薄得過紙。
紙上桃花薄更可知。
君呀。你既寫花容先要曉得花的意思。
青春難得。莫悞花時。
我想絕世風流都無乜好恃。
秋風團扇怨在深閨。
寫出萬葉千花都為情一箇子。
唔信你睇侯公子李香君。唔係情重點得
　　遇合佳期。

Song 93
船頭浪

船頭浪。合吓又分開。
相思如水湧上心來。
君呀。你生在情天。奴長在慾海。
拍天連水。水與天挨。
我哋紅粉點似得青山長冇變改。
你睇吓水面個殘花。事就可哀。
似水流年。又唔知流得幾耐。
須要自愛。
許你死後做到成佛成仙亦未必真正自在。
罷咯。不若及時行樂共你倚遍月榭風臺。

Song 94
聽烏啼

斷腸人怕聽烏啼。
啼成咁辛苦想必為借一枝棲。

邊一個唔想望高飛大抵唔係乜易嚌。
況且你滿身毛羽尚未生齊。
鵲呀。做乜你淨係替人哋填橋。總唔曉
　　得自幾贔屭。
兩頭頻撲你嗰搵的挨依。
今日風露咁清涼。林木咁阻滯。
須要早計。
莫話烏頭轉白正知到世事難為。

Song 95
梳髻

頭路撥開梳過一隻髻。
等佢知頭知路早日開嚟。
髻心須要侵頭髮。
把定心頭怕乜是非。
札住髻根聯住髻尾。
我重要跟郎到尾正有的心機。
花管帶花通到髻底。
等我花債還通。管得你帶我去歸。
重要花伴髻。髮邊藏住月桂。
正係月老與及花神都重保祐我哋兩個白
　　髮齊眉。

Song 96
還花債

想必緣份已盡。定係花債還齊。
債還緣盡。惹起我別慘離悽。
我哋兩個人咁情癡。再不估情不到底。
想起吓從前個種風月好似夢斷魂迷。
起首共你相交。你妹年紀尚細。
共你細談心曲怕聽水上鳴雞。
只估話日子咁長你同妹設計。
點想你夫妻情重。帶不得賤妾回歸。
累得我斷梗飄蓬無乜倚繫。
細想吓飄流無定只着要搵的挨棲。
今日人哋講我哋薄情。唔係亦都似係。
總係同輩咁多姊妹。點曉得我心事咁難
　　為。
我身上着呢件青衫。都是憑眼淚洗。
唔係計。
君呀。你是必硬着心腸唔多愿睇。
故此自從聽見話我去咯。此後總總唔嚟。

Song 97
點清油

清油半盞點着幾條心。
君呀。你心事咁多時。叫我點樣子去尋。
睇你心頭咁猛亦都唔禁浸。
你試睇吓個盞清油尚有幾深。
恐怕越浸越乾油越緊。
點似得心少油多慢慢斟。
你唔怕我譜。
莫學無人恨。
你重要剔起心頭正好做人。

BIBLIOGRAPHY

A Buddhist Dictionary of Terms and Concepts. Tokyo: Nichiren Shoshu International Center, 1983.

Baudelaire, Charles. *Poems, Correspondences. 1821–67.*

Bynner, Witter. *Three Hundred Poems of the T'ang Dynasty 618–906.* English translation and Chinese text. Taipei: Man Sing, 1963.

Ch'en, Kenneth K S. *Buddhism in China. A Historical Survey.* Princeton, New Jersey: Princeton University Press, 1964.

Chang Hsin-hai. *The Fabulous Concubine.* Hong Kong: Oxford University Press, 1986.

Clementi, Cecil. *Cantonese Love-songs.* Translated with introduction and notes. Oxford: Clarendon Press, 1904. (The Chinese text of these songs is printed in a companion volume.)

Cooper, Arthur. *Li Po and Tu Fu.* Penguin Books, 1973.

Eberhard, Wolfram. *A Dictionary of Chinese Symbols.* London and New York: Routledge & Kegan Paul, 1986.

Eitel, Ernest John. *Handbook of Chinese Buddhism.* A Sanskrit–Chinese Dictionary with vocabularies of Buddhist terms and a Chinese index by K Takakuwa. Tokyo, Sanshusha, 1940.

Eliade, Mircea. *The Myth of the Eternal Return.* Translated from the French version by Willard R Trask. New York: Bollingen Foundation Inc., 1954.

Fletcher, W J B. *Gems of Chinese Verse.* Shanghai: The Commercial Press Ltd., 1932.

Fletcher, W J B. *More Gems of Chinese Poetry.* Shanghai: The Commercial Press Ltd., 1933.

Giles, Herbert Allen. *A Chinese Biographical Dictionary.* Taipei: Literature House, 1968.

Ho, Kenneth P H. *The Nineteen Ancient Poems.* Hong Kong: Kelly & Walsh, 1977.

Humphreys, Christmas. *The Popular Dictionary of Buddhism.* Curzon Press, 1976.

Jung, C G. *Man and His Symbols.* London, 1964.

Kiu Yin-nung 喬硯農. 廣州話口語詞的研究, *Gwong Jau Wa Hau Ue Chi Dik In Kau* (*Wah K'iu Ue-Man Ch'ut-Paan-She yan hong*). Hong Kong: Overseas Chinese Languages Publishing Company, 1966.

Kwan Kit Choi. *A Dictionary of Cantonese Colloquialisms in English*. The Hong Kong: The Commercial Press Ltd., 1990.

Lam Yue-tong. *Gems From Chinese Literature Rendered Into English*. Hong Kong.

Larsen, Jeanne. *Brocade River Poems. Selected works of the Tang dynasty courtesan Xue Tao*. Translated and introduced by Jeanne Larsen. Princeton, New Jersey: Princeton University Press, 1987.

Lau, Sidney. *A Practical Cantonese–English Dictionary*. Hong Kong: The Government Printer, 1977.

Ling, T O. *A Dictionary of Buddhism*. Introduction by T O Ling. (The text of this book has been taken from *A Dictionary of Comparative Religion*. Edited by S G F Brandon. New York: Charles Scribner's Sons, 1972.)

Liu, James J Y. *The Poetry of Li Shang-yin, A Ninth-Century Baroque Chinese Poet*. Chicago: The University of Chicago Press, 1969.

Lu Shu-xiang and Xu Yuan-zhong (Editors). *Gems of Classical Chinese Poetry in Various English Translations*. Hong Kong: Joint Publishing Company, 1988.

Mayers, William Frederick. *The Chinese Reader's Manual*. Reprinted. Taipei: Literature House Ltd., 1964.

Nakamura, Hajime. *Ways of Thinking of Eastern Peoples: India–China–Tibet–Japan*. Honolulu, Hawaii: East–West Center Press, 1966.

New Larousse Encyclopedia of Mythology. Introduction by Robert Graves. Translated from the French *Larousse Mythologie Generale* by Richard Aldington & Delano Ames. 17th Impression. The Hamlyn Publishing Group Ltd., 1983.

Soothhill, William Edward and Hodous, Lewis: *A Dictionary of Chinese Buddhism*. Kegan, Paul, Trench, Trabuer & Co. Ltd., 1976.

Stutley, Margaret and James. *A Dictionary of Hinduism — Its Mythology, Folklore and Development 1500 BC – AD 1500*. London and Henley: Routledge & Kegan Paul Ltd., 1977.

The Chinese–English Dictionary. Hong Kong: The Commercial Press Ltd., 1979.

The New Encyclopaedia Brittanica, 1987.

Thomas, Edward J. *The History of Buddhist Thought*. Reprinted. London: Routledge & Kegan Paul Ltd., 1967.

Turner, John A. *A Golden Treasury of Chinese Poetry*. Compiled and edited by John J Deeney. A Renditions Book. Reprinted. Hong Kong: The Chinese University of Hong Kong, 1979.

Webster's Third New International Dictionary. Springfield, Massachusetts: Merriam–Webster Inc., 1961.

Wieger, Leon. *Les Pères du Systeme Taoiste*. Paris: Cathasia, 1950.

Williams, C A S. *Manual of Chinese Metaphors*. Shanghai: The Commercial Press Ltd., 1920. (First AMS edition: 1974.)

Wu Juntao: *Tu Fu — A New Translation*. Hong Kong: The Commercial Press, Ltd., 1981.

Yang, Wei-Lin (Editor). *The Summary of Buddhist Terminology in English*. Taipei, Taiwan: Wen Szu Publishing Company, 1982.

Zeng Zifan. *Colloquial Cantonese and Putonghua Equivalents*. Translations by S K Lai. Hong Kong: Joint Publishing Company, 1986.

INDEX

A stroke (/) after the number of a Song indicates Part 1, Part 2, etc. of that Song, e.g., Song 1/2 means, Song 1 (Part 2).

Advice, spurned, *Song 17*
Appearance, outward, *Songs 1/2; 7*
Autumn, *Songs 11/1,3,4; 12/6; 21; 22; 30; 31/1; 35/2,5,6; 36; 63; 74/3; 76/2; 89*
'Autumn Joy', *Song 47*
Avalokitesvara, *Intro. p. 37*
　function of, *Intro. pp. 33, 37*
　meaning of name, *Intro. p. 37*
　the female, *Intro. p. 39*
　traits of both sex, *Intro. p. 39*
Azalea, *Song 11/3*

Baak Gui-yi, *Songs 11/4; 12/4; 51*
Baan Gei, *Song 26*
Baudelaire, Charles, *Intro. p. 12*
Bees, *Songs 11/5; 18; 35/6; 37; 74/2*
Beet, red, *Song 82*
Birds, *Song 4*
Blossoms, peach, *Song 37*
　red, *Song 12/2*
　willow, *Songs 11/1; 32; 35/2*
Blue Bridge, *Song 74/4*
Bodhisattva, nature of, *Intro. pp. 32–34*
Body, only one, *Song 80*
Bo-yuk, *Songs 25; 79/1*
Brahma, *Intro. p. 26*
'Bridge of Sighs', *Pref. 8*
Buddha, life of the historical, *Intro. p. 23*
　meaning of the word, *Intro. p. 24*
　teachings of, *Intro. p. 26*
　the Laughing, *Intro. p. 23*
　the legend of, *Intro. p. 23*
Buddha Amitabha / Amitayus, *Intro. p. 36*
Buddhism, *Intro. p. 19*
　arrival in China of, *Intro. p. 20*
　background of, *Intro. p. 25*
　translation of its scriptures, *Intro. pp. 20, 21*
　concept of 'emptiness' in, *Intro. p. 22*
　expansion of, *Intro. p. 20*
　Hinayana, *Intro. p. 31*
　hindrance to expansion in China, *Intro. p. 21*
　influence on Chinese culture, *Intro. p. 21*
　Mahayana, *Intro. p. 31*
　Theravada, *Intro. p. 31*
Buddhism, *Songs 7; 11/3; 47; 72; 85; 93*
Butterflies, *Songs 12/6; 13/2; 35/2,6; 45; 48; 49; 50; 54; 67*
Butterfly dream, *Song 38*

Cham Yeung, the River, *Songs 12/4; 74/3*
Chan Mei-gung, *Song 11/4*
Chi Wan, *Pref. 8; Song 47*
Ching Ming Festival, *Song 47*
Chiu Dak-yin, *Song 33*
Chiu Gwan, *Song 11/1*
Choi Yung, *Song 11/4*
Chrysanthemum, *Songs 35; 74*
Chui Woo, *Song 37*
Clouds and rain, *Song 12/5*
Country, the fragrant, *Song 62*
Courtesan(s), *Intro. p. 7*
Cowherd & Spinning Girl, *Songs 12/3; 18; 36; 43; 82*
Creepers, *Song 87*
Crows, cawing of, *Song 94*
Crows' Bridge, *Songs 18; 82*

Death, *Songs 3; 46*
Desires, causes of, *Intro. p. 27*
Dharani, *Song 17*
Dharma, *Intro. p. 33*
Discipline, mental, *Intro. p. 28*
Dissipation, *Song 67*
Do Foo, *Songs 28; 86; 88*
Do Gwong, *See Emperor*
Do Muk-yi, *Pref. 6*

Do Si-hung, *Pref. 9*
Dream of the Red Chamber, *Songs 3; 79/1*
Dreams, *Songs 8; 9; 12/3; 16; 22; 27; 28; 38; 47; 51; 52;*
Duckweed, *Songs 12/4; 35/2; 52; 54; 69*
Dust, red, *Songs 30; 40*

Eight characters, the, *Song 81*
Eliade, Mircea, *Intro. p. 14*
Emperor Do Gwong, *Intro. p. 5; Pref. 1*
'Emptiness' in Buddhism, *Intro. pp. 22, 29*
Entertainment, houses of, *Intro. p. 6; Songs 11/1; 17; 32; 35/2; 40; 44; 47; 69; 78; 85*
Euphemisms, *Intro. pp. 7–9, 13*
Eyes, unfeeling, *Song 58*

Famous flowers, *Song 11/4,5*
Fan, peach-blossom, *Song 92*
Fan Yam, *Pref. 2*
Fans, *Songs 26; 35/5; 89*
Farewell *See 'Parting'*
Fate, *Songs 2; 5; 6; 8; 9; 11/1; 12/5; 13/1; 14; 34; 35/4; 38; 40; 44; 55; 65; 66; 72*
  frail, *Songs 39; 73; 75; 92*
  ungenerous, *Songs 6; 35/5; 81*
Feelings, as paper, *Songs 22; 92*
Fish, *Song 65*
Fish, twin, *Song 58*
Flower and powder groves, *Song 71*
  withered, *Song 5*
Flower-boat, *Pref. 2*
Flower-debt, *Songs 6; 11/5; 13/1; 25; 31/1; 47; 95; 96*
Flowers, *Songs 8; 13/1,2; 18; 21; 34; 37; 39; 49; 54; 74/2*
  famous, *Song 11/1,4,5*
  grave of hundred, *Song 11/1,2*
  life of, *Song 31/1*
  symbolism of, *Intro. p. 17; Song 90*
  wild, *Song 44*
  world of, *Songs 7; 13/1; 60*
Flowers and powder, *Songs 11/1; 66*
  and willows, *Song 1/2*
Fong Yuen-ling, *Song 80*
Fragrant country, the, *Song 62*
Fragrant soul, the, *Song 21*

Garments,
  green, *Songs 12/4; 60*
  wet, *Song 12/4*
Gautama, Siddhartha, *Intro. p. 23*
Geese, *Songs 17; 30; 64*
  letter-carrying, *Songs 6; 16*
  lone-flying, *Song 28*
  wailing of, *Song 64*
Go Tong Mountain, *Song 12/5*
Gong Yim, *Song 74/1*
Good deeds, *Song 1/1*
Goose Pagoda, *Song 59*
Grave of 100 flowers, *Song 11/1,2*
Groves, flower, *Song 35/3*
Gwong Hon, *Song 34*
Gwoon Yam, *Intro. pp. 10, 20, 23, 33, 37–39; Song 7*

Hair, dressing the, *Song 95*
Hang Yeung, *Songs 16; 28*
Happiness, *Song 1/2*
Hau Chiu-jung, *Song 92*
Hau Ngai, *Song 24*
Heart, a single, *Song 61*
  a true, *Song 2*
  only one, *Song 25*
Hinduism, *Intro. pp. 21, 25, 26, 29, 34*
Hoh Moon, *Pref. 2*
Hon Fung, *Song 35/5*
Hop Foo, the River, *Song 16*
Hung Fat Nui, *Song 62*

Ill-fate, *Song 37*
  and Passion, *Song 14*
Ill-fated, *Songs 11/1-5; 35/2*
Immortals, land of, *Song 31/1*
Impatience, *Songs 19; 34*
Inconstancy, *Songs 1/2; 13/1; 35/1; 89*
Infatuation, *Songs 1/2; 10; 14; 41*
Iris, the, *Song 90*
Isles of the Blest, *Songs 11/5; 55*

Jade and fragrance, *Songs 11/4; 31/2; 33; 39; 48*
Jade, personage of, *Song 18*
Jau Bo, *Song 11/3*
Jau, the critic, *Pref. 9*
Jeng Yuen-woh, *Song 59*
Jeung (measurement), *Song 50*
Jeung Chiu, *Intro. pp. 17, 19*

Jeung Gau-ling, *Intro. pp. 15, 16*
Jeung Hin, *Song 12/3*
Jeung Kiu, *Song 11/1*
Jeung Toi, *Song 12/2*
Jeung Toi willow, *Song 35/2*
Jiu Ji-yung, *Pref. 1; Intro. pp. 4, 6, 9*
Jiu Fei-yin, *Song 26*
Jong Ji, *Song 38*
Juk Faat-laan, *Intro. p. 20*

Karma, *Intro. pp. 20–22, 26, 29, 30, 32, 33; Songs 9; 35/3,4; 66; 72*
King of Hell, *Song 47*

Lam Doi-yuk, *Songs 25; 79/1*
Lam Yue-tong, *Intro. p. 17*
Lament, *Song 58*
Lamp bowl, *Song 97*
Lamp, oil & wick of the, *Song 97*
the lonely, *Song 91*
Lamp-snuff, red, *Songs 73; 91*
Laurel Garden, *Song 5*
Lau Seung-lin, *Song 3*
Lei Baak, *Song 91*
Lei Heung-gwan, *Song 92*
Lei Seung-yan, *Songs 6; 12/3*
Lei Sin, *Song 59*
Lei Yeuk-si, *Song 62*
Letters, *Songs 8; 11/4; 15; 29*
Li (measurement), *Songs 22; 51*
Life, emptiness of, *Songs 5; 8; 9; 35/1; 71; 83*
shortness of, *Song 82*
wasted, *Songs 5; 70*
Lotus, *Songs 11/3; 15; 35/4; 38; 60*
Lotus River, the, *Song 12/5*
Love, *Song 23*
bonds of, *Songs 49; 53*
cable of, *Song 84*
knot of, *Song 55*
spurned, *Songs 5; 11/2; 12/4; 17; 19; 27; 30; 31/2; 35/4,6; 46; 52; 56/3; 68; 76; 79/2; 83; 96*
tree of, *Songs 35/5; 54*
Lover, a fickle, *Songs 2; 4; 29; 37; 61*
a single-hearted, *Song 2*
Lovesickness, *Song 85*
Lui Boon-jung, *Intro. p. 12*
Lust-debt, *See 'Flower-debt'*

Ma Gwoo, *Pref. 8*
Maang Seung, *Song 16*
Maitreya, *Intro. pp. 23, 38*
Maitreya Buddha, *Pref. 8*
Man Gwaan, *Song 26*
Mandarin drake and duck, *Songs 3; 12/6; 35/4; 38; 60; 76/2; 79/1; 88*
Mara (Buddhist devil), *Intro. p. 24*
Marriage, *Songs 10; 68; 71*
Mei Sang-go, *Song 74/4*
Milky Way, *Songs 12/3; 18*
Ming, Emperor, *Intro. p. 20*
Mirror, *Songs 21; 33*
flowers in the, *Song 33*
the broken, *Song 81*
Mist and flowers, *Songs 12/1; 14; 31/1,2; 34; 45; 46; 47; 57; 87*
Mo Ling ford (Utopia), *Song 57*
Mok Sau, *Pref. 8*
Mong Foo Sek, *Song 75*
Moon-cassia, *Song 95*
Moon, *Songs 14; 21; 23; 24; 26; 27; 32; 34; 39; 74/4*
the old man in the, *Songs 14; 24; 95*
seventh night of seventh, *Songs 18; 43; 82*
symbolism of the, *Intro. p. 14*
Morality, *Intro. p. 24*
Moth, *Songs 50; 58; 73; 88*

Naam Bo, *Pref. 6*
Naam Po, River, *Song 74/1*
Neo-Confucianism, *Intro. p. 21*
Ng Gong, *Song 33*
Ngok Luk-wah, *Song 12/3*
Nim No, *Song 12/4*
Nineteen Ancient Poems, The, *Intro. pp. 11, 15*
Nirvana, *Intro. pp. 14, 27, 30–33, 36*

Oh Hau, *Pref. 8*
Oriole, *Songs 4; 73*
Oriole's song, *Song 4*

Pa Bridge, *Pref. 8; Song 76/2*
Paper, tissue, *Song 90*
Parlour, flower, *Song 18*
Parting, *Songs 8; 9; 11/1,2; 12/6; 23; 27; 35/5; 36; 43; 52; 56/1-6; 62; 63; 75; 76/1; 86; 93*

Parting tears, *Songs 56/2,3*
Passion, *Songs 1/2; 3; 11/2,3; 12/1-6; 13/1; 14; 18; 20; 35/1,3; 50; 51; 53; 73; 75; 86; 89; 92*
　and grief, *Song 67*
Passion-flower, *Song 90*
Passion's fibres, *Songs 60; 83*
Path, Eightfold Right, *Intro. pp. 27, 30*
　The Middle, *Intro. pp. 26, 27*
Peach blossom, *Song 37*
Pearl Lady, the, *Song 35/6*
Pearl River, the, *Pref. 2, 8; Song 71*
Pears and lungans, *Song 90*
Peking, *Song 73*
Peony, *Song 32*
Phoenix, a widowed, *Songs 64; 88*
Pipa, *Songs 12/4; 31/5; 35/6; 52; 74/2*
Pooi Hong, *Song 74/4*
Powder, red, *Songs 60; 66; 72*
Predestination, *Songs 5; 14; 35/4*
Princess Lok Cheung, *Song 33*
Pure Land, the, *Intro. pp. 35–37*

Raft on autumn tide, *Song 12/3*
Ransoming self, *Songs 6; 46*
Re-birth, *Intro. pp. 14, 20, 26–31, 36, 37*
Retribution, *Song 11/2*
Reward, *Song 1/1*
Rose-complexioned, *Songs 48; 72; 74/2*
Rouge and powder, *Songs 48; 93*

Sai Si, *Pref. 4*
Sai Wong Mo, *Song 24*
Sakyamuni, *Intro. pp. 24, 25, 34, 36–38*
Sap-neung, *Song 11/1*
Sea of bitterness, *Song 70*
　of desire, *Pref. 1*
　of sorrow, *Pref. 8; Song 1/1*
Sek Lak, emperor, *Song 11/3*
Sell-smile Village, *Song 7*
Separation, *Songs 12/4; 14; 73; 74/1*
Seung Ngoh, *Songs 24; 34; 74/4*
Seung, The River, *Songs 16; 35/4*
Seven Sisters, The, *Song 43*
Shadow, (My), *Song 91*
Si-hung To, *Pref. 5*
Si-Ma Seung-yue, *Song 26*
Sik Si, *Song 35/5*
Silken fabric, weaving, *Song 90*
Sin-debt See 'Flower-debt'

Single-hearted, *Songs 2; 68*
Single-heartedness, *Song 90*
Sit To, *Pref. 9*
Siu Ching, *Songs 11/1; 12/1*
Siu, The River, *Song 16*
Six Roots (of perception) *Song 85*
So Neung, *Pref. 8*
So Toi, *Pref. 3, 9*
So Wai, *Song 58*
Songs without feeling, *Song 59*
Sorceress Mountain, *Songs 12/5; 51*
Sorrow, *Songs 1/1,2; 12/2; 15; 35/3,6; 54; 77; 78*
　city of, *Song 1/2*
Sorrows, (dispel your), *Song 1/1,2*
Soul, the fragrant, *Song 21*
Spinning Girl & Cowherd, *Songs 12/3; 18; 36; 43; 82;*
Spring, *Songs 4; 11/2; 12/2; 13/2; 22; 35/2; 36; 48; 54; 57; 59; 74/1; 76/2; 86; 88*
Spring dream, *Song 18*
Stars, the three, *Pref. 2*
Steadfastness, *Songs 10; 81*
Suen Saan, *Song 79/2*
Suet Yi, *Pref. 9*
Suffering, human, *Intro. pp. 24, 27*
Suicide, *Songs 3; 47; 68*
Sung Yuk, *Songs 12/5; 74/3*
Support, lack of, *Songs 14; 21/1; 35/6; 37; 40; 46; 47; 48; 68; 69; 73; 76/2; 77; 85*
Sutra,
　The Lotus, *Intro. pp. 33, 34, 37, 38*
　The Pure Land, *Intro. p. 36*
Swallows, *Songs 8; 12/2*
Swan, *Pref. 6*

Taoism, *Intro. pp. 21, 22, 35, 36*
Tathagata, *Intro. p. 27*
Tears, *Songs 9; 15; 16; 17; 34; 40; 48; 52; 58; 71*
Tender Village, *Song 53*
Third Sister, *Song 3*
Three lives, *Song 60*
Tong Yuen Jung, *Song 34*
Transiency, *Songs 34; 35/3*
Tree,
　elm, *Song 11/1*
　juniper, *Song 5*
　laurel, *Songs 5; 33; 34*

palm, *Song 61*
phoenix, *Song 11/4*
pine, *Song 11/4*
plum, *Songs 11/1,5; 12/3*
single-hearted, *Song 61*
willow, *Songs 1/2; 11/2; 22*
Tripitaka, *Intro. pp. 22, 35*
Truths, The Four Noble, *Intro. p. 27*

Union, phoenix-like, *Song 18*
Unpitied, *Song 6*
Unsubstantiality, *Songs 11/3; 12/3; 37; 54*
Upanishads, *Intro. p. 25,*

Vedas, *Intro. pp. 25, 26*
Village, The Gentle, *Song 1/2*
Vinegar, *Song 80*
Virtue,
    cultivation of, *Songs 8; 9; 11/5*
    life of, *Song 13/1*
Virtues, The Ten, *Intro. p. 24*
Virtuous woman and passionate man, *Song 42*

Wai City, *Pref. 6*
Wai Jong, *Intro. p. 10*
Wai Ying-mat, *Pref. 9*
Wan Ying, *Song 74/4*
Weather and human affairs, *Song 43*

Well, the Golden, *Song 11/1*
Western region, the, *Song 85*
Willow, *Song 86*
    a blighted, *Song 5*
    the magic, *Song 35/2*
    the passionate, *Song 76/1,2*
    the weeping, *Song 63*
Willow groves, flower streets, *Song 77*
Wind and dust, *Song 12/2*
    and moon, *Songs 13/1; 96*
Wisdom, intuitive, *Intro. p. 28*
Words, unfeeling, *Song 67*
World, a burdensome, *Songs 20; 44*
    the dusty, *Song 72*
    the flowery, *Songs 7; 13/1; 60*
Wong Cheung-ling, *Song 11/1*
Wong Fooi, *Songs 20; 37*
Wong Wai, *Song 11/2*

Yan Chat-chat, *Song 11/3*
Yan Gwai-ying, *Song 20*
Yeung Gwaan, *Songs 11/2; 63; 86*
Yeung Gwai-fei, *Song 11/1*
Yeung Jau, *Pref. 6*
Yeung So, *Songs 33; 62*
Yim Guan-ping, *Song 12/3*
Yim Loh Wong, *Song 47*
Yue Yeung, *Pref. 4*
Yuen Jong, *Intro. p. 39*
Yung Moon, *Pref. 7*